Plays in American Periodicals, 1890–1918

PALGRAVE STUDIES IN THEATRE AND PERFORMANCE HISTORY is a series devoted to the best of theatre/performance scholarship currently available, accessible and free of jargon. It strives to include a wide range of topics, from the more traditional to those performance forms that in recent years have helped broaden the understanding of what theatre as a category might include (from variety forms as diverse as the circus and burlesque to street buskers, stage magic, and musical theatre, among many others). Although historical, critical, or analytical studies are of special interest, more theoretical projects, if not the dominant thrust of a study, but utilized as important underpinning or as a historiographical or analytical method of exploration, are also of interest. Textual studies of drama or other types of less traditional performance texts are also germane to the series if placed in their cultural, historical, social, or political and economic context. There is no geographical focus for this series and works of excellence of a diverse and international nature, including comparative studies, are sought.

The editor of the series is Don B. Wilmeth (EMERITUS, Brown University), Ph.D., University of Illinois, who brings to the series over a dozen years as editor of a book series on American theatre and drama, in addition to his own extensive experience as an editor of books and journals. He is the author of several award-winning books and has received numerous career achievement awards, including one for sustained excellence in editing from the Association for Theatre in Higher Education.

Also in the series:

Undressed for Success by Brenda Foley
Theatre, Performance, and the Historical Avant-garde by Günter Berghaus
Theatre, Politics, and Markets in Fin-de-Siècle Paris by Sally Charnow
Ghosts of Theatre and Cinema in the Brain by Mark Pizzato
Moscow Theatres for Young People by Manon van de Water
Absence and Memory in Colonial American Theatre by Odai Johnson
Vaudeville Wars: How the Keith-Albee and Orpheum Circuits Controlled the Big-Time and Its Performers by Arthur Frank Wertheim
Performance and Femininity in Eighteenth-Century German Women's Writing by Wendy Arons
Operatic China: Staging Chinese Identity across the Pacific by Daphne P. Lei
Transatlantic Stage Stars in Vaudeville and Variety: Celebrity Turns by Leigh Woods
Interrogating America through Theatre and Performance edited by William W. Demastes and Iris Smith Fischer
Plays in American Periodicals, 1890–1918 by Susan Harris Smith

Plays in American Periodicals, 1890–1918

Susan Harris Smith

palgrave
macmillan

PLAYS IN AMERICAN PERIODICALS, 1890–1918
© Susan Harris Smith, 2007.

First published in 2007 by
PALGRAVE MACMILLAN™
175 Fifth Avenue, New York, N.Y. 10010 and
Houndmills, Basingstoke, Hampshire, England RG21 6XS
Companies and representatives throughout the world.

PALGRAVE MACMILLAN is the global academic imprint of the Palgrave Macmillan division of St. Martin's Press, LLC and of Palgrave Macmillan Ltd. Macmillan® is a registered trademark in the United States, United Kingdom and other countries. Palgrave is a registered trademark in the European Union and other countries.

ISBN-13: 978–1–4039–7765–6
ISBN-10: 1–4039–7765–8

Library of Congress Cataloging-in-Publication Data

Smith, Susan Harris.
    Plays in American periodicals, 1890–1918 / by Susan Harris Smith.
        p. cm.—(Palgrave studies in theatre and performance)
    Includes bibliographical references and index.
    ISBN 1–4039–7765–8 (alk. paper)
        1. American drama—19th century—History and criticism. 2. American drama—20th century—History and criticism. 3. Journalism and literature—United States—History. 4. American periodicals—History. 5. Literature and society—United States—History. 6. Politics and literature—United States—History. 7. Politics in literature. 8. Social problems in literature. I. Title.

PS345.S65 2007
812′.5209—dc22   2007061460

A catalogue record for this book is available from the British Library.

Design by Newgen Imaging Systems (P) Ltd., Chennai, India.

First edition: July 2007

10 9 8 7 6 5 4 3 2 1

Printed in the United States of America.

For Phil . . . as always and forever

Contents ✑

List of Illustrations   ix
Preface   xi
Acknowledgments   xix

1. Varieties of Dramatic Experience   1
2. Cultures of Social Distance and Difference   35
3. Women as American Citizens   77
4. Cultural Displacement   117
5. Dis/Contented Citizens   149

Appendix: Plays in Periodicals   191
Works Cited   197
Index   213

List of Illustrations ∾

1.1 Frederic Dorr Steele for Arnold Bennett's
The Honeymoon (*McClure's* 1911)   30

1.2 Two illustrations by W. Glackens for Helen Green's
In Vaudeville (*McClure's* 1910)   31

2.1 May Wilson Preston for Bernard Shaw's *Pygmalion*
(*Everybody's Magazine* 1914)   42

2.2 Henry Raleigh for Bernard Shaw's *Great Catherine*
(*Everybody's Magazine* 1915)   44

2.3 Lucius Hitchcock for John Corbin's "How the Other
Half Laughs" (*Harper's* 1898)   64

2.4 Wallace Morgan for Helen Green Van Campen's *"Life
on Broadway": The Disillusions of Flossie* (*McClure's* 1913)   68

3.1 Florence Scovel Shinn for May Isabel Fisk's *Her
Tailor-Made Gown* (*Harper's* 1904)   83

3.2 Edward Penfield for John Frederick Bangs's *A Proposal
under Difficulties* (*Harper's* 1895)   98

3.3 Two photographs for Edwin Milton Royle's
The Squaw-Man (*Cosmopolitan* 1904)   109

Preface ✑

ONE NATION DIVIDED

This book examines a hitherto neglected body of work, plays published in periodicals. To put it simply, between 1890 and 1918 over one hundred and twenty five dramatic texts (American, English, Irish, and Anglo Indian) were published in fourteen American general interest periodicals ranging from elite publications such as *The Atlantic Monthly* and *Scribner's* to more popular venues such as *McClure's* and *Everybody's Magazine* to progressive magazines such as *Arena* and *Forum*. One key assumption I bring to this work, in concert with other critics, is that the periodicals and the plays in them collectively were an important site of public deliberation, contestation, and intellectual circulation, at once interlocking and in tension. My particular focus on the plays is meant to fill a striking gap in American literary history and to widen the dramatic canon; though most of these plays have received virtually no critical attention, they are as rich in historical and contextual complexity as the more-examined fiction and essays that comprise the literary canon of this period. Therefore, plays published in periodicals are as much part of the study of periodical literature as of dramatic history.

To that end, I consider the plays both individually and as a unique body of work. There are several compelling reasons to do this. First, histories of drama do not consider most of the plays at all. Second, of the plays that do get consideration, their publication in periodicals goes almost unnoticed. Third, no one has considered the presence of drama in American periodicals of this period as a body of work, and only some of the plays have had any notice as individual works. The same is true for histories of periodicals even though drama did the cultural work of the periodical's mission; even the slightest of the plays reveals the attitudes and values working in concert with the prose and poetry selections.

Finally, even though some of the plays are not written by Americans nor are on the face of it on an ostensibly American subject, every play was published in an American magazine because, I will argue, it accomplished some Americanist editorial objective. Therefore, I consider all the plays as doing the cultural work of American periodicals, work that was central to the American project of self-conscious class and nation formation, a project marked by a tension between the desire to be singularly and exceptionally "American" and the equally compelling urge to remain part of what William Dean Howells called "the Larger England," an extended community bound together by a shared code and a shared language. One of the interesting aspects of this unresolved struggle is the transatlantic circulation of American periodicals, which marks the coexistence of attempts to distinguish American culture from European culture and of a desire to be an integral participant in the international arena. Ultimately, the emergence of the United States as a global and imperial power can be understood as part of this effort to forge bonds among the dominant classes of "white" nations.

There are many arguments for accepting this historical periodization not the least of which is that various accounts of both political and dramatic history persuasively make this cut. For many cultural historians these three decades, framed by the Cuban conflict and World War I, comprise the Progressive and Populist era, a time of sweeping reforms and anxiety over the consolidation of business enterprises and monopolistic control, the subversion of frontier individualism, and the perceived threat to American democratic social structure by rising immigration. Furthermore, the drama was engaged powerfully with many of these issues, including the commodification of culture, the production of social stereotypes, the anxiety over labor struggles, social and ethnic strife, and the reluctant participation in the Great War. One important point for this study is that the commercial theatre between 1896 and 1915 was dominated by the Theatrical Syndicate, a domination challenged in 1915 by modernism. As such, the drama of this period, whether written for the stage or the page, shared several characteristics, summed up by Ronald Wainscott as "a dedication to environmental reality, the presentation of a believable society (both rural and urban), and carefully crafted language deemed appropriate for the time, place, and characters of the play. Although social issues would appear periodically in some of these plays, what kept most far from the frontiers of Ibsen was their approach to dramatic structure, selection of sensational event, and conventional conclusion to the central problem of the play. Nearly all of the American work that ventured into topical material in these years verified 'traditional values' of the age" ("Plays" 264). One way to understand the historical and dramatic relationship is to access the class-based "structure of feeling" (to invoke Raymond Williams's term) that invigorated the social-political transitional work of the failed Reconstruction period.

The periodicals under consideration, despite their range, from conservative to progressive, voiced and shaped the concerns of a very specific group, best summed up as white, Anglo-Saxon, non-immigrant, and middle class or what Richard Ohmann in *Selling Culture: Magazines, Markets, and Class at the Turn of the Century* calls the "PMC," the professional-managerial class. That class created its own mythic heritage and space, a space overwhelmingly white, in which characters of color are marginalized and stereotyped if they appear at all, in Benedict Anderson's well-known phrase, an "imagined political community." The drama participated instrumentally in this imaginative construction of an Anglo-Saxon legacy, a mythic history of whiteness, unity and imperial destiny born of a determination to close the sectional wound between post-Civil War Southern and Northern factions. Not only did the racial superiority of Anglo-Saxons go unquestioned but also the necessity to reproduce within one's own race and class was insisted upon. Finally, it is important to bear in mind the thoroughly integrated commercial basis of periodical publication; most periodicals were commercial commodities dedicated to advertising goods and promoting consumerism as necessary for national economic growth and cultural advancement.

The most comprehensive general history of periodicals is still Frank Mott's multivolume *A History of American Magazines*, though studies of individual periodicals such as Harold Wilson's *"McClure's Magazine" and the Muckrakers* and Arthur John's *The Best Years of the "Century"* and general overviews such as John Tebbel's *The American Magazine: A Compact History* amplify and update Mott's work. In all of these, however, there is virtually nothing about the dramatists or their work though, ironically, a great deal of space was given in the periodicals to debates about the theatre, to theatre reviews, and to concerns about achieving a distinctly American and "literary" drama as well as to the plays themselves. Though Mott notes that there was extensive commentary on and coverage of the drama, the stage, and shows of all kinds in the periodicals, and that "an important element in the formula for a successful cheap magazine always was a department of pictures of actresses, accompanied by a page or two of stage gossip," he says nothing of the dramatic texts published in the magazines (*History 1885–1905* 255).

Plays in periodicals also have gone unrecognized in cultural studies both of literature and drama. More recent studies of periodicals, for instance Richard Ohmann's *Selling Culture: Magazines, Markets, and Class at the Turn of the Century* (1996), Nancy Glazener's *Reading for Realism: The History of a U. S. Literary Institution, 1850–1910* (1997), and Matthew Schneirov's *The Dream of a New Social Order: Popular Magazines in America 1893–1914* (1994), focus on fiction and nonfiction, leaving poetry and drama largely unexamined, in order to investigate other concerns pertinent to this study as well: the cultures of letters, the operations of bourgeois culture, the forms of engagement with social issues, and the dominance of realism. Studies of American drama for this period also are largely silent on the matter of drama in periodicals. In Brenda Murphy's *American Realism and American Drama, 1880–1940*, only Hamlin Garland's *Under the Wheel* is mentioned other than Howells's work, which receives extensive treatment. Alan Ackerman in *The Portable Theater: American Literature & the Nineteenth-Century Stage* likewise attends to Howells's work but to none of the other plays in this study. Ronald Wainscott in *The Emergence of the Modern American Theater, 1914–1929* mentions Shaw's *Androcles and the Lion* and Marion Craig Wentworth's *War Brides* but only in passing. Of the one hundred and twenty-five plays under consideration in this study, one-quarter were published in *Harper's Monthly* (the lion's share of these are attributed to William Dean Howells and two *farceurs*, John Kendrick Bangs and May Isabel Fisk). Of the others, twenty were in *Forum*, sixteen in *McClure's*, twelve in *Scribner's*, eight in *Century*, three each in *New England Magazine*, *Bookman*, *North American Review*, and *Everybody's*, two each in *Cosmopolitan*, *Arena*, and *The Atlantic Monthly*, and only one each in *Lippincott's* and the *Critic*. Obviously, despite their shared general characteristics, the magazines had their own nuanced proclivities, biases, and cultural agendas and different relationships with drama and theatre.

With the exception of the well-known Europeans—Yeats, Shaw, Galsworthy and Lady Gregory—and one American, William Dean

Howells, most of the dramatists, though they were well-known to their contemporaries (though not necessarily as playwrights) are not as familiar today. Of the seventy dramatists all but twelve were American. Of the one hundred and twenty-five plays, fifty-one were written by women and most of the women were American. Thirty-two plays are set in the past (Biblical, Anglo-Saxon "England," Puritan America, Ancient Greece, and France during the Revolution), eighty-two are set in the present, and five in the future. Of the sixty-nine that are set in America, with one exception (Hamlin Garland's *Under the Wheel*), all have urban settings; the rest are set elsewhere (usually Europe). Twenty-seven of the plays are in verse and sixty-six are illustrated. Of the one hundred and twenty-five plays only about seven could be described accurately as dramaturgically "experimental."

Because the voices were as often raised in discontent as in content, a contentment haunted by ill-concealed anxiety, I describe the writers as "dis/contented." Specifically, I want to think of the periodicals as a "site," a socially constructed phenomenon with peculiar types of often strained relations operating within it, relations that were the foundations of a collective identity for a particular class, a self-identified "Anglo-Saxon" middle class in a dynamic and unstable state of turmoil and anxiety. This study will trace and analyze both the unified fronts predicated on a certain degree of unity and conformity that provided temporary contentment and the genuine disagreements within the class about culture and politics, which produced irruptions of discontent. A wide range of opinions are voiced in the drama, from the most virulent dismissal of immigrants to well-intentioned engagement with progressive causes; all are framed by middle-class objectives, not the least of which was to locate and naturalize the leadership of the nation by that class alone. As I will stress, the drama in particular was a powerful agent in the attempt to establish and sustain difference and distance between the middle and the lower classes and between the Anglo-Saxon and the various "Others."

The general goals and rationales of the project are set up in chapter 1, "Varieties of Dramatic Experience": to capture what Raymond Williams calls the "felt sense" of life for the privileged middle-class readers in America who were invested in the production of what Benedict Anderson describes as "the national imaginary," an imaginary that fostered American racism, consumerism, nativism, and imperialism, themselves extensions of what William Dean Howells's approved of as the "Larger England."

The chapter sets forth the varieties of dramatic literature readers would have encountered in the periodicals with particular attention to class.

Chapter 2, "Cultures of Social Distance and Difference," examines the strategies used to create a distinct social audience in a closed cultural zone: the inter- and intratextuality of periodical literature as it pertained to the drama; the dependence on specific cultural knowledge; the total exclusion of African Americans as citizens or subjects in the drama; the voyeuristic framing of immigrants; and the creation of a privileged consumer-reader class. That class generated numerous ways of naming themselves, their culture, and their values: respectable, genteel, cultivated, and traditional; values reaffirmed by the plays. It is a class decidedly and insistently in the middle, portraying itself as above working and poor people and below wealthy and aristocratic people, circling the wagons against all Others.

This middling conservatism is dramatized in the most gendered group of plays, those about women. Chapter 3, "Women as American Citizens," considers the ways in which women were positioned to reject suffrage and accept conservative expectations of marriage, particularly within their own class, how women (but not men) were ridiculed lightly for their "feminine" foibles and how women were presented as "naturally" charitable. Marriage within one's own class was presented as necessary for social stability and the reproduction of Anglo-Saxons as essential to combating the "race suicide" that was threatening the "civilized" citizens and imperiling the nation's strength.

One way for a periodical to secure an elite cultural zone, the demonstrable sign of being "civilized," was to resort to the traditional "high" cultural forms, genres, and themes that were accepted markers of refinement and good taste. Chapter 4, "Cultural Displacement," proposes that though verse plays and plays on religious, historical, or mythological subjects made claims to such "higher" ground, aesthetically and morally, this was a strategy, first, to enable the dramatization of suicide, adultery, fallen women, and sexual depravity, second, to naturalize religious miracles, indulge in extreme sentimentality, and romanticize racism and monarchism, and, third, to de-nationalize and naturalize the plays of Irish and East Indian playwrights to serve "American," specifically nationalist, needs.

In conclusion, chapter 5, "Dis/Contented Citizens," looks at the plays that were openly critical of contemporary American social and political issues—particularly the economic abuse of laborers, "white slavery" (prostitution), monarchy, and World War I—noting the culturally conflicted work of "progressive" polemical pieces purporting to support a demographically broad democracy. The discontent was not just thematic; the most inventive dramaturgy marks many of these plays that participate in the emergent Modernist experiment.

Therefore, situating the plays in their original periodical context establishes both their autonomy as works of literature and their participation in the complexities of the cultural conversations transpiring in the monthly press. Furthermore, the varieties of dramatic experience speak not only to an aesthetic range, from conventional melodrama to experimentation with "modern" forms, but also to the extensive cogent engagement with political and social issues that characterize the thematic concerns. As I have said, the work of this project is driven by the need to bring to attention plays that, individually or collectively, deliberately or unconsciously, have been overlooked and to locate that work in their periodical context, a context that emphasizes a shared history and cultural alliances but also countenances a focus on social and political differences and divisions marked by race, ethnicity, gender, and class. By considering the plays in their periodical context, we can hear the authority with which they spoke to their readers and can better understand and reassess their impact on the culture they were so instrumental in both reflecting and producing. It is, of course, impossible to reconstruct the entire historical and cultural fabric within which the plays operated but it is possible to listen to each voice participating in the cultural conversation. Because most of these plays will be unfamiliar to contemporary readers, examination of the cultural work necessitates detailed recapitulations of the themes and subject matter of each play. This avoids the danger of positing a distinct and coherent ideology but does encourage marking the rhetorical practices and strategies, dramaturgical devices, and thematic patterns that recur.

Acknowledgments ⌒

My thanks are few but heartfelt: to Don Wilmeth for his consistent support and eagle eye, Nancy Glazener for her thoughtful and insightful interventions, and Jim Burke for the photographs. And, of course, Phil who is always by my side.

1. Varieties of Dramatic Experience ~

I begin this examination of dramatic texts in American general interest periodicals at the turn of the twentieth century with a contentious question that I hope will be answered by the work itself, namely, "Why bother?" Literary histories ignore their presence and plays are no longer published in such periodicals; nonetheless, periodicalized dramatic literature played a significant role in the social constitution of the middle class as citizens and consumers. The cultural hypothesis that modalities of feeling are social and public, not only personal or private, was introduced by Raymond Williams in *Marxism and Literature* in 1977. This concept, which he termed "structures of feeling," has become central to methodologies that relate the extraordinariness of imaginative literature to the ordinariness of cultural processes and that attempt to understand their connections to a historical period. As he explained, "we are concerned with meanings and values as they are actively lived and felt . . . not feeling against thought, but thought as felt and feeling as thought: practical consciousness of a present kind, in a living and inter-related continuity" (132). Crucially, Williams stressed the ways in which literature articulated an alternative to dominant views and, thus, to the politics of social order and social change.

Raymond Williams also reminds us, in *The Long Revolution*, that the most difficult thing to grasp in studying any particular period is the "felt sense" of the quality of life at a particular place and time, a sense of the ways in which particular activities combined into a way of thinking and living (47). The felt sense of life I want to recover is that of a privileged group of Americans at the turn of the last century, from 1890 to 1918, a time in which a new social order, managed by the growing middle class, a professional-managerial class, engaged in the project of achieving a "modern" and "national" cultured status through the activity of reading, which was a consumer activity. The consumption of culture encouraged and enabled the reader-consumer to bask in an expanded world of goods to be purchased, behaviors to be examined, and lands to be claimed for nation building. The coast-to-coast consolidation of America was secured through the agency of the railroad system and consequent articulation of wealth and power as the national desiderata. The new American national identity, a modern identity promoted by mass culture, mass advertising, and mass anxiety, was one of patriotic material advancement at home and rationalized righteous expansionism abroad. It was also highly unstable, an imagined formation erected precariously on wishful assertion rather than discernible fact.

At the turn of the twentieth century, the middle class understood itself to have definite cultural commitments to self-improve as both readers and consumers, to participate in and contribute to an America that was presented to them as a cultural and political success dependent upon their full cooperation and adherence to a narrowly circumscribed national norm. The axiom of social harmony upon which a post–Civil War nation depended was predicated on class cooperation if not co-option. Benedict Anderson's definition of nation is, by now, quite familiar; in *Imagined Communities* he says that nation is "an imagined political community— and imagined as both inherently limited and sovereign. It is *imagined* because even the members of the smallest nation will never know most of their fellow-members, meet them, or even hear of them, yet in the minds of each lives the image of their communion" (6). The rise of the nation-state was, as Anderson argues, driven by a growth of "national consciousness" that was enabled by the print medium. Though America ostensibly was one nation, in fact it was divided between a literate class and others (some native-born, some immigrant) who were illiterate or poorly educated in English. For the print medium this distinction was a foundation on which the community of the nation-state could be constructed. Etienne Balibar calls such a community a "fictive ethnicity," noting the "great competing routes to this: language and race usually operate together, for only their complementarity makes it possible for the 'people' to be represented as an absolutely autonomous unit" (96). At stake at the American turn of the century, so its dominant class was told, was the survival of the Anglo-Saxon race, the race that William Dean Howells characterized as the "Larger England," an extended community bound together by a shared code and a shared language (*Laureate*).

The construction of national identity and values was carried out not only in legislation, such as the Immigration Act of 1881, which assigned responsibility for assessment to the federal government and allowed a medical examination, for example *Plessy v. Ferguson* (1896), that legitimized racial segregation; the Naturalization Act of 1906 in which knowledge of English became a requirement; the restriction of Japanese in 1907, and the 1917 Literacy test, but also in the periodicals that collectively were an important location for public contestation, deliberation, and intellectual circulation about race and immigration. The drama in periodicals, I argue, was complicit to a large degree in the formation of a racially restrictive, ethnically exclusionary, and Protestant Anglo-American identity, often modeling such behaviors and attitudes for the readers while reflecting the foundational unsettled anxiety about the issues.

Benedict Anderson also argues that the construction of the imagined nation-state of America required not only "republican institutions, common citizenships, popular sovereignty, national flags, anthems, etc." but also the necessary corollary, "the liquidation of their conceptual opposites: dynastic empires, monarchical institutions, absolutisms, subjecthoods, inherited nobilities, serfdoms, ghettos, and so forth" (81). Such "official nationalism," he continues, was a highly effective "anticipatory strategy adopted by dominant groups which are threatened with marginalization or exclusion from an emerging nationally-imagined community" (101). One reason the dominant group felt an urgent need to promote an official nationalism was that, at base, it did not feel unified. As David Blight forcefully demonstrates in *Race and Reunion*, his history of the aftermath of the Civil War, in fact the nation was not grounded in shared civic ideals because "a segregated society demanded a segregated memory." Consequently, "the many myths and legends fashioned out of the reconciliationist vision provided the superstructure of Civil War memory, but its base was white supremacy in both its moderate and virulent forms. This concerted effort to "forget" what had transpired and to introduce a national mythology that yoked reunion with racism he calls "segregated historical memory" (361). One of the prominent means of promulgating the myths and legends of civic union was through the wide-spread distribution of print media directed at the middle-class consumer.

At the turn of the century in America, one of the ubiquitous vehicles in the realm of print media was the periodical: technological advances having made possible the dissemination of both "quality" and "pulp" magazines to a wide audience. The target audience for periodicals interested in drama was driven by a passion for self-improvement and education; they supported the lyceum and Chautauqua movements, home-study correspondence courses, morally uplifting fiction, and special interest clubs. The quest for self-improvement was not new; Burton Bledstein notes that mid-nineteenth-century Americans depended on the "guidebook, the manual, handbook, or book of reference in order to function—*by the book*—" (10). Periodicals also filled that function. According to Frank Mott, between 1860 and 1900 as the American population doubled, the number of daily newspapers grew from 387 with an average circulation of 12,000 and doubled again between 1890 and 1915. Also American periodicals grew, from 700 in 1865 and peaking at 5,500 in 1900, during which time more than a thousand new magazines were founded. Carolyn Kitch's estimations also speak to staggering growth; she maintains that "in 1865, there were nearly 700 hundred titles with a total circulation of about four million; forty years later, in 1905, there were some 6000 magazines with a total audience of sixty-four million, averaging four magazines per household. By the same year, ten American magazines had readerships in excess of half a million" (*History 1885–1905* 4). The fortunes of all periodicals during this period rose and fell with the stock market but the cheaper and more "popular" periodicals such as *McClure's, Munsey's,* and *Cosmopolitan* gained in strength as they sold increasingly more advertising; that is, they were directed to the reader as consumer. The consequence was a huge audience of readers and it is not too much to claim that the popular or "general interest" magazines revolutionized mass communications between 1893 and 1918. In 1893, S. S. McClure established *McClure's* to compete with the four quality or genteel periodicals, *Atlantic Monthly, Harper's Monthly, Scribner's,* and *Century,* and it was also the year in which Frank Munsey cut the price of his magazine to ten cents.

In *The End of American Innocence,* an early intellectual history of the cultural and political legacy of the turn-of-the-century "custodians of culture" and the "revolution" against them between 1912 and 1917, Henry F. May speaks powerfully to the tensions and debates carried on in the periodicals as well as in other public forums. Although May falls too easily into the evolutionary Victorian/Modern dichotomizing formulation that marks many cultural histories, he argues that three central doctrines characterized American discourse: the certainty and universality of moral values, the inevitability of progress in America, and the importance of traditional literary culture. May locates one of the primary modes of instantiation and dissemination in the magazines. "In the early twentieth century," he explains, "more I think than in any other period and much more than at present, every shade of American opinion and every level of culture had its magazine" (404).

Therefore, one way to recover Raymond Williams's "felt sense" is to examine the periodical magazines that middle-class literate people read for pleasure and edification. It would be hard to overstate the importance of the periodical press at this time. Periodical literature was instrumental in disseminating everything from models of domestic decorum to expansionist ideology; it played a significant role in the popularization of national identity with its congruent theories of race and responsibility. Amy Kaplan points to the growing dominance of mass markets in newspapers, magazines, advertising and book publishing which "created a national market which constructed a shared reality of both information and desire. The new media promised a coherent and a cohesive world in place of older forms of cultural authority" (*Social Construction* 13). The expression and legitimization of codes of conduct, consumer values, and conventional expectations comprised, to reinvoke Raymond Williams's term, a "structure of feeling" that was requisite to social control and nation building. From this perspective, it could be argued that periodicals were agents of social control, that they were instrumental in setting up ideals, norms, and boundaries, both conceptually in describing and delimiting "types" of behavior, from the social to the national, and actually in documenting and dramatizing threats of disruptive disorder to the status quo. They were, in Lyn Pykett's term, "active shapers" of culture. The periodicals often represented the opinions of one dominant figure; for instance, Henry Alden Mills was the editor of *Harper's* from 1869 until his death in 1919 and, similarly, the founder of *Arena*, B. O. Flower, held sway during the periodical's entire run, from 1889 until 1909. Furthermore, the periodicals had weight if not gravitas because the presence of known authors conferred cultural authority on the periodicals as much as the cultural authority of the periodicals sanctioned the ideas of lesser-known writers. Close examination of periodical literature reveals the discursive forces that contributed to the larger American narratives about immigration, progressivism, and nation formation.

Though all this speaks to a seeming cohesive homogeneity, I also want to read with heterogeneity in mind and to suggest that there was not necessarily a consensual position on any one issue. For instance, I want to resist assertions presuming prewar stasis, such as Paul Fussell's diagnosis that before the First World War, "the values appeared stable and . . . the meanings of abstractions seemed permanent and reliable" (21). I want to leave behind a tyranny of exceptional monolingualism and disinter the cultural conversations and disparate voices too often buried under the assumption that the dominant and privileged group necessarily participate unqualifiedly in totalizing assertions about national or class hegemony. I do want to test the hegemonic argument because it provides a useful point of entry into the way a particular group, in this instance, the middle class, was understood to cohere as it strove for authority in and control of political and cultural life and how it attempted to marginalize and denigrate subordinated groups. I am not an apologist for the racism, nativism, or imperialism of this period but, at the same time, I want to avoid a position of self-righteous criticism of the past for failing to meet current standards of political correctness.

Each periodical had different political allegiances and cultural goals and the plays reflect those variables just as much as the essays and fiction. I hope to demonstrate that a range of opinions were aired and that, despite what contemporary readers would condemn as retrograde attitudes, many writers, to a large degree, were engaged with serious issues often in as enlightened or progressive a way as the periodicals and the times allowed. Though most writers stayed within the normative bounds, some protested social and political wrongs. My objective is not to attempt to construct a shaping historical narrative, rather it is to point to critical divisions within what might appear to be a homogeneously bland unified front of middle-class Americanness, divisions manifested through the dramatized voices of "dis/contented citizens." The varieties of dramatic experience speak not only to the aesthetic range, from conventional melodrama to experimentation with "modern" form, but also to the plays' cogent engagement with political and social issues. Finally, it should be understood that the dramatic constructs are just that—imaginative constructs, not mirror images. The readers, too, are constructs created by the magazines. Ronald Zboray aptly calls such a collective readership "a fictive people" being imagined as becoming culturally adept and upwardly mobile through the agency of the magazine. Hamlin Garland in his autobiography, *Roadside Meetings* (1930), characterized this period as marked by "a bitter and accusing mood . . . a time of parlor socialists, single-taxers, militant populists, Ibsen dramas, and Tolstoyian encyclicals against greed, lust, and caste" (*Roadside* 126). Recently, Louis Menand in *The Metaphysical Club* has characterized the period from 1898 to 1917 in the United States as "a period of adjustment to life under industrial capitalism . . . . The Spanish–American War, in 1898, in which the United States acquired the Philippines in what seemed an almost reflexive gesture of imperialism, exposed [William James] thought, the soul of modern America: its mindless drive toward expansion, conglomeration, massification" (372).

In 1921, the U.S. Congress passed the Emergency Quota Act, a law restricting European immigration to three percent per annum of each European nationality already resident in the United States. Desmond King has argued, in *Making Americans*, that the act marked the culmination of an exclusionary process of nation formation dating back to the restrictionist agenda developed in the 1880s. Broadly speaking, from the Chinese Exclusion Act of 1882 to the Emergency Quota Act in 1921, the U.S. immigration policy, bolstered by the eugenicists' anxieties and nativists' hysteria about "racial degeneration" and "race suicide," privileged an Anglo-Saxon conception of U.S. identity, which "also helped solidify the second-class position of nonwhites, notably African Americans, already exposed to segregated race relations" (3). By a congressional decision, the American identity would be white, Anglo-Saxon, and preferably Protestant because 70 percent of the immigrants would come from the United Kingdom, Ireland, and Germany. Gail Bederman in *Manliness & Civilization* argues that "between 1890 and 1917 as white middle-class men actively worked to reinforce male power, their race became a factor which was crucial to their gender. In ways which have not been well understood, whiteness was both a palpable fact and a manly ideal for these men" (5).

Alexander Saxton refers to the 1890s in particular as "the decade of hegemonic crisis," arguing that a number of historians, including Martin Sklar and Richard Slotkin, concluded that the decade was "a watershed between the citizens' lower case *r* republicanism of the older America and the new capitalized Republicanism that was ushered in by the 'incorporation of America' " (351). He also observes that Richard

Hofstadter applied the term " 'psychic crisis' " to the decade, a crisis Saxton demonstrates spread across the social spectrum. He concludes that works by writers as different as Stephen Crane and Ignatius Donnelly shared "dark visions," evidence that suggests, "in Gramscian terms, a breakdown of ruling-class hegemony: the moral and cultural authority of the ruling class appeared to have become too selective, too self-serving, to justify a broad social order" (352). In the face of a crumbling order, the nation needed heroes, Saxton argues, pointing to Theodore Roosevelt's regiment in the Cuba campaign as "an almost perfect scale model for the politics of Social Darwinism," a politics that combined the "white egalitarianism with imperial authority and Christian mission" and "swept the heights of American national consciousness" for the next half century (376–77).

In terms of literary, and especially dramatic history, as Thomas Postlewait notes in his revisionist assessment, most critics since the 1930s have held that "the period between 1880 and 1920 becomes the age of transition—an awkward, adolescent age when the drama, struggling to shed its exuberant youthfulness, begins to achieve adulthood" ("From" 43). For example, Montrose Moses, in his history of the drama from 1860 to 1918, quotes Bronson Howard's observation that American writers suddenly discovered themselves as a body of dramatists in about 1890 and notes that "it was on this occasion that Howard founded the American Dramatists Club" (272). For Arthur Hobson Quinn, 1890 marked "the beginning of an era" characterized by humanitarian realism (*From the Beginning* 158) and 1915 as the beginning of the regenerative force of the Little Theatre movement (*From the Civil* 160). Postlewait offers a corrective interpretation of the period, resisting the dominant historical acceptance of the odious and onerous binarism of melodrama versus realism, refusing "evolutionary and antagonistic narratives," and arguing instead for greater attention to the complexities of genre ("From" 53). Even though, as Alan Ackerman argues, "two distinctive dramaturgies both pervade thinking about theater and shape social notions of social life from roughly 1830 to 1900"—melodrama and realism, the American plays published in periodicals actually cover a wide diversity of styles (xiii). Nonetheless, they are still far from the innovative experiments of contemporaneous European dramatists such as Maeterlinck, Jarry, and Strindberg, who were published in *Poet-Lore*, the only periodical to embrace radically new work and ideas.

Many of the periodicals that published drama fall under the aegis of Nancy Glazener's designation "The *Atlantic* Group" in *Reading for Realism : The History of a U. S. Literary Institution, 1850–1910*. Her list (exclusive of periodicals already out of print by 1890) includes: *The Atlantic Monthly* (1857–present), *The Critic* (1881–1906); *The Forum* (1886–1930); *Harper's Monthly* (1850–present); *Lippincott's* (1868–1916); *The Nation* (1865–present); *The North American Review* (1815–late 1930s); *Scribner's Magazine* (1887–1939); and *The Century* (1881–1930). All but *The Nation* published plays. Glazener groups these magazines together because they "shared contributors with the *Atlantic* and with each other, endorsed each other's cultural authority, and based that authority in similar understandings of class-inflected cultural trusteeship" and consequently could be understood as constituting a "market" (257). This commonality, she argues, is best understood not as "genteel" or "upper-middle-class" but, more accurately, as "bourgeois" (259). The exercise of that cultural authority was managed in part by the deployment of realist dramaturgy. I understand realism as defined by William Demastes and Michael Vanden Heuvel as "a form that renders information as a measure of a system's order . . . . Early realist theatre sought to produce complete descriptions of reality in order to eliminate uncertainty, disorder, and complexity. It qualitatively assessed what information was valuable and what information was extraneous 'noise,' highlighting the former and suppressing the latter so that the data ultimately presented was taxonomic, linear, and transmitted with optimum clarity" (261). In other words, class-inflected cultural control assured a smooth representaion of an ordered existence, a voicing of the contentment that was an essential element of the national imaginary.

As well as the eight periodicals in "The *Atlantic* Group," I include six other periodicals of importance: the progressive, reformist *Arena* (1889–1909) and the more "middle brow" and investigative magazines such as *McClure's*, *Cosmopolitan*, and *Everybody's* as well as *Bookman* and *New England Magazine*. All the "quality" magazines suffered in the mid-1890s as a consequence of the economic depression of 1893 and stiff competition from the new, cheaper magazines. For instance, *Century's* circulation fell from 200,000 to 75,000 whereas the circulation of *McClure's*, *Munsey's*, and *Cosmopolitan* rose. The introduction and consequent popular and economic success of the ten-cent magazine (*McClure's*, *Munsey's*, *Cosmopolitan*, and *Argosy*) in the marketplace with

McClure's in June 1893 was followed by a flood of imitators; by 1903 they comprised about 85 percent of the total circulation of magazines in America. The competition from the ten-centers put pressure on the entire magazine market in two ways. First, the monthly magazine market jumped from four monthlies with a circulation of 100,000 or more in 1885 to twenty with a total circulation of more than 5.5 million by 1915. Second, the ten-cent monthlies' success with writing on social reform forced the "quality" periodicals (*The Atlantic, Scribner's, Century,* and *Harper's*) to engage more with those issues (Tebbel 165–67).

Though these were not the only magazines to publish dramatic texts, they were the most significant in terms of engaging with serious cultural issues affecting class and nation formation. For instance, I am excluding periodicals that focused on Christmas plays, plays for amateurs, and plays for children. Also, because I consider only general interest periodicals and not special interest magazines, I do not examine what Mary Ellen Zuckerman calls "The Big Six" women's magazines of the late nineteenth century: *Delineator, McCall's, Ladies' Home Journal, Woman's Home Companion, Good Housekeeping,* and *Pictorial Review.*

It is also worth noting the work of publishing plays done by two other periodicals, which are not part of this study. The first is *Poet-Lore* (1899–1920), which, between 1890 and 1899 alone, published thirty-seven plays by the following: Annunzio, Björnson, Dreyer, Fiske, Gorky, Giitzkow, Hauptmann, Hyde, Maeterlinck, Musselman, Noguchi, Schnitzler, Strindberg, Suderman, Wilbrandt, and Wildenbruch. Among the plays readers would have encountered were *Uncle Vanya, The Seagull, Miss Julie,* and *Salomé.* Clearly this body of work is markedly different from the plays in the general interest American periodicals and presumably reached a different or overlapping readership.

In his survey of the early years of *Poet-Lore,* Melvin Bernstein describes the two founders, Helen Archibald Clarke ("C") and Charlotte Endymion Porter ("P"), as "indefatigable literary people" (Very 10). Clarke (1860–1926) was a musician and scientist who dramatized Browning's poems and Porter (1859–1942) was a specialist in French theatre, the president of the American Drama Society founded in Boston (1909) to organize a civic theatre, and the person responsible for the "first" American translations of the European plays in *Poet-Lore* (Very 11). Bernstein stresses the significance of *Poet-Lore*: "no other American periodical regularly published translations, especially of drama" (Very 15).

To read a monthly magazine, twenty-five cents per copy, which was dedicated to Browning, Shakespeare, and the comparative study of literature, Bernstein argues, was "to collaborate toward the creation of the new world of emergent women, positivism, beneficent Social Darwinism, a vague liberalism, and an understanding of the supranational art of literature" (Very 14). Bernstein credits *Poet-Lore* with a liberal "cosmopolitanism and internationalism" and with "trying to rescue the American reader's imagination from the parochialism of both modernism and nativism" (Very 14). Certainly the women had a firm belief that universal literacy was an essential "part of the faith of democracy" and that everyone should be able to have access to the "bounty of poets" (Very 50). Most of the periodicals in this study were more parochial than cosmopolitan, more nativistic than international, and more intent on preserving the status quo than in creating a new world.

The second periodical, *Current Literature*, I exclude from this study for two reasons: first, because until July 1905, it published only short theatre reviews and observations on the drama and, second, because it published only excerpts from plays, never the full text. Up to this point, *Current Literature* had been, for the most part, a reprint journal, when, under the revitalizing editorship of Edward Wheeler in 1905, it made a regular feature of publishing excerpts of plays and by 1908 had a circulation of 50,000. Every month, in a section entitled "Music and Drama" (literature being aligned with art in another section), *Current Literature* featured a condensation and excerpts from a contemporary play prefaced by an evaluation that was often highly critical and judgmental. At the beginning, the excerpts were all from European writers such as Schnitzler, Bahr, and Ibsen, but in December 1906, three scenes from William Vaughn Moody's *The Great Divide* were printed and the periodical became transatlantic in its coverage. Though the plays often were chosen because they were successful on the stage, *Current Literature*'s interest in the drama was both as a cultural phenomenon ("why is *this* play popular?") and as a social corrective (there was a heavy commitment to "muck-raking" drama). For instance, in December 1908, reviewers were puzzled by the attractions of Denman Thompson's *The Old Homestead* ("What is the cause of the phenomenal success of this rustic and Christmasy melodrama?") and in May 1910 they introduced the reader to the American version of John Galsworthy's *Strife*, a "powerful labor play," relocated to Pittsburgh. Looking at only one or two such summaries would neglect the larger cultural mission of the periodical's claim to social responsibility, a responsibility demonstrated by their choice of plays.

One could profitably study the genealogy of modern drama as manifested by the excerpts and commentary in *Current Literature* and, within those confines, create a lineage of (largely) politically engaged (though not "politically correct") and (largely) Anglo-American plays. In "The Theatrical Muck-Raker Answered" (1909), *Current Literature* invokes Jane Addams's praise for the American dramatist eager to attack serious social problems and reminds its readers that they "are not unaware of the ethical note so strongly sounded in the American drama and so persistently ignored by its critics" (669). An examination of their offerings shows *Current Literature* to be only partly correct about its self-appraisal. In 1912, for instance, a reader of *Current Literature* would have been introduced to summaries and analyses of the following: Graham Moffatt's *Bunty Pulls the Strings* (a Scottish comedy at the expense of Scots); George Broadhurst's *Bought and Paid For* (a sensational marital melodrama); Charles Kenyon's *Kindling* (raking the muck of New York tenement life); David Belasco's *The Return of Peter Grimm* (a psychic ghost play); the Hungarian Lengyel's *The Typhoon* (on "The Yellow Peril"); A. E. Thomas's *The Rainbow* (if Strindberg were saccharine); Edward G. Hemmerde and Francis Neilson's *Butterfly on a Wheel* (an exposé of English divorce courts); Edward Locke's *The Case of Becky* (a psychic melodrama about a woman with multiple personalities); Arnold Bennett and Edward Knoblauch's *Milestones* (how the progressives of today are the reactionaries of tomorrow); Eugene Walter's *Fine Features* (flays the self-indulgent American woman); George Bernard Shaw's *Fanny's First Play* (Shaw's tribute to himself); and Bayard Veiller's *Within the Law* (the American police system fails to protect starving shop girls from the urban underworld). The format is always the same: the evaluator is anonymous, the play is introduced succinctly and sharply in a few paragraphs followed by a plot summary and then five to six pages of excerpts, the interest clearly being on the thematic substance and on the "story."

The periodicals had specific positions on the drama, positions that reflected their cultural aspirations. For instance, when the first number of *Scribner's Magazine* appeared in January 1887, there were already three American general "quality" monthly periodicals: the *Atlantic Monthly*, which had no illustrations, 144 pages, a circulation of 12,500, and a claim to a polite literary tradition; the *Century*, which was lavishly illustrated, had 160 pages, a circulation of over 220,000, and a claim to covering both literature and current events; and *Harper's New Monthly Magazine*, which also was illustrated, had 168 pages, a circulation of 185,000, and a cultural level just below that of its two competitors. Each sold for thirty-five cents a copy or four dollars a year. *Scribner's* sold for twenty-five cents a copy because the editor from 1887 to 1914, Edward Burlingame, who had been educated in American and European universities, packaged popular topics in a "literary" treatment and had by the mid-1890s established *Scribner's* as a profitable "quality" magazine (Mott, F., *1885–1905* 717–32). In terms of the drama, "quality" meant not much of it and what there was of it either was written by largely recognizable "literary" figures such as Edith Wharton and John Galsworthy, both of whom published two plays in *Scribner's*, or took up serious themes such as war (Andrews's *The Ditch*) or religion (Sherwood's *Vittoria*). Even the lightest play *Scribner's* published, Merington's *A Gainsborough Lady*, a series of *tableaux* with verse, was unimpeachably inoffensive.

The *Forum*, on the other hand, was a serious periodical dedicated to progressive politics; it did not publish fiction or poetry, was not illustrated, and between 1905 and 1918 published twenty plays covering a diverse range of writers such as Yeats, Lady Gregory, and Rabindranath Tagore as well as plays about prostitution (*Tiger* and *Chinese Lily*) and against the war (*"Law"* and *The Inconveniences of Being Neutral*). In particular, *The Forum* went after moral hypocrisy. For instance, Nina Wilcox Putnam's *Orthodoxy* (1914) targeted religious hypocrisy by voicing the "secret minds" of worshippers occupied with everything except worship. Likewise, the only two plays published in *Arena*, Hamlin Garland's *Under the Wheel* in 1890 and Newell Dunbar's *Das Ewigweibliche (The Ever-Womanly)* in 1904, did serious political and cultural work.

Does this collection of plays published in American periodicals constitute a distinct and separate body of work from what was being produced on-stage? Though that would be too great a claim and too sweeping a generalization, nonetheless there are critical points of difference worth noting. In his history of post–Civil War to World War II theatre, Thomas Postlewait sets forth eight key determinants of American theatre: the expansive entrepreneurial capitalist system of production and distribution, the representation of women, the complex relationship between stage and screen, the star system, ethnicity, theatrical touring, the demographic shift from a rural to an urban society, the primacy of stories of successful struggle and happy resolution, and blackface performance ("Hieroglyphic" 131–35). How do the plays in periodicals "map" onto this template? Whether one includes the non-American plays or not, there are marked differences, in large measure because Postlewait concludes that the emerging theatre was part of "a process whereby a democratic or mass culture enters into a new kind of spectatorship, an optical culture defined by the reign of the eye and the seduction of images" ("Hieroglyphic" 188). The obvious salient differences between the stage and page, I will argue, depend on the difference between a play to be read and a play to be produced and, in some instances, the degree to which the readers were willing to perform the material in their parlors. Certainly the plays in periodicals are the products of entrepreneurial publishing enterprises, variously represent women and, to a lesser degree, ethnic "types," and share an urban focus. But even many of the American plays take on serious problems and do not resolve easily. As well, the startling absence of African Americans as playwrights or characters marks the most significant difference between periodical and production practice. If the theatre of this period was primarily visual, the drama in periodicals was primarily verbal and aural. Though often complemented by illustrations, the American plays as well as the foreign plays dramatize situations through accessible language and dialogue. For all these reasons, it is possible to mark dramatic literature, American or otherwise, in American periodicals as a singular body of work, a separate canon, needing to be understood in its primary context as part of periodical culture.

It is worth noting another difference: the writers Montrose Moses cites as representing American drama from 1888 until 1900—Bronson Howard, James Herne, Steele MacKaye, David Belasco, William Gillette, Augustus Thomas, and Clyde Fitch—are absent from the periodicals as dramatists. What was true of the nineteenth century was also true of the early twentieth century; the American stage successes of the day were not represented by their work as dramatists in the periodicals (though Europeans were). None of them published a play in the periodicals though they were present as subjects of discussion about the drama and theatre or their productions were reviewed. Therefore, it is possible to make a distinction between plays that were seen in theatre and plays that were understood to be read as dramatic texts in the periodicals.

How significant were the American playwrights in the periodicals? *The Cambridge History of English and American Literature* (1907– 1921) bibliography lists twenty-two American playwrights as "the most important dramatists of the period between 1860–1918": George Ade, David Belasco, Dion Boucicault, Bartley Campbell, Henry Guy Carleton, George M. Cohan, Rachel Crothers, Augustin Daly, William C. DeMille, Clyde Fitch, William Gillette, Edward Harrigan, James A. Herne, Howard Bronson, William Dean Howells, Charles Hoyt, Charles Klein, Percy MacKaye, Steele MacKaye, Brander Matthews, Edward Sheldon, and Augustus Thomas. Of this pantheon, only William Dean Howells appeared as a playwright in the American periodicals. Likewise, most of the American dramatists who published in the periodicals cannot be found in the standard histories of drama from Quinn to Bigsby. The distinguished European dramatists such as Shaw, Galsworthy, and Yeats were better represented though histories of drama are silent on their presence in American periodicals. In fact, many of the dramatists in the periodicals would have been well-known to their readers because they often were widely published in the periodicals. For instance, between 1900 and 1904, Josephine Dodge Daskam Bacon, author of *The First of October (Harper's* 1904) and *The Twilight of the Gods (Forum* 1915), published sixty-two poems and essays and was the subject of six profiles in several periodicals. Likewise, George Abiah Hibbard, author of *A Matter of Opinion (Scribner's* 1900), published countless short stories in *Harper's, Scribner's, Century, The Saturday Evening Post* and *Everybody's Magazine.*

Most of the dramatists were either American or English, though with the onset of the war, national identity mattered less. Some dramatists appeared in periodicals on both sides of the Atlantic, and some awareness of transatlantic circulation and transmission of periodical materials is necessary, of course, for a complete understanding of the process of cultural dissemination. Frank Mott, in his history of American magazines, points to the fact that as early as 1886 *Harper's, Century,* and *Scribner's* were dominating the market in England (*History 1885–1905* 229). Given the range of subject matter, it is clear that many of the dramatists understood their work to be addressing global and modern issues. Additionally, though I refer to the authors in this study as "dramatists," because I am considering only the plays they published in these periodicals, it should be understood that most of the authors wrote in several genres and, in many cases, the distinction would not have meant very much either to them or their readers. Two examples will serve. Edith Wharton published two plays, *Copy* and *Pomegranate Seed*, in *Scribner's* but contributed extensively to American periodicals as a short story writer. Another case in point is John Galsworthy whose *Little Dream, Hallmarked*, and *The Sun* were the only three plays he published in this group of periodicals but who, like Wharton, contributed in other genres to American periodicals. Often writers appeared early in their careers as playwrights but went on to be better known for other work. Sada Cowan published two plays in *Forum, Illumination*, a monologue, in 1912, and *In the Morgue* in 1916, but would be much better known later for her screenwriting; between 1919 and 1939, she wrote thirty-two filmscripts, from *The Woman Undercover* to *Stop, Look and Love*. Lester Luther, author of the minimalist anti-war *"Law"* published in *Forum* in 1915, was a character actor in 1940s films including *Adam's Rib, The Red Menace*, and *Masquerade in Mexico*. Nina Wilcox Putnam, whose *Orthodoxy* was published in *Forum* in 1914, became well known for her work in *The Saturday Evening Post* and *Cosmopolitan* between 1919 and 1932 as well as for her children's books such as *Sunny, Funny Bunny* and, later, film scripts.

One might expect the five great European moderns—Ibsen, Strindberg, Chekhov, Shaw, and Yeats—to have a strong presence in the periodicals; however, though Ibsen was the most discussed of the European dramatists, none of his work appeared in the periodicals under consideration. Neither did the plays of Chekhov and Strindberg, who otherwise also received a lot of attention through reviews and essays. The more general stance against those writers was explained by John Corbin in 1907: "As for the plays from the Continent, two influences combined to invalidate them. The growth of native feeling in our audiences rendered the old method of false and specious adaptation powerless; and, with the growth of realism and the literary sense abroad, the plays themselves were becoming more and more difficult to transpose into terms of American life . . . . The newer order of dramatists—Ibsen, Sudermann, Hauptmann, Capus, Brieux, Donnay, Lavedan and others—were on the whole impossible, at once because of their greater intellectuality, their more local and individual presentation of life, and the gloominess or unmorality of their themes" (635). There were exceptions, though. As a poet understood to be dramatizing the "Celtic folk," Yeats was uncontroversial and, more important, could be appropriated for American nativist ends; two of his plays, *The Shadowy Waters* and *The Hour-Glass,* appeared in *North American Review* and *The Green Helmet* in *Forum.* Shaw also proves to be an exception as three of his comedies, *Androcles and the Lion, Pygmalion,* and *Great Catherine* appeared in *Everybody's Magazine* during the period he was under attack for his views on the war.

Obviously one cannot tell the story of drama in periodicals without considering the reader. Considerable work has been done on the subject of the reader of periodicals, though not the reader *of drama* in those periodicals. Of the reader of nineteenth-century periodicals in general, the editors of *Nineteenth-Century Media and the Construction of Identities* argue that regular engagement with periodicals "made the nineteenth-century reader part of a clearly definable, and defining, textual community with its own ideologies, social aspirations, and cultural assumptions" managed by a press that was "able both to reflect and to mediate social consciousness" (Brake et al. 3). This group of readers and consumers Richard Ohmann characterizes as the "professional-managerial class," Richard Brodhead as the "postbellum elite," and Nancy Glazener as "bourgeois." It is important to keep in mind that because each periodical created and maintained its own "textual world," a reader who read several magazines could enter multiple worlds, facing not necessarily comfortable homogeneity but possibly diversity of forms, discourses, and ideologies. That said, nonetheless the periodicals under consideration assumed a certain social formation, characterized especially by a high degree of literacy and cultural awareness, and should be understood to be part of the cultural divide between "high" and "low brow" that Lawrence Levine has argued is characteristic of late-nineteenth-century American culture, a culture I mark as conflicted between being part of Howell's "Larger England" and being singularly, exceptionally "American." Be that as it may, in the plays, at least, there are no difficult concepts to grasp and, in terms of foreign languages, only a few foreign words appear occasionally and their context is sufficient for comprehension.

Historically, dramatic texts were less prevalent than other forms. The construction of the antebellum American reading public has been amply detailed in *A Fictive People* by Ronald J. Zboray, who stresses the reading public's preference for fiction over fact as it negotiated both national and individual identity. Michael Lund in *America's Continuing Story* makes a similar argument for a later period, 1850–1900, giving primacy to the national magazine industry, which "helped preserve regional and ethnic identity through fiction published in its pages at the same time that it asserted a national identity in the broad range of its subject matter and the great reach of its distribution" (111). In fact, I would argue that readers of periodicals approached dramatic texts not primarily as play scripts to be performed but more as "stories" in dramatic form amplified by illustrations and narrative stage directions. The readers and writers clearly were members of the culturally empowered, the educated and literate class actively engaged in the production and dissemination of authoritative positions on economic, political, and social questions. For want of a better term, for the most part, they were "middle class."

Though gender, race, and even to a large degree ethnicity were accepted as transparent categories during the transitional late nineteenth century, class was a mobile and unstable category; it had many markers and was processual, a way of defining oneself in relation and opposition to others. Of all the cultural work being done by the drama in the periodicals, this proves to be of paramount concern and the slipperiest to define. Stuart M. Blumin suggests that the "ascendancy" or "elevation" of an evolving and expanding group of "the middling sort" in the mid-nineteenth century became more finely articulated by the turn of the century because of "widening differences between the worlds of non-manual and manual work, the expansion of middle-class suburbanization, and the resumption and expansion of social and economic conflict that was phrased in class terms" (13). That attempted consolidation through discursive differentiation did not produce stable definitions; Phillip Barrish underscores the instability when he states that the middle class "felt constitutively insecure" (19). Sociologists Melanie Archer and Judith Blau conclude that the nineteenth-century middle class was "characterized by heterogeneity and a historically shifting social composition" (21). In Gramscian terms, class becomes hegemonic by attaining self-awareness of itself as a class, a process that necessitates distinguishing itself from others and by representing its interests and values as "natural." I do not argue that the middle class achieved static and absolute control but I do suggest that the drama in periodicals articulated class-specific assumptions and aspirations that were marked off from other (read "lower") classes as well as ethnic and racial groups. Each descriptor—white, Anglo-Saxon, American, non-immigrant, middle class—reinforces the other and attempts to create a coherent identity reinforced by the cultural work of the periodicals. It is important to remember that the controversies and differences aired in the periodicals are class specific; the middle class was a class arguing with itself, not a class trying to persuade or make connections with outsiders. This cultural work I call the dramatization of difference and distance.

According to Martin J. Burke, the great diversity of classifications and disagreement about class relations in late-nineteenth-century America was expressed in great detail in the Senate's 1883 investigations of the "Relations between Labor and Capital" at hearings designed to map out the semantic field of class and classes: "Over eight hundred pages of testimony from [workers and employers] demonstrate that there was not in 1883, any more than there had been in 1783, a single 'language' or lexicon of class in American public discourse" (160). Even specific terminology, which included "working class," "laboring class," "non-laboring class," "class rule," "class struggle," "oppressors and oppressed," "producers," "non-producers," "upper" and "lower class," "capital" and "ruling class," "privileged" and "permanent class," was the cause of definitional and interpretive agreement. Burke observes that by the turn of the century, the imagery of the "producing class," represented politically and symbolically by the Knights of Labor in the 1880s and which emerged in a rhetorical contest against the "nonproducers" in the Populist campaigns of the 1890s, "gave way to the dichotomies of the 'working class' versus 'capitalists,' and to the tripartite division of 'upper,' 'middle,' and 'lower' classes" but that "the ambiguities of this popular usage were no more readily clarified than those of the usage of the social critics" (161). It is not surprising, therefore, that "class" is understood by implication and is not openly discussed in the drama in the periodicals. At the same time, however, this indeterminacy frames and shapes the dramatic representations of class; the plays actively participate in the articulation, mediation, and management of class difference.

I use "middle class" much as Richard Ohmann describes it in *Selling Culture* as the "PMC," the professional-managerial class, a group he notes amounted to over a million people in 1880 (or seven percent of the population) and 3.5 million (or twelve percent) by 1910 (118–19). Small though the percentages were, this class exercised significant cultural influence especially over matters of consumption, taste, and the struggle to achieve the desired end of assured homogeneity and stability. Finally, though until recently class has provided the analytical frame for the historical account of men and gender for women, I want to stress class as primary for both, though I will mark gendered differences when relevant.

The readers of drama in the periodicals under consideration were understood to be familiar with the conventions of dramatic literature and, also, with a range of related issues. Dramatic criticism in periodicals, especially that concerning the nature and future of a specifically American drama, had a long history. Some of the most significant essays that were published prior to the last decade of the nineteenth century include James Kirke Paulding's "American Drama" in the *American Quarterly Review* (1827); contributions made by Augustin Daly, Edward Harrigan, John Grovesnor Wilson, Steele MacKaye, Bronson Howard, William Gillette, and William Winter to "American Playwrights on the American Drama" in *Harper's Weekly* (1889); and Dion Boucicault's essays for the *North American Review* between 1877 and 1899. The critics were united in a powerful desire to promote an indigenous American drama of high quality. Boucicault in "The Future American Drama" opened with this salvo: "There is not, and there never has been, a literary institution, which could be called the American Drama" (641). Daly's opening assertion was the same: "I do not consider that there is any such thing as an American school, or as American drama" (Daly et al. 97). This idea was expanded upon by Bronson Howard: "We now have simply a number of Americans writing plays in the English language" (98).

Though I focus primarily on dramatic texts in the context of the cultural work of the periodicals, it is important to remember that a significant context for reading plays was the extensive discussion about theatre as a business, an educational instrument, and as an art and numerous forms of interest in individual dramatists, traditional and modern, American and European. From 1896 to 1915, American dramaturgy was marked by a commitment to the commercial theatre under the control of the Theatrical Syndicate and, as a consequence, the stage was dominated by domestic comedies of manners, the realistic mirroring of the audience, an adherence to traditional values, and only a tentative engagement with serious social issues. The periodicals had hundreds of essays on these subjects and readers were exposed to a variety of critical opinions. From 1890 to 1899, Alfred Hennequin, James A. Herne, Thomas Dickinson, Hutchins Hapgood, and Brander

Matthews were the most prominent theatre critics. One of the most important statements on the drama at this time was Herne's "Art for Truth's Sake" in the *Arena* (1897). From 1900 to 1904, the prominent critical voices included Clayton Hamilton, Brander Matthews, Henry Arthur Jones, William Dean Howells, William Archer, Edmund Gosse, and Montrose J. Moses and from 1905 to 1909, Clayton Hamilton, James Huneker, H. A. Jones, William Archer, John Galsworthy, Arthur Symons, and Percy MacKaye established the critical norm.

Interestingly, dramatic texts comfortably inhabit both the literary and cultural milieu of periodicals—there are no apologies, no defensive postures, no ambivalences, no anxious rationales for inclusion of the genre. Drama is simply one of the many forms of creative expression— short story, novel, essay, poetry, illustration—that comprise the texture of a magazine. Sometimes a play is quite clearly marked in its presentation as a text to be read not performed, but at other times, it is clearly intended for a performance. Sometimes that performance is imagined to be by amateurs and confined to the home, at other times it is understood that the play has been or could be performed on a professional stage. The term itself—drama—proves to be slippery. In the periodicals, a dramatic text may be the conventional and familiar combination of scene, characters, and dialogue, but it may also be only a dialogue or a monologue or a plot summary combined with dialogue or an extended descriptive reading accompanied by excerpts.

Readers of periodicals were exposed also to a wide variety of dramatic styles: plays could be one-act, full-length, or merely a sketch of a page or two; they could be the broadest farce or parody in colloquial prose or the "highest" tragedy in elevated language; they could be in blank or rhymed verse or prose; they could be conventional melodramas or romances or "modern" experiments; they could be historical or contemporary; they could be plain text or illustrated with line drawings or photographs. This rich profusion contributed to the readers' broad understanding of the "dramatic." I have already noted Postlewait's expansionist revision of the standard assessment of the period in which he argues for greater attention to the complexities of genre ("From" 53). Certainly, even if one looked only at the American plays in the periodicals, a wide range of styles and subjects are evident. For my purposes, the essential point is that readers of periodicals were exposed to wide varieties of dramatic experience as well as to extended discussions about the merits and demerits of both drama and theatre as well as hundreds of reviews of productions. Readers were dramatically if not theatrically literate.

Furthermore, the theatre itself and its worn-out dramatic conventions were the subjects of several plays: John Kendrick Bangs's *The Fatal Message* (*Harper's* 1896), Tudor Jenks and Duffield Osborne's *The Baron's Victim* (*Harper's* 1898), Sir William S. Gilbert's *Trying a Dramatist* (*Century* 1911), *"Fanny's Second Play"* (*Bookman* 1912), and Helen Van Campen's *The Musical Comedy Rehearsal* from her " 'Life on Broadway' " series (*McClure's* 1913). All of these assume a working knowledge of, if not also weariness with, the stale conventions of melodrama, life on the other side of the proscenium arch, the lower-class position of those who work in the theatre, and the biases of critics. As Bruce McConachie has established, "melodrama was ubiquitous in American culture between 1820 and 1870," and readers of newspapers and periodicals also would have been exposed to portraits of actors and to reviews of productions (ix). That readers were expected to appreciate the "inside" jokes of these plays suggests a degree of familiarity if not sophistication about theatre and drama and, perhaps, a desire for something different.

Bangs's *The Fatal Message* sets up the comic struggles of a group of amateurs rehearsing a dreadfully clunky melodrama, a scene no doubt familiar to readers from their own drawing rooms. Tudor Jenks and Duffield Osborne's *The Baron's Victim* is a much cleverer piece in that the characters speak directly to the audience, critiquing "the mellow drama" as they perform it. For instance, the maid explains that her "duty is to amuse the audience while they are coming late, slamming seats, and rustling their programmes. I have nothing to say, because if I had it couldn't be heard until the theatre parties settle down and keep quiet; hence I merely dust around until the entrance of dummy number two" (645). This metatheatrical romp takes on everything from bad acting to clichés of speech to audience reactions, also scripted. Sir William S. Gilbert's *Trying a Dramatist* puts a play called "Lead" on trail in a criminal court where it is charged by the actors with every conceivable crime from having long and tedious speeches and unrealistic scenes to not being an adaptation from a French play. At the end, the judge decides that the author has been mistreated by the actors and the theatre manager and that in future he should have a direct control over the production of his work. Helen G. Van Campen also makes fun of actors in *"Life on Broadway": The Rehearsal of a Musical Comedy* in which vain, talentless, and egocentric character types (Bill Bawler, Sadie Skitter, Vera Volante) bicker about how many lines they will get and how far down stage they can be; the satire is underscored by May Wilson Preston's illustrations, which depict the coarseness and vulgarity of the cast. Van Campen, as Helen Green, also wrote comic prose pieces, leaning heavily on dialect, about Vaudeville for *McClure's* and the dramatizations were similar, marking a distinct class separation between vaudeville and "legitimate" theatre. In *In Vaudeville*, for instance, a "wop" performer and his "peop," his troupe of chimpanzees, disturbs a boarding house despite the man's insistence that "My companee are educate. They lady an'gentlemans" (395). *Fanny's Second Play* imitates George Bernard Shaw's poke at English theatre critics in *Fanny's First Play*, by setting up equally unimaginative American critics trotting out their predictable assessments: "Ava Dixon" adores anything Belasco produces, "William Novemdecember" bemoans the death of Shakespeare, and "Fenemey" likes only plays by foreigners and roasts all plays by Americans, especially young ones. Taken collectively, these plays dramatize the subjects of concern extensively debated in the essays in the periodicals such as the need for good American drama, the difference between a "high" culture and a "low," the need for critical fair mindedness, and the tyranny of managerial control.

The simplest full dramatic form in the periodicals is the monologue, a narrative form closest to the character-based short story with which the reader would have been very familiar. Sada Louise Cowan's *Illumination* in *Forum* (1912) is a highly emotional, introspective interior monologue by a young woman on the eve of a serious operation deeply regretting a life not lived to the fullest. She describes the comings and goings of the medical personnel as the night passes in highly compressed time and faces the morning in dread and with a plea to God. Neith Boyce's *Maddalena Speaks* in *Forum* (1914) is in a similar vein, though in this monologue other characters are understood to be present and speaking to Maddalena, an Italian wet nurse who has been "sold" by her husband to an Englishwoman whose baby she has poisoned. An indictment of the rich, the monologue points up the sharp discrepancies between two women, both new mothers who ought to have much in common; money, in effect, creates such distance that the wealthy woman does not accord the wet nurse any human dignity: "But you never thought I had a heart!," Maddalena cries out to the Signora, "I was only a poor animal, and you had bought me" (106). Boyce (1872–1951), married to Hutchins Hapgood, was part of the Provincetown circle and the author of four plays, *Constancy* (1914), *Enemies* (1916), *The Two Sons* (1916), and *Winter's Night* (1916). She would have been known to readers of periodicals as the author of poems, some novelettes (*Provident Woman* and *Undertow* in *Lippincott's*), as well as short stories and essays in *McClure's, Harper's Weekly*, and *American Magazine*.

In a similar vein, the townspeople and clergy in Nina Wilcox Putnam's one-act *Orthodoxy* in *Forum* (1914) voice only their "secret minds," "the private thought of the moment," in a savage indictment of religious hypocrisy (801). Contrasting actions with words, Putnam dramatizes the false piety of a community corrupted by commercial goals; the minister preaches greed: "Happy is the man that findeth cunning and getteth unscrupulous" and the congregation replies: " For the merchandise of it is begotten of the merchandise of silver, and the gain thereof, fine gold" (812).

Monologues more often served comic ends. May Isabel Fisk wrote twenty-two monologues, nearly all of them spoken by a self-absorbed, selfish middle-class woman, for *Harper's* between 1903 and 1914. Clearly Fisk imagined or hoped that these comic pieces might also be performed because each one is marked "stage rights reserved." Also a light comedy mocking women's unstoppable loquaciousness, Marguerite Merington's *A Gainsborough Lady: A Christmas Masque* (*Scribner's* 1902) could easily have been performed by amateurs because the actors, framed as subjects in paintings, have only to gesture not act, and the rhyming verse, spoken only by the woman, would have been easy to memorize. Likewise, *Special Delivery* (*Harper's* 1904) by Van Tassel Sutphen was written for one performer. A woman believing herself to be meeting a painter for her first sitting mistakenly enters another man's room with an invisible chaperone to whom she talks, snoops through his things, believes herself to be have been betrayed, and finally discovers that she is in the wrong room. All of these monologues are lavishly illustrated, offering the reader models of dress and display; the addled snoop in *Special Delivery*, for instance, is portrayed in six "attitudes" in an elaborate hat, embroidered gown, pearls, a fur muff, and trailing fur boa, presumably to stir acquisitive interest in the reader/consumer.

Deportment and decorum were significant values for the middle class, and because plays offered models of social intercourse, they added an important dimension to the cultural work also being promoted by books of etiquette. The "tale *dialogue*" in which two or more speakers interacted was a prominent feature of the periodicals. Henry James's dramatic career could be said to have started in the periodicals with the dramatic form. In April 1869 his short dialogue, *Pyramus and Thisbe*, appeared in *Galaxy, Still Waters* in the *Balloon Post* in April 1871, and *A Change of Heart* in the January 1871 issue of the *Atlantic Monthly*. James favored dialogue or, more exactly, as an unhappy reviewer said, " 'polite conversation' but failed to write it in such a way as to include the audience as well as the actors." Furthermore, as another critic noted, he imitated French comedies (Tucker 220). *An Animated Conversation* in *Scribner's* (1889) is a case in point. It opens with a classic Jamesian wry observer who sets the scene in a lengthy narrative introduction and then turns to dialogue for dramatizing the lack of common sense and intellect of his characters. The narrative is an acerbic commentary on those who believe themselves to hold "ideas," but the play is lifeless and stiff; arch and empty banter lacking dramatic tension pass for action. Clearly such lifeless stuff was too far removed from the readers' interests or experience to be successful.

William Dean Howells fared better with the drama in general and the "tale *dialogue*" in particular because he had a broader dramatic range and an abiding commitment to invigorating American drama with realism. As Brenda Murphy explains: "Howells tried to put realism into the dramatic form itself, and although most of his plays are either farces with simple linear structures or straightforward comedies, he also experimented with the discussion play (*Out of the Question*), the drama of pathos (*Bride Roses*), the philosophical dialogue (*The Mother and the Father*), the burlesque (*Saved: An Emotional Drama*), and two original forms he called the 'mystery play' (*The Impossible*) and the 'farce tragedy' (*Self-Sacrifice*)" (*American Realism* 71). Many of Howells' plays also are dialogues. *Self-Sacrifice: A Farce Tragedy* (*Harper's* 1911) is a series of exchanges between pairs of shifting characters, never more than two to a scene. *Indian Giver* (*Harper's* 1897) and *A Previous Engagement* (*Harper's* 1895) follow a similar pattern of conversations among a changing roster of characters. As Ackerman notes, "Howells is totally uninterested in 'dramatic' plots" (143). There is very little physical description or stage business, the emphasis being almost solely on character and revealing the intentions, emotions, and anxieties expressed in common speech and decorous behavior, but the plays are lively, have accessible characters and familiar discourse, and are brightened with humor. In Edith Wharton's *Copy: A Dialogue* in *Scribner's* (1900), an exercise in unspoken longings, two famous middle-aged writers parry about their romantic past together with the object of retrieving the love letters for their memoirs.

It is worth noting that the dialogue and setting format also was used in (or was modeled on) published interviews. For instance in a "Real Conversation" between William Archer and the playwright Mrs. Craigie (John Oliver Hobbes) in the *Critic* (1901) the "scene" is her drawing-room, the "period" is tea-time, and the "characters' lines" are formatted as if the piece were a play. From this perspective, a social conversation could be understood as "theatre," formal, scripted, and "dramatic" which the reader would enter as if reading a play, and, conversely, a dramatic dialogue could be readily appreciated as a social "text" that the participant could "read." In this way, dramatic dialogues and social intercourse as represented in the periodicals were mutually reinforcing and, of course, any danger of (or opportunity for) authentic, unmediated behavior was eliminated.

Anthony Hope's *A Life Subscription*, one in the "Dolly Dialogue" series in *McClure's* (1901), represents a simple commercial response to commercial success. According to *McClure's* chronicler, although some of the magazine's fiction paralleled in theme and seriousness the factual articles, McClure did not hold fiction to the same stringent criteria as the investigative articles (Wilson, H. S., *McClure's Magazine and the Muckrackers* 116). As a consequence, all he asked was that it be interesting and exciting, hence the proliferation of stories about firemen and train engineers, the importance of railroads being key in the American modern imaginary. McClure was also savvy about picking up English writers; the novels and stories of Robert Louis Stevenson, Rudyard Kipling, Arthur Conan Doyle, and Anthony Hope (Hawkins) met the criteria for entertainment. Initially, Hope made his reputation with the Ruritanian romance *The Prisoner of Zenda* (1894), but he also had a huge success with the *Dolly Dialogues*, a series of witty sparring between Miss Dolly Foster (later Lady Mickleham) and Mr. Samuel Carter. First published during 1894 in the *Westminster Gazette*, the *Dolly Dialogues* were collected as a book in London in 1899 and in America in 1901 (Mallet 82). Light, romantic, and sophisticated, the dialogues are marked by triviality and underlying sexual tension as the couple cleverly deflects any open statement of feeling. The charm lies in the clearly nuanced verbal play between a couple who understand how the material and sexual aspects of their bourgeois respectability must be negotiated even though they are loathe to admit to it. The dialogue in *A Life Subscription* is one of the additional pieces Hope wrote for *McClure's* to answer the demand for his insatiable audience; not only did Hope publish the *Dolly Dialogues*, he also performed them.

Another significant experience of the dramatic text was the "directed" reading. The first dramatic text to be published in *Scribner's Magazine* was *An Animated Conversation* by Henry James in March 1889. Though James begins with a long conventional narrative paragraph in which he sets up the conceit that the narrator is reporting what was told to him by one of the interlocutors, he quickly moves into dialogue, with this rationale: "The colloquy took a turn which, little dramatic though it may appear, I can best present in scenic form" (371). The typical Jamesian narrator—analytical and distanced—is removed but not before he has carefully set up the reader as "judge" of an exchange that he has introduced as lacking "general sense." This kind of prefatory material was the exception. A more common version of such a "directed" reading occurred in the hybrid form, the extended critical summary combined with excerpts from the play itself. Five examples of such extended directive readings that can be found in the periodicals include: of Ibsen's *Brand* in 1890 and *John Gabriel Borkman* in 1897, of Arthur Schnitzler's *The Wife* in *Current Literature* in 1905, and of Lord Dunsany's *The Gods of the Mountains* in 1914.

Wilbur Cross's reading of Ibsen's *Brand* in *Arena* (1890) provides the "service" of an "outline" as well as a correction of the prevailing condemnation of Ibsen's work by praising Ibsen for his "fearless" diagnosis of social ills (81). Cross turns the dramatic poem into a lengthy prose narrative; the result is a very detailed, very prosaic transcription of the action of the play. In Cross's hands, *Brand* becomes a short story, nothing more. The *Arena*, a progressive periodical, presumably would have only been concerned with the social message and not the art, dramatic, literary, or theatrical of the poem. William Carpenter's more complicated summary and interpretation of Ibsen's *John Gabriel Borkman* in *Bookman* (1897) is in three parts. First there is a long plot summary of the play, which concludes with an excerpt between Mrs. Borkman and

Ella from the end of the play; second, there is an interpretation of the symbolism and an explanation of the play's social lesson; third, there is an appraisal of the play's literary merits. "*John Gabriel Borkman* is a play that reads as well as the Norwegian papers say it acts," Carpenter notes, praising the play's construction, use of language, and verisimilitude (159). Clearly Carpenter's expectation is that because readers are unlikely to see a production, they are more likely to encounter only the dramatic text and, therefore, he is at pains to preserve both the thematic and literary qualities.

Charles Vale's "Lord Dunsany's Gods" in *Forum* (1914) is an extensive appreciation prompted by three readings of Lord Dunsany's *The Gods of the Mountain*, first produced in London in 1911 and just published in the United States in a modern drama series edited by Edwin Björkman. Following the editor's lead, Vale reads the play, excerpting lengthy passages and pointing to the "deep and rich symbolism," the elements of "modern psychology," and the ways in which the play suggests both "the intimate unity and appalling vastness of life" (784). Vale responds to the play and others in the collection only as a reader, not as a potential theatregoer. The periodical reader, of course, has no opportunity to make his or her own judgment because Vale is selective and directive. In this way, the play is reviewed as a novel would be.

Current Literature published many such directed readings. One example will suffice: the conclusion to Arthur Schnitzler's *The Wife* was excerpted in November 1905. The prefatory introduction sets Schnitzler up as "the Austrian Hauptmann," positions him as "a modern of moderns," alerts the reader that he is "half decadent" but always "polished and graceful," and advises that he deals with " 'dangerous' subjects without offending the most delicate susceptibilities." His subject matter is explained: he writes about two kinds of women, the "average type, which appears in a most unenviable light," and her opposite, "endowed with intellectual qualities that are almost masculine." The reader is assured that though Schnitzler accepts the second type with "approbation" it is "never with admiration." Finally, the reader is given an assessment of Schnitzler's achievements by his biographer, Dr. Hans Landsberg, who positions the poet as one above seeking " 'blind success and sordid gain" and whose art is " 'noble and glorious' " (Anonymous, "Arthur" 553). Therefore, when the reader gets to the play, she knows how to interpret Olga as well as the dead Eveline.

This lengthy description of summaries and excerpts is part and parcel of a necessary understanding not only of the variety of dramatic materials readers would have confronted but as well of the way in which a play might be "packaged" for the readers. One of the most significant aspects of that "packaging" was the illustration. Of the 125 dramatic texts in this study, 66 were illustrated, though some periodicals, notably the *Forum*, did not illustrate plays. The illustrations took several forms from the most prevalent, the line drawing or full illustration, to the infrequent photograph. None gave any indication of a stage; the plays were illustrated in the same way as the short stories and novels, that is, the characters are "naturalized" in their domestic settings.

When a play was illustrated, the images were integral to amplifying and directing reader's response as well as setting the tone. For instance, the Parisian poster style, studied frivolity, and cosmopolitan sensibility of Edward Penfield would have alerted readers to the spirited sophistication of Van Tassel Sutphen's *First Aid to the Injured* in *Harper's* (1896). Furthermore, because illustrators usually worked for several periodicals, their images and styles would have been familiar. For instance, Everett Shinn, a member of the New York realists' "Ash Can School," produced light, insubstantial drawings for *McClure's*, *Hearst's*, *Everybody's*, and *Century* but A. B. Frost was best known for the naturalistic hunting and shooting illustrations he made for *Harper's*, *Scribner's*, and *Life*. Seeing that Arnold Bennett's *The Honeymoon* in *McClure's* (1911) was illustrated by Frederic Dorr Steele, who was known for his *The Return of Sherlock Holmes* frontispieces for *Collier's* (1903–1905), the reader correctly would anticipate an adventure involving the upper class (see figure 1.1). An upper-class situation also was signaled when a play was illustrated by Charles Dana Gibson, Howard Chandler Christy, or their imitators depicting the "aristocratic" Anglo-Saxon. The illustrations of the lower classes in particular underscored the sharp social difference and distance the middle class wanted to maintain. W. Glackens's sketches for Helen Green's *In Vaudeville*, for instance, depict a boarding house owner as a heavy, sour-faced woman under which is the caption "A party has a right to add more tong [tone] to their own joint" (392). The final image shows the house in chaos because eight chimpanzees are running wild (see figure 1.2). Clearly, no respectable middle-class home would ever be inhabited by such coarse and vulgar creatures, human or animal, and the whole is presented as

Figure 1.1   Frederic Dorr Steele for Arnold Bennett's *The Honeymoon* (*McClure's* 1911)

comic nonesense. As well as conditioning the readers' responses, illustrations also allowed readers to "edit" their choices and to be spared any surprises. The illustrations work in much the same way as the directed readings, eliminating any possibility for "incorrect" interpretation.

When the illustrator was credited and established, the name also carried implications of associated cultural value for the play. For instance, Olive Tilford Dargan's verse play, *The Woods of Ida: A Masque* in *Century* (1907), set forty years before the fall of Troy, is introduced by a "Greek" frieze and illustrated with three paintings by Sigismond de Ivanowski. In a reversal of the normal practice, Jehen George Vibert (1840–1902)

"'A PARTY HAS A RIGHT TO
ADD MORE TONG TO THEIR
OWN JOINT'"

Figure 1.2   Two illustrations by W. Glackens for Helen Green's *In Vaudeville* (*McClure's* 1910)

wrote *The Sick Doctor*, scenes appropriating Molière's hypochondriac and his doctor, to dramatize his painting of the same title for *Century* (1896). The little comedy was one of three such exercises, the others being "The Delights of Art," in which a painter carries on a dialogue with Phoebus, and "Coquelin as 'Mascarelle,' " in which a painter talks through the process of developing a character.

Occasionally, illustrations also served as templates for amateur productions and, more often, for models of correct behavior. Marguerite Merington's *A Gainsborough Lady*, a verse printed in a center column, is flanked by the poses the man and the woman hold during the woman's monologue. The stage direction, "Gentleman disclaims the epithet," is depicted in the adjacent sketch (66). The illustrations for Gleason's *Signal Service* show how a young man in evening dress should stand at ease against a fireplace mantel, how a flirting lady holds her fan, and exactly how much distance should be maintained between a couple sharing a sofa. The illustrations to the play, therefore, serve two functions simultaneously, one dramatically situtational, the other prescriptively social. The illustrations accompanying the plays complement the cover art, the photographs, and the advertisements in the periodicals, all of which formed a dense network of images designed to convey social values.

Finally, it could be suggested that the illustration for a play, in so far as it replicated a *tableau*, participated in the development of moving pictures. Ben Brewster and Lea Jacobs have written convincingly about the influence of *tableaux* on early filmmaking as signaling "a set of functions performed by the stage picture: to punctuate the action, to stress or prolong a dramatic situation, and to give a scene and abstract or quasi-a llegorical significance" (35). Two early examples of the union of pictorial representation and play anticipated film: Alexander Black's "Photography in Fiction: 'Miss Jerry,' The First Picture Play" in *Scribner's* (1895) and "The Camera and the Comedy" in *Scribner's* (1896).

With *Miss Jerry*, Black (1859–1940) created what he called a "picture play," a partnership of monologue and photographs, but which *The Critic* noted "might with equal justice be called an illustrated short story" (249). Black wanted "to illustrate art with life" by using photographs and, more than that, make the text secondary to the pictures. By combining a fictional story with pictures of "the actual life of the city," Black wanted to make the pictures "analogous to the action of a play" (348). The goal was to free the text from the necessity of description and to concentrate on the characters' thoughts and words and to halve the reading time for a novelette. On the page, the text of *Miss Jerry* occupies one-third to the pictures' two-thirds. Each page has about three illustrations running parallel to a column of text, a conventional melodramatic romance. Despite Black's stated intentions, of the thirty-three pictures only four are set outdoors and the rest are quite conventional stage *tableaux*. The last photograph is of the "cast" lined up for a "curtain call." In "The Camera and the Comedy," Black describes the problems facing the construction of *A Capital Courtship*, which was produced in April 1896. He clearly knows that his work is transitional, "pending the perfection of the vitascope, the cinematograph, and kindred devices," and is challenged by the need to correctly balance the text with the photographs (606). The essay, illustrated with photographs of President Grover Cleveland in his office, focuses exclusively on the problems challenging the photographer and offers the reader no accompanying story.

In sum, the dramatic genres, the competencies required to read them, and the very language of the drama participate directly in the layered coding of the periodicals. All are part of the bourgeois project of nation formation, the production of a class and race that attempt to secure exclusivity as well as dominance and that are predicated on a univocal agreement about what constitutes the core national unit. The nationalization of this core community is dependent on a shared culture and the commerce that sustains it. But the more imagined this community is shown to be, the more unstable and anxious it proves to be at base; the more closely one examines the voices joining in the national conversation, the more its conflicted, discontented, and polyvocal nature surfaces. The "fictive ethnicity," to reinvoke Etienne Balibar's term, is predicated on the socialization of individuals, on the transference of social class to nationality, on the naturalizing of one racial community, and on language as the national language. The plays in periodicals are part of an ideological apparatus producing both Anglo-Saxons and speakers of "correct" English as the desirable and necessary citizens of an America under siege. Despite the veneer of unified beliefs and practices, in many instances, the "felt sense" of the nation proves to be anxiety and conflict thinly dramatized as harmony and unity.

2. Cultures of Social Distance and Difference ❧

Frank Mott's "reflection theory" of the periodicals as "mirrors" of society, as Scott E. Casper has noted, has given way to "a more reciprocal vision of the relationships among magazines (and their editors and publishers), authors and literary works, and reading publics" (262). Therefore, one way to read the dramatic texts in periodicals is to contextualize them as entertaining and edifying literature being brought to the attention of a reading public, a largely bourgeois, upper- and middle-class audience, in contiguity and conversation with the essays, poems, fiction, illustrations, and advertisements in the "highbrow" and "middlebrow" periodicals as well as the "quality" and "ten-cent" magazines. In this context, an important critical task is to try to recover what was at stake for the reader and for the nation in the publication and circulation of dramatic texts in periodicals and to determine how they participated in and were instrumental in producing the national imaginary. Of particular interest are the ways in which the plays established their own cultural zone, which marked social distance and difference, separating Americans into groups according to race, ethnicity, and especially class. When readers entered this privileged zone, they temporarily participated in an artificially stable but inherently troubled and threatened network of closed social relations, a fictive nation of secure exclusion.

In *Cultures of Letters: Scenes of Reading and Writing in the Nineteenth-Century*, Richard Brodhead likens the cultural zone produced by the "quality journals" (*Atlantic Monthly, Century Magazine*, and *Harper's Monthly*) to the classical museum or symphony orchestra, "a strongly demarcated high-status arena for high-artistic practice," part of the arsenal of a social elite arbitrating cultural (especially genteel) values (124). Certainly the readership was understood to be "cultivated" people not the working class. It was a privileged, leisured class still marked by Europhilia and, to an even greater degree, Anglophilia. Brodhead argues for an understanding of the "shared social space," of the ways in which literary production is bound up with a "distinct social audience," an audience identified not only by its "readerly interests" but also by "other unifying social interests as well" (4–5). Though Brodhead's particular concern is with the "quality" journals, the same argument could be made about the progressive journals such as *Forum* and the "ten-centers" such as *McClure's*. Each likeminded group constituted a "zone" of shared concerns, concerns that often overlapped with the contiguous "zones." I take seriously Brodhead's dictum that "nineteenth-century literary genres we are used to thinking of as free standing were not autonomous in their original cultural production but formed mutually supportive parts of a concerted textual program" (131). That "program" I understand to be at the very least a convergence of four primary cultural concerns: "American" nationalist cohesion, Anglo-Saxon racial identity and supremacy, Protestant middle-class formation, and the consolidation of the middle class as "cultivated" consumers. And all of these are marked by a tension between the desire to be singularly and exceptionally "American" and the equally compelling urge to remain part of what William Dean Howells called the "Larger England." The individual elements of this convergence and tension are not always as transparent as one might imagine and, with the passing of time, it becomes increasingly difficult to recapture the immediate pressing concerns of a particular cultural moment.

Dramatic texts, like all other texts in periodicals, including the advertisements, occupy part of that complex cultural matrix. There are two things to keep uppermost in mind. First, there are no "innocent" appearances in periodicals; every article, essay, poem, or play participated in the periodical's mission and was shadowed by an editorial agenda, which, for most periodicals, was supported by advertising. It is important to remember that periodicals were commodities and that many of them were thick with advertisements. In an examination of the rise of periodical studies, Sean Latham and Robert Scholes stress what they term "the hole in the archive," documenting the stripping that took place when magazines were bound in book form for libraries. They cite as one startling example *McClure's Magazine* for September 1898, which has nearly 100 pages of advertising, about the same as the number of pages devoted to text. Without the advertisements, however, the contemporary reader loses the full context and the cultural conversation. The loss is significant: "modern culture was created from a still-obscure alchemy of commercial and aesthetic impulses and processes. And this mixture was most visible in magazines . . . . The shift, at the turn of the nineteenth century, from periodicals supported by circulation to periodicals supported by advertising was crucial for modern culture" (521).

Another case in point is the *Century*, which was edited by Richard Watson Gilder from 1881 until his death in 1909. In 1890, the *Century's* circulation was about 200,000 and the advertising filled about 100 pages per issue. Under Gilder's leadership, according to Arthur John, *Century* "became a rallying point for conservatives seeking to stabilize and guide American society in a period of stress and change" (120). *Century*, along with *The Atlantic Monthly, Scribner's Magazine,* and *Harper's Monthly*, was a gatekeeper of culture, moral codes of conduct, gentility, Puritanism, and national optimism. Even in the years of vigorous Progressivism, the *Century's* position was "detached rather than participatory . . . descriptive rather than accusatory" (John 251). In the 1890s, the *Century's* position on the American stage was that it was seriously degraded, that feverish and unwholesome plays plagued social stability, and that the only remedy lay in returning to the ideal standards of the past and cultivating the classic drama.

Given this fixed position of elegiac conservatism, it is hardly surprising that most of the plays published in the *Century* between 1896 and 1915 are safe, "high" culture artifacts. J. G. Vibert's *The Sick Doctor* (1896) spins off of Molière, Josephine Daskam's *The Wanderers* (1901) is a romantic verse set in eighteenth-century Europe, Olive Dargan's *The Woods of Ida* (1907) is a masque about Troy in verse, and Louis Parker's *A Minuet* (1915) is a romance in verse set in Revolutionary France. The three comic plays, W. S. Gilbert's *Trying a Dramatist* (1911) and Tudor Jenks's *At the Door* and *Parried* (1899), uphold traditional values. The most politically engaged play, Marion Craig Wentworth's *War Brides* (1915), is also the most melodramatic and traditional of all the war plays published in the periodicals.

On the other hand, *Forum* gave a great deal of space to reform issues. Its editorial policy was guided by four principles: the publication of distinguished specialists on any given topic, the use of the symposium to encourage debate, the balancing of weighty material with lighter pieces, and meticulous editing. *Forum* featured extended political discussions on prohibition, feminism, divorce, civil service, prisons, and socialism as well as articles on *belles-lettres*, movements in the arts and literature, religion, and education. The twenty plays *Forum* published were all seriously engaged with social and political issues such as prostitution (Paula Jakobi's *Chinese Lily*) to feminism (George Middleton's *The Man Masterful*) to war (Laurence Vail's *The Inconveniences of Being Neutral*).

The problem for the contemporary reader is understanding exactly what is at stake with each essay or play, within each periodical, and among the periodicals. The turn-of-the-century periodical readers, on the other hand, might have been aware of at least some of the issues driving selection because those readers could have followed issues within a periodical and across periodicals. Three examples from the essays must serve. First, an issue might be debated within one periodical. For instance, in the July 1894 issue of *McClure's Magazine*, Hamlin Garland's "Homestead and Its Perilous Trades" was directly responded to by "L. W." in "Homestead as Seen by One of Its Workmen." Second, a response could be explicit across periodicals. For instance, after William Randolph Hearst bought *Cosmopolitan* in 1905, he ran a series of articles by Otheman Stevens in 1910 in defense of Mexico and its government, clearly designed, Mott points out, as "a reply to the 'Barbarous Mexico' articles in *Everybody's* and motivated by Hearst's Mexican interests" (493). Third, a response might have been implicit across periodicals. For instance, B.O. Flower wrote on Simon Pokagon, a prominent Native American, in "An Interesting Representative of a Vanishing Race" (*Arena* 1896), but a reader would have needed to go to the *Forum* for Simon Pokagon's own perspective in "The Future of the Red Man" (1897). This kind of complicated interlocking textual referentiality and dialogic exchange, a commonplace to the original readers, may be lost to contemporary readers and needs to be foregrounded in recovery work such as this project undertakes. It is imperative to keep this diversity uppermost because such conflicts and discussion are evidence of the rich polyvocal nature of the periodical culture.

For examples from the drama, I turn to the three plays of George Bernard Shaw published by *Everybody's Magazine: Androcles and the Lion* (September 1914), *Pygmalion* (November 1914), and *Great Catherine* (February 1915). Though Don Wilmeth and Christopher Bigsby say that Shaw received the same negative reception as did Ibsen, citing the *Sun* newspaper's characterization of his work as " 'a dramatized stench' " (5), Shaw was a ubiquitous presence in American periodicals from *Arena* and

The Atlantic to *Munsey's* and *McClure's* between 1890 and 1918 both as an author and as the subject of portraits and positive essays and reviews. *Everybody's Magazine*, founded in 1899 under the editorship of John O'Hara Cosgrave, was fully committed to investigative, or what Theodore Roosevelt testily called "muckraking," journalism (Regier 1). Between 1902 and 1912, *Everybody's Magazine* published many important exposés by well-known writers including Frank Norris on agricultural business practices, Upton Sinclair on the meat industry, Ambrose Bierce on the Navy, and Lincoln Steffans on organized business. According to Frank Mott, by 1903, *Everybody's Magazine* had a circulation of 150,000 and continued to be concerned with social injustices perpetrated by big business. The most famous assault was a series by Thomas Lawson, "Frenzied Finance," which ran for three years (July 1903–February 1908). Boosted by that success, circulation rose to over half a million by 1908 though it fell to nearly half that by 1911, a level that it maintained through the war years (*1905–1920* 72–87).

The three Shaw plays published in *Everybody's Magazine* are among his "amusing" plays but are also didactic, a feature that would have had clear appeal to the rising middle class engaged in self-improvement. More important, the publication of these plays came at a critical moment for Shaw. On June 28, 1914, Archduke Franz Ferdinand was assassinated at Sarajevo, and in five weeks Europe was at war. On November 7, 1914, Shaw published, in the *Nation*, "An Open Letter to the president of the United States of America," and a week later, a pamphlet entitled "Common Sense about the War" appeared as a supplement to the *New Statesman* for November 14, 1914 (Valency 329). Though the pamphlet was mainly a protest against militarism, it included some remarks in defense of German culture quickly appropriated by the German propaganda agencies and, as Valency observes, "the effect on Shaw was disastrous" (330). Shaw's plays were blacklisted, he was shunned by many newspapers, and he was declared *persona non grata* by the Dramatists League. Not only was every Englishman against him, as Henry Arthur Jones told him, but Americans, too, were appalled: "former President Theodore Roosevelt called him a 'blue rumped ape' and lumped him with 'the unhung traitor Keir Hardie' among a 'venomous' herd of socialists, all 'physically timid creatures.' " Granville Barker, in New York producing *Androcles and the Lion*, reported to Shaw that " 'You are not so loved here as you were' "

(Holroyd 354). That did not seem to trouble *Everybody's Magazine*, which had its own agenda for publishing Shaw.

Everybody's Magazine took the position that the United States should support Britain against Germany and favored compulsory military training. Former president Theodore Roosevelt contributed a prowar article, "America—On Guard!" in January 1915, Samuel Hopkins Adams wrote an essay on the dangers of German propaganda and American disloyalty, and the magazine created a new department, "The Poetry of the War." In January 1916, *Everybody's Magazine* published a symposium, "America's Neutrality as England Sees It." Among the twenty-one contributors were H. G. Wells, G. K. Chesterton, Mrs. Humphrey Ward, William Archer, and George Bernard Shaw. Shaw's contribution was terse, pragmatic, and pointed: "Neutrality is nonsense. 'Crushing Germany' is also nonsense . . . . The future lies with an alliance to which Britain, Germany, France, and the United States will be the first and indispensable allies" (12).

The first Shaw play to appear in *Everybody's Magazine* (1914), *Androcles and the Lion* could be understood as a "toga play," which the historian of the popular phenomenon explains was a term coined in 1895–1896 to identify "melodramas enacting conflict, persecution, and clashes in values and beliefs between early Christians or proto-Christians and their Roman oppressors" (Mayer x). In 1880, Lew Wallace's *Ben-Hur, a Tale of Christ*, closely followed by Henryk Sienkiewicz's *Quo Vadis?* firmly established religious melodrama as a popular genre. In Shaw's play, when the Christian heroine, Lavinia, loses her faith on the eve of her sacrificial martyrdom, she discovers God within herself and, though no longer loyal to Christ, she is willing to die for the divine individualist principle within herself. Shaw's polemic is couched in the sweet package of the comic fable. *Everybody's Magazine* was illustrated with Peter Newell's comic, cartoonish line drawings and more realistic photographs from the London production in which the echoes of pantomime are evident. Readers coming to the play certainly would have been familiar with Peter Newell, a famous illustrator of children's books such as *Topsys and Turvys* and a comic newspaper series, *The Naps of Polly Sleepyhead*, published in 1906 and 1907, and, as a consequence, would expect a light, fantastic play. *Androcles and the Lion* was first produced in Berlin in November 1912, in London in September 1913, and in New York in January 1915. Thus its American publication as "a fable play" in *Everybody's Magazine* preceded its American production. The preface written in December 1915, a Fabian interpretation of the New Testament in which Shaw denounced war and proposed a political policy based on non-Pauline Christian principles, did not appear in *Everybody's Magazine* nor did the appended epilogue about social evolution. The absence of preface and epilogue kept the play safely within the realm of entertainment and conservative Christianity.

Pygmalion, first produced in German in Vienna in October 1913, in London in April 1914, and in New York in October 1914, was hugely successful and was published simultaneously in *Everybody's Magazine* and in England in *Nash's and Pall Mall* in November 1914. One striking difference between the two is in the illustrations. The English version opens with a seated, opporturing Eliza, her basket at her feet, reaching up to proffer a flower to a standing man in an overcoat and hat; the scene is dark and realistic. The American version was illustrated by May Wilson Preston, well-known for her satiric cartoon sketches and for her suffragist work and illustrations. Her first depiction of Eliza, drawn in bold, energetic strokes, shows her standing alone, holding her basket, smiling and reaching out to an unseen potential customer. In short, the "American" Eliza is bold and vital, a proto-suffragette, compared to her more abject English counterpart.

Soon *Pygmalion* was being performed all over Europe in a variety of languages, making Shaw both prominent and wealthy. Shaw added a short preface about speech and class status when it was published: caste should be based on character and ability, not birth, and once free of class restrictions, the individual can rise: "social mobility is indispensable to the evolutionary process" (Valency 318). There was no preface or epilogue in *Everybody's Magazine*, but it did include Eliza's scandalous lines from the end of Act III: "Walk! Not bloody likely! (*Sensation.*) I am going in a taxi" (598). For good measure the lines were repeated as a caption to an illustration of the scene (see figure 2.1). One way to understand the appeal of the play to an American, middle-class audience of consumers is to turn to the ubiquitous critical observation that *Pygmalion* is a play about education. For instance, Maurice Valency observes, "Eliza learns not only how to produce upper-class sounds, but also, as a necessary by-product, how to be a self-sufficient and self-reliant person, traits for which she has already shown extraordinary native aptitude" (316–17). Because a culturally legitimating marker of class was good diction and correct speech, elocution, correspondence,

Figure 2.1 May Wilson Preston for Bernard Shaw's *Pygmalion* (*Everybody's Magazine* 1914)

and verse-recitation manuals were popular at this time. The advertising in *Everybody's Magazine* suggests a strong tie to self-improvement and self-education in matters of speech as well as general and vocational education; the index to advertisements for December 1914 lists thirty-one schools under "educational" including three for stutterers and one for "language phone method."

Class distinctions also mattered to the same audience. Part of the appeal of the play was, as Holroyd says: "the way in which the science of phonetics could pull apart an antiquated British class system" (325). "At a speech to the National Liberal Club in 1913, Shaw had called for a constructive social scheme for the creation of gentlemen—not the sham gentlemen of hereditary qualifications who lived in idleness, but a new breed of moral gentlemen who claimed a handsome dignified existence and subsistence from their country, who gave in return the best service of which they were capable and whose ideal was to give to their country more than they received from it" (Holroyd 327). As to the problematic ending, for the play's first publication in book form in 1916, Shaw added a sequel about Eliza's marriage, not to Henry Higgins but to Freddy Eynsford-Hill, and continued to revise the ending until he wrote the final version in 1939. In *Everybody's Magazine*, the play ends with Professor Higgins's assurance to his mother that Eliza will return to him after buying the tie and gloves as he ordered her to do when she left. Therefore, the play participates in the social norm promoted by the periodicals because Eliza's flirtation with real independence is cut short as—it was with so many American "girls"—in the periodicals by an appropriate marriage.

In November 1913 *Great Catherine* had a short run at London's Vaudeville and was not well received; the American premiere was in New York in November 1916, but the play had been published with a prefatory "apology" in *Everybody's Magazine* in February 1915. The appeal to democratic Americans is clear from Maurice Valency's characterization of the play as "an amusing and reasonably useful skit based on the notion that an English gentleman of traditional cut belongs in a museum among the respected vestiges of antiquity" (Valency 333). In the author's prefatory "apology," Shaw explains that his Catherine is Byron's Catherine. The small epigraph, tucked into Henry Raleigh's lively line illustration on the first page reads only: " 'In Catherine's reign, whom glory still adores.'— Byron" (193). To appreciate the significant ironic implications of Shaw's remarks, however, readers would have to have known that the next, and essential, line from *Don Juan* was "As greatest of all sovereigns and whores." Stripped of the necessary directive link between aristocratic whoring and politics, the play could pass as merely an inoffensive merry

"IN CATHERINE'S REIGN, WHOM
GLORY STILL ADORES." —*Byron*

Figure 2.2   Henry Raleigh for Bernard Shaw's *Great Catherine* (*Everybody's Magazine* 1915)

romp of comic stereotypes through the decadent court of eighteenth-century St. Petersburg. No doubt it did for the readers who did not know their Byron but the play would carry a pointed political message for those who did (see figure 2.2).

As with *Androcles and the Lion* and *Pygmalion*, the comic dimensions of *Great Catherine* are emphasized by the illustrations. The illustrator, Henry Raleigh, would have been as well-known to the readers as were Peter Newell and May Wilson Preston. He had worked as a sketch artist for the *San Francisco Examiner* and, after coming to William Randolph Hearst's attention, moved to New York and worked for *Harper's Bazaar, Saturday Evening Post*, and *Collier's* as well as *The American Weekly*, a Sunday supplement with a huge circulation and a predilection for scantily clad showgirls and tales of murder and suspense. Raleigh's illustrations of the court buffoonery and of the English diplomat's ineptness work in harmonious tandem with Shaw's introductory "apology" in which he refers to the "furious harlequinade with the monarch as clown" and the "Englishman as a fool" (194). For a democratic American public, such anti-monarchist sentiments, displacing class problems onto Europe, would have been most welcome.

The second thing to bear in mind about plays in periodicals is that the writers had specific cultural expectations of their readers; they could and did anticipate and play off a knowledge base now largely lost to the contemporary reader but that needs to be recovered for a better appreciation of the complex cultural work being done by the plays. I want to offer three examples of dramas that relied on readers to possess cultural literacies, and I deliberately have chosen work that might seem transparent at first glance: Margaret Cameron's *The Committee on Matrimony*, Marie Manning's *Nervous Prostration*, and Barrett Wendell's *Ralegh in Guiana*. The first, Margaret Cameron's one-act comedy, *The Committee on Matrimony* in *McClure's* (1903), opens with a relatively lengthy discussion between a courting couple, Robert and Phyllis, about Kipling's views on marriage, a discussion that sets the theme for the rest of the play. Robert begins with an encomium on Kipling's merits as a decorous writer: "he's keen and direct, with an apparently inexhaustible fund of humor and command of the English language that is simply marvelous. Moreover, he never goes into mawkish, morbid analysis of the commonplace, nor does he write unhealthy books which—to use his words— 'deal with people's insides from the point of view of men who have no stomachs' " (659). When Phyllis teases him about quoting Kipling as he would the Bible, Robert reaches for a book and reads aloud to her, insisting that "one can't open one of his books without finding something worth reading." Because Robert takes the passage to be sarcasm and Phyllis takes it to be straightforward, an argument is triggered between them that becomes the subject of the play, which continues with no further direct reference to Kipling.

That Robert does not identify the particular book by Kipling he is reading from suggests that the *McClure's* reader would know the passage: " 'How can a man who has never married; who cannot be trusted to pick up at the sight of a moderately sound horse; whose head is hot and upset with visions of domestic felicity, go about the choosing of a wife? He cannot see straight or think straight if he tries; and the same disadvantages exist in the case of a girl's fancies. But when mature, married, and discreet people arrange a match between a boy and a girl, they do it with a view to the future, and the young couple live happily ever after' " (659).

Margaret Cameron indeed could assume that her readers would recognize the passage as being from "Kidnapped," one of the stories in *Plain Tales from the Hills* (1888), because Kipling was one of what Frank Mott calls the "literary fevers of the nineties" ("Literary Fevers" 183) and William Dean Howells's "laureate of the Larger England." The lines, in fact, are from the opening paragraph of the story, though the first few sentences, which clarify that the Indian practice of arranged marriages between children is the actual subject, are deleted for the play. The second paragraph of "Kidnapped," in which the feasibility of a Matrimonial Department with a Jury of Matrons is described, has a direct bearing on Cameron's play, but the story would have been so well-known to her readers that she doesn't need to quote it or even refer to it; it would have been common currency. In fact, given that Kipling reached the zenith of his popularity in American in 1899, Robert and Phyllis are marked as mainstream and conventionally correct and not "corrupted" by "modern" ideas.

The Kipling "craze," enabled by the rampant piracy of texts that prevailed before the international copyright agreement went into effect in July 1891, was fed by the serialization of his novels (*The Light that Failed* in *Lippincott's* in 1891, *Naulahaka, a Story of West and East* in *Century* in 1891–1892, *Captain's Courageous* in *McClure's* in 1896, and *Kim* in *McClure's* in 1900–1901), extensive work by Kipling and notes and anecdotes about him in the periodicals, the vogue for his verse and verse set to music, and the common currency of his "tags" such as "East is East and West is West, and never the twain shall meet." Kipling, with his message of Anglo-Saxon supremacy, was a welcome and ubiquitous presence in American periodicals, but his strongest showing by far was in *McClure's*, which, between 1893 and 1906, ran forty-four pieces as well as the two serialized novels. Clearly *McClure's* had a commercial as well as an ideological investment in keeping Kipling's name and cultural value alive in readers' minds. As clearly, Cameron could count on her opening invocation of Kipling not only to culturally position her couple but also to accrue the benefits of connections with a popular and respected writer. The reader could proceed with the play in full confidence that the treatment would be light, the language correct, the idea comprehensible, the discussion polite, and the whole, despite a titillating venture into alternate behaviors, ultimately would sanction a conservative position on marriage.

My second example is a minor, one-act sketch in *Harper's Monthly* (1912), *Nervous Prostration* by Marie Manning (1873–1945). It also might be easy to pass by, but to do so would be to overlook the cultural freight it carries and on which it depends, to say nothing of the author's prominence and authority. Set in the reading room of a resort hotel, the play satirizes the middle-class obsession with "Nervousness" and "Higher Thought." The characters, all recognizable social types, from "First Lady with a Gift for Personality" to "A Motor Enthusiast in Exile" to "The Gentle [bicycle] Speeder," discuss their symptoms of and remedies for nervousness. Their total absorption in the consumption of remedies, from riding a velocipede to applying varieties of therapeutic services, marks nervousness not only as a psychophysiological illness but also as a desirable consumer "commodity," so much so that the play ends with a "Hotel Child" requesting its own "little nervous prostration" because "every one here's got it" (644). This little farce of course depends on the reader's familiarity (whether through actual or vicarious experience) with resort hotels and social types belonging to a privileged class but, more importantly, it is essential that the reader also know about the two fads being ridiculed.

The first, Neurasthenia (literally "nerve weakness"), was introduced in medical literature for the first time in 1869, but became increasingly common through the end of the century and reached a fever pitch in 1903. The "father" of Neurasthenia, George M. Beard, M.D., the author of *American Nervousness* (1881) and *Sexual Neurasthenia* (1884), developed a theory of mental and physical health that depended in turn on theories of bodily energy understood to be "economic." People were assumed to have a certain amount of "nerve force" or nervous energy that was subject to strict bodily economy; if too severely "taxed," the body would become "bankrupt" and nervous. Beard blamed Thomas Edison in particular for much of the problem, citing his electric light as a modern invention that threatened the natural circuitry of the body (Pena 102).

Tom Lutz has amply documented the late-nineteenth and early-twentieth-century phenomenon of "Neurasthenia" in *American*

Nervousness, 1903. "Neurasthenia," he argues, "was a sign of modern life" (4). It was also a class marker because it was supposedly a disease of the leisure class, of "brain workers," of artists and connoisseurs, affecting only the most " 'advanced' races, especially the Anglo-Saxon" (6). Lutz offers many examples of Neurasthenic characters in contemporary fiction, among them: the maddened narrator in Charlotte Perkins Gilman's story "The Yellow Wallpaper" (1892), Edna Pontellier in Kate Chopin's *The Awakening* (1899), Curtis Jadwin in Frank Norris's *The Pit* (1903), Martin Eden in Jack London's *Martin Eden* (1909), and Eugene Witla in Theodore Dreiser's *Genius* (1915). Lutz documents the ways in which Neurasthenia participated in the creation of middle-class hegemony: "In medical, literary, and popular discourse, Neurasthenia had class and racial implications and was closely allied to the discourses justifying dominant American culture, and Anglo-American high culture in particular" (6).

The disease once had been taken very seriously. For instance, Edward Wakefield's "Nervousness: The National Disease of America" in *McClure's* (1894) describes Dr. Weir Mitchell's cure for the afflicted "white races" who must be saved "for the sake of humanity, for the sake of morality, for the sake of patriotism" (307). No less an august thinker than William James had engaged the problem. In "The Gospel of Relaxation" in *Scribner's* (1899), one of his *Talks to Teachers on Psychology and to Students on Some of Life's Ideals*, James had counseled a course of mental and physical hygiene for tense Americans, especially Annie Payson Call's "Power through Repose" system in which the stressed female subject learned to condition her thought and relax by riding bicycles.

But by 1912, when Manning's play was published, a cultural shift had occurred. Lutz notes that the new rhetoric of America advocated the expenditure, not the conservation, of energy and points to Theodore Roosevelt's loss of the presidency to Woodrow Wilson, "a man whose most famous campaign speech was 'The Liberation of a People's Vital Energies' " (288). Manning's characters, therefore, are unfashionably out of step with the modern world, throwbacks to the fads of a previous decade and risible in their self-absorption. Because the play is a slight piece of entertainment, it offers nothing more than gentle ridicule underscored by the commitment of one of the ladies to "Higher Thought" or "New Thought," also a fad of the 1890s.

"New Thought," founded on the transcendental doctrine of the immanence of the divine within each individual, advocated the exercise of optimism, mental control of health, and existence on high spiritual planes. Owing something to theosophy, Christian Science, and primitive psychiatry, "Higher Thought" soon had its own publishing industry; Mott notes that no fewer than eight magazines exclusively were devoted to the subject (*1741–1905*, IV: 283–84). "Higher Thought" or "New Thought" also was described in detail in two articles in 1896 and 1899 by Horatio Dresser in *Arena* setting forth the "philosophy and practice of the mental cure" which, he counseled readers, had won "an assured place among the progressive factors of our time" ("Mental Cure" 131). Advocating the mental cure as "a product of American thought" that developed "individualism" and "self-reliance," Dresser believed that this would play its part "in the evolution of the race" (135–37). In his longer explanation, "What is the New Thought?," Dresser pits New Thought against the "materialism of the age" and invokes Ralph Waldo Emerson as its "the great prophet" (30–31).

To return to the play, whether Manning is mocking a character for her fatuousness or for the belief itself is not clear, but the reader of the mainstream *Harper's* would probably not also be the reader of the reformist *Arena*, and Manning's comic dismissiveness would discourage any serious consideration of Dresser's progressive argument. Manning's primary target is the self-absorbed woman who abandons herself to fads and fancies and, unlike the presumed reader, is not mindful of the comic contradiction in advocating high thoughts at a resort hotel. Any real bid to be "modern" or engaged with something beyond oneself is muted by the gentleness of the satiric barb, which reprimands but does not offer an alternative mode of social behavior. Manning's position would have carried a great deal of weight with her reader because by the time "Nervous Prostration" appeared in *Harper's* in 1912, Manning, a career journalist, was well-known as "Beatrice Fairfax." "Dear Beatrice Fairfax" was America's first personal advice column, which made its debut on July 28, 1898, in William Randolph Hearst's *New York Evening Journal*. It was an instant success, ran for decades, and elicited over a thousand letters a day from readers. Manning's authority on social matters was an established fact for the reader.

My third example is a verse play, Barrett Wendell's *Ralegh in Guiana* (1897), which immediately lays claim to lofty matter because it imitates a Shakespearean tragedy in that the "high" characters speak in iambic pentameter and the "low" characters in prose. Wendell had already staked his claim to this historical territory with a scene in verse, *Rosamond* in *Scribner's* (1890), in which an irate and vengeful Eleanor of Aquitaine brings Rosamond de Clifford to an acceptance of her guilt in her illicit liaison with Henry Plantagenet. Though she first defends her love with Henry, Rosamond, moved by Eleanor's argument about the sanctity of a consecrated marriage and shamed by her sin, accepts the poison Eleanor forces on her. Wendell offers little to his reader by way of context beyond placing the Queen and Rosamond at Woodstock and Henry in France, clearly expecting his reader to be knowledgeable about English history in general and the peccadilloes of royalty in particular. The fanciful revisioning of the encounter offers the reader a corrective narrative and a comforting moral quite in keeping with the magazine's conservative line on marriage: Eleanor of Aquitaine did indeed love Henry and her marriage was indeed a consecrated state. Furthermore, Wendell alerts the reader to the dangers of romantic mythologizing when Eleanor concludes the play with a prediction: men will shed tears over Rosamond, "loved, unforgotten," whereas she will be remembered as "unloved, forsaken" (788).

   Ralegh in Guiana assumes substantive knowledge of English history and, more significantly, also aggrandizes what was in fact a personal and political disaster. It dramatizes Sir Walter Ralegh's last expedition, the tragic voyage to the Orinoco in the winter of 1617–1618 just prior to his execution back in England in October 1618, In 1596, Ralegh had published *The Discoverie of Guiana*, an account of his adventures the previous year to claim for Queen Elizabeth "a Countrey that hath yet her Maydenhead" but under James I Ralegh came to be charged with treason and imprisoned for twelve years (Harlow 73). His only chance for freedom was to prove his value to James thereby assuring him of the occupation of a valuable territory by bringing home a cargo of ore from Guiana. Whether or not Ralegh deliberately deceived the king with assurances that Guiana was covered with gold and silver, he staked everything on the voyage. The attempt was a disaster; Ralegh's partner, Keymis, shot himself when he was unable to reach the Spanish mine, and Ralegh returned to England, a doomed man. There were several consequences: his nobility at his execution made him a martyr for liberty and, even though the raid failed, V. T. Harlow points out, "the prominence which Ralegh had given to [Guiana] from 1595 onwards did much to encourage extensive colonizing enterprises . . . . The story of Ralegh in Guiana is essentially a part of the history of British expansion as that of Ralegh in Virginia. *In both cases he worked for the commercial and political aggrandizement of his country"* (my emphasis; cvi).

Though the play obviously can be read as the dramatization of an English adventurer dedicated to the expansion of English global properties and power, it also can be understood as an argument for American foreign expansionism and as a model for American Anglo-Saxon manhood. The nineteenth-century displacement of Britain by the New World as the new empire depended in large measure on a rhetoric of imperial self-definition built on the foundation of rigorous Anglo-American industry and masculinity in opposition to fears about the wholeness and stability of the nation in the face of diverse ethnic immigration. By 1897, Barrett Wendell (1855–1921) had been teaching at Harvard since 1880, where he championed a general humanist education over a scholarly one for the students. Kim Townsend in *Manhood at Harvard* details Wendell's concerns: that American literature was not worth serious attention; that the most "manly" texts were from the English sixteenth century; that America's young men were becoming feminized; and that moral action rather than " 'introspection . . . idealistic inaction' was the only path to a noble and successful life' " (138–39). Wendell could have been understood to have a "right" to imitate Shakespeare and to advocate national ideals; his 1894 *William Shakespere* [sic] had been well received in reviews in the *Atlantic Monthly, Dial, Nation,* and *Poet-Lore.* In *The Atlantic Monthly* review, Wendell praises Shakespeare: " 'these plays show themselves the work of one who at least sympathetically has sounded the depths of human suffering . . . . Throughout is a profound fatalistic sense of the impotence of man in the midst of his environment; now dispassionate, now fierce with passion, this sense—which we called a sense of irony—pervades every play from Julius Caesar to Coriolanus' " ("Comment" 560). These lines can serve as a template by which to read Wendell's encomium to Ralegh, who is depicted as having remained faithful to James I despite having endured twelve years in prison charged with treason. Wendell accepts and amplifies the popular conception of Ralegh as a cultural icon, a man who popularly represented an ideal Elizabethan, a man who was not only a courtier but also a statesman, scholar, soldier, sailor, and man of letters. In the play, Ralegh stoically endures the death of his son, speaks always as a "gentleman," defends Queen Elizabeth's actions against the Spanish, and, most important, takes the long view of history: "England shall remain, / Long after James, and we, with all that live / To-day, lie rotting" (Harlow 780). Ralegh, therefore, represents the ideal model for Anglo-Saxon manhood, an ideal Wendell believed America sorely needed.

That the play ends with Ralegh lamenting the darkening of Elizabeth's golden England by the taint of Scottish blood goes to the second related issue implicitly raised in the play. The question of "tainted" blood was particularly relevant at this moment in the history of American immigration. In 1891 the Bureau of Immigration had been established under the Treasury Department to federally administer all immigration laws except the Chinese Exclusion Act, Congress added health restrictions, and pogroms in Russia caused large numbers of Jews to immigrate. In 1894 Congress created the Bureau of Immigration, and the Immigration Restriction League was organized to lead the restrictionist movement for the next twenty-five years and to enforce a distinction between "old' (northern and western Europe) and "new" (southern and eastern immigrants). Between 1890 and 1900, more than three and half million immigrants were admitted. Immigration was extensively debated in periodicals as anxiety over Anglo-Saxon "race suicide" escalated: a consequence of the surge in nativism that characterized the decade or so after 1885. Maldwyn Allen Jones observes that nativism had come "to life again for the first time since the Civil War with the Haymarket bomb outrage in Chicago in May, 1886" (217). Wendell, too, had aired his apocalyptic vision of an America under siege. In "*Stelligeri*," an essay on America's need to be guided by a "pure, simple, aspiring" ideal from the past," Wendell invoked Harvard's marking of dead classmates with the phrase, "*E Vivis cesserunt stelligeri*," "they that bear the stars haved [*sic*] passed from among the living." For Wendell, the need for superior men was urgent because America's "floodgates are opened. Europe is emptying itself into our Eastern seaports; Asia overflowing the barriers we have had tried to erect on our Western coast; Africa sapping our life to the southward. And meantime the New England country is depopulated, and the lowlands drained by the Mississippi are breeding hordes of demagogues" (16).

Besides the lesson in moral manliness and the anxiety over Anglo-Saxon racial purity, there was a third serious contemporary political issue that must have resonated with the readers of Wendell's play, namely President Grover Cleveland's support in 1895 of Secretary of State Richard Olney's attempts to get Great Britain to submit to arbitration over the border dispute between its colony of Guiana and Venezuela. Nearly all the leading magazines and reviews covered the issue in articles or symposia and, as Mott observes, "by no means all were on the side of President Cleveland and Congress" (227). Cleveland, who was not a supporter of American imperial expansionism, also opposed support for anti-Spanish rebels in Cuba and the annexation of Hawaii. America's reaction to and involvement with this international incident between Great Britain and its colonies was closely aligned with a domestic incident of great significance, the Pullman Railroad strike of 1894, which brought Eugene Debs to national attention and led directly to his conversion to Socialism. The strike ended with the intervention of the United States Army under the direction of then-attorney general Olney, who was also a pivotal agent in the Venezuelan dispute. In a review of recent historical events for *Scribner's* in April 1896, E. Benjamin Andrews described "the Venezuelan Excitement" thus: "The vigor shown by Mr. Olney when Attorney-General, in enforcing law and order during the Chicago strike, he now displayed in conducting foreign affairs . . . . He insisted, on the ground of the Monroe Doctrine and of our essential sovereignty upon this continent, that Great Britain should submit to arbitration a long-standing boundary dispute with Venezuela" (487). Wendell's play clearly supports Elizabeth's consolidation of her power by taking action against the Spanish and James's right to "his broad Guiana" (778) because "the manly law of England should prevail" and "the whole wide world is England's" (783).

Wendell's play, therefore, could have been read as advocating an expansionist American foreign policy, a policy also predicated on racial supremacy and national superiority. Finally, Wendell and Theodore Roosevelt, who exulted in the Spanish–American War over Cuba, what he called his "splendid little war," may have shared political views. An introduction by Roosevelt, calling on college graduates to do the manly thing and avenge the American citizens murdered on the high seas by the Germans and "our women raped in Mexico," precedes one driver's account of the American Ambulance Field Service in Lorraine published in *Outlook* (1915) (125). That Wendell shared Roosevelt's views is indicated by the fact that in the subsequent publication of Field Service as a book, *Friends of France* (1916), Wendell's verse serves an epigraph to Roosevelt's introduction:

> Though desolation stain their foiled advance,
> In ashen ruins hearth-stones linger whole:
> Do what they may they cannot master France,
> Do what they can, they cannot quell the soul. (61)

Given the periodicals' complex involvement with current issues, whether conservative or progressive, one might expect the plays to be fully engaged with compelling and urgent national problems as well as with passing fads and fancies. During the time under consideration in this study (1890–1918), the United States faced the "closing of the frontier" and the end of the "Indian problem," yawning discrepancies between rich and poor, industrial strife and strikes, a severe four-year economic depression (1893–1897), the Spanish– American War, the disgrace of urban tenement housing, calls for regulation of big business, mandated segregation, and rising tides of immigration to name but the most obvious. This was also the investigative or "muckraking" period of journalism (1902–1912), which coincided with Theodore Roosevelt's presidency. Furthermore, the United States, with its entry onto the world stage as a rapidly developing imperialist power, was consolidating an international as well as a national identity. Given that all these subjects were discussed and debated as well as fictionalized extensively in the periodicals, one might expect them to have been the subjects of the plays as well. Therefore, I think there is very reason to think of a periodical as a "shared social space" in Brodhead's terms, that is, that every form of literary production is "bound up with a distinct social audience: in its production each addresses and helps call together some particular social grouping, a portion of the whole public identified by its readerly interests but by other unifying social interests as well" (5). In particular, I want to place the drama at the center of that "shared social space" and tease out some of the radiating connections from the plays, not the least of which is the question of who was welcomed into that space, who was excluded and why. In fact, one of the most interesting things about studying the plays as a body of work is the degree to which the drama did and did not participate in those debates; the work of the drama does not always "map" neatly onto the work done by the fiction and the essays in the periodicals.

Perhaps the most glaring difference is the startling and disturbing omission of African Americans, either as playwrights or as characters in plays, even though the periodicals under consideration published work by Booker T. Washington, Frederick Douglass, Paul Laurence Dunbar, W. E. B. Du Bois, and Charles Chesnutt as well as short stories and articles on a diverse range of racial issues. Though the world dramatized in the plays published in American periodicals is decidedly "white," a highly artificial construction, it is always shadowed by the absence of the Negro. Of the 125 plays under consideration only one, Paula Jakobi's *Chinese Lily* (*Forum* 1915), includes an African American character, "colored" Annie, a prostitute who is described only as "evil looking." Therefore, for all intents and purposes, African Americans were not "marginalized," they were erased totally from a significant body of literature in American periodicals that both produced and expressed the national "whiteness" by ignoring many of its citizens. Of this phenomenon, John R. Gillis observes that "national memory is shared by people who have never seen or heard of one another, yet who regard themselves as having a common history. They are bound together as much by forgetting as by remembering" (7). By way of example he points to the post–Civil War monument building in the North and South, constructions that were "icons of whites only. Post–Civil War American identity was forged by forgetting the contributions of African Americans to the military effort, forgetting even what the struggle had been about" (10). Alice Fahs in *The Imagined Civil War* observes that "the memory of the Civil War as the shared bravery of white soldiers was used to underwrite ideas of the nation as a whites-only brotherhood" (315). Benedict Anderson made a similar point: of the 1880s he notes that "a vast pedagogical industry works ceaselessly to oblige young Americans to remember/forget the hostilities of 1861–65 as a great 'civil' war between 'brothers' rather than between—as they briefly were—two sovereign nation-states" (201). Finally, Desmond King argues that the removal of Asians and African Americans from consideration in discussions of citizenship was tied to the power of eugenic theories and practices and to the primacy of the struggle between the "old" (Northern) and the "new" (Southern) Europeans.

In the face of this phenomenon, it is important to remember that such a strong absence indicates massive anxiety. Janet Gabler-Hover, focusing on the " 'shadow of the negro' " in the *Century* in the 1880s, finds that there was a "strong psychological pull toward ethnic homo-geneity and a resistance and a denial of racial difference" (240) and that, as a consequence, "even through omission the African American presence is manifested in American literature" (254). In the drama in the period-icals the entire issue is side-stepped; the servants and laborers, especially in the comedies, are "ethnic" (usually Irish or German), not African American. Though the plays ostensibly present realistic depictions of society, I want to recall the idea of suppressing " 'extraneous noise,' " which Demastes and Vandel Heuvel set forth as one characteristic of early realist theatre (261). The exclusion of African Americans underscores the larger cultural dominance of whiteness or "Anglo-Saxonism" in the conceptualization of Americans enacted through the differential allocation of social and material privileges along racialized lines.

Given the massive anxiety about race in general and the "Negro problem" in particular at this time, perhaps it is not surprising that the drama in periodicals produced a wholly imaginary "pure" white nation for its readers. Gary Gerstle in *American Crucible: Race and Nation in the Twentieth Century* observes that the two shaping constructs that "animated the nation's communal imagination" were "civic nationalism" and "racial nationalism" (5). If civic nationalism posited a belief in the fundamental equality of all, a "democratic universalism," racial nationalism, in contradiction, conceived of America "in ethnoracial terms, as a people held together by common blood and skin color and by an inher-ited fitness for self-government" (4). Noting that this ideal, encoded in a 1790 law limiting naturalization to "free white persons," a law that, despite a modification in 1870, remained in force until 1952, was evidence of America's yearning to be a white republic; Gerstle points to the far-reaching consequences: "from the perspective of this racialized ideal, Africans, Asians, nonwhite Latin Americans, and, in the 1920s, southern and eastern Europeans did not belong in the republic and could never be accepted as full-fledged members. They had to be expelled, segregated, or subordinated" (5).

Louis Menand in *The Metaphysical Club* offers another possible explanation: "It is possible to . . . say that the price of reform in the United States between 1898 and 1917 was the removal of race from the table. When the Populist Party was founded in 1892 with a platform that included demands for an income tax, government ownership of railroads, and laws to protect unions, its leaders set out to recruit black voters. By 1906 the Populists had become the party of white supremacy. In *Plessy v. Ferguson*, in 1896, the Supreme Court sanctioned apartheid; in *Williams v. Mississippi*, in 1898, it sanctioned the disenfranchisement of Southern blacks . . . . White Americans were free to appropriate the rhetoric of abolition and emancipation, but they were not free to apply the situation of black Americans" (374). David Blight shares much the same view. In *Race and Reunion* he details the creation of a national mythology, a core master narrative of reconciliation and white supremacy, being driven by the need to rewrite the Civil War between 1863 and the semicentennial in 1915: "The Southern victory over Reconstruction replaced Union victory in the war and Jim Crow replaced the Fourteenth Amendment in their places of honor in national memory." "A segregated society," he acidly observes, "demanded a segregated historical memory" (361).

Of this striking absence, Ronald Wainscott in his assessment of the drama of this period observes that with a few exceptions, "race relations played a limited role in the plays of this period, although many plays included jokes or comments about African American characters in small roles, especially step-and-fetch-it type servants" ("Plays" 280). However, in the dramatic texts in periodicals, there is a significant difference: the comic servants are "ethnic," not African American. Wainscott notes that the playwrights of these decades were concerned with "environmental reality, the presentation of a believable society (both rural and urban) and carefully crafted language deemed appropriate for the time, place, and characters of the play" as well as "dramatic structure, selection of sensational event, and conventional conclusion to the central problem of the play. Nearly all of the American work that ventured into topical material in these years verified 'traditional values' of the age" ("Plays" 264). And, as Blight, Menand, Gerstle, and others explain, the new "tradition" demanded an American united in reconciliation, reunion, and unified purpose undergirded by the assurance of white supremacy.

Recently, Gavin Jones, in *Strange Talk: The Politics of Dialect Literature in Gilded Age America* (1999), has demonstrated late-nineteenth-century America's obsession with vernacular American English: "Readers could not get enough of black dialect, Appalachian dialect, Pike County dialect, Maine dialect, New Yorkese dialect—every region was mined for it vernacular gold, and every predominant ethnic group was linguistically lampooned in popular poetry and prose" to such an extent that "new literary genres developed: the dialect poem, the dialect story, the dialect novel" (1). Though the periodicals were filled with such materials, the plays in the same periodicals remarkably are committed to either a colloquial, educated middle-class norm (what Alan Trachtenberg calls the "discourse of respectability") or a "high," "poetic" language (189). There are very few exceptions—Hamlin Garland's *Under the Wheel*, William Dean Howells's *Bride Roses* and *The Impossible. A Mystery Play*, Edwin Milton Royle's *The Squaw-Man*, Booth Tarkington's *Mr. Antonio*, nine short social satires by Helen Green Van Campen, and two monologues by May Isabel Fisk—but, for the most part, the plays in periodicals are in conventional, grammatically correct English. It is, of course, impossible to know if dramatists deliberately avoided the "low" vernacular or if the absence of dialect plays in the periodicals should be attributed to the fact that there were simply fewer plays proportionately to stories, novels, and poems and, therefore, the odds on dialect plays appearing also were low. But it seems more probable that the cultural anxiety about theatre itself and the questionable "literary" merits of American drama were the primary motivation. By keeping the level of discourse "high" and also by publishing plays in verse, periodicals marked the plays they published as being "safe" from the "lower" dramatic forms such as burlesque, vaudeville, and minstrelsy and produced yet another "imaginary," that of an uncorrupted dramatic canon.

There is another, related, possible explanation that could account for the anomaly of the "missing" African American presence in the drama in periodicals. Clearly, in many instances, it was assumed that the plays would be read not only silently but also aloud and even performed in the home; the textual evidence suggests that there was every expectation that the performers would conform to normative social behavior. To depart from that normative mode would be to court disaster. Here we must recognize the transformative power of mimesis with reference to Michael Taussig's *Mimesis and Alterity* in which he posits a "two-layered" process, "a copying or imitation, and a palpable sensuous, connection between the very body of the perceiver and the perceived . . . . On this line of reasoning, contact and copy merge to become virtually identical" (21). Though Taussig's argument at this juncture is focused only on the visual and the mimetic, I would argue that to physically imitate, as well as give voice to, the Other and, as a necessary corollary, to call up political and social circumstances especially those shrouded in a shameful recent past, might have been too dangerous, too threatening an activity for the periodical reader and amateur performer.

To summarize, in general the periodicals had a conservative, nation-building agenda predicated at worst on nativist, Anglo-Saxon supremacy and at best on sentimental humanitarianism. Even *Arena* and *Forum*, for all their moralistic, didactic, progressive, and reformist intentions, did not stray too far from the center. One could argue that a democratic society whose public space is a normalizing commercial culture denies individuality, that under the weight of homogenization the autonomous self shrinks into a socialized self without much originality or vitality. On the other hand, the claim of the periodicals was that they actively contributed to the production of cultural energy and social progress and, further, that the individuals became complete only as members of the whole when they engaged in the pursuit of the yoked democratic desirata: economic prosperity and social cohesion. From this perspective, though the culture may have been in a transformational phase, the individual and the collective were secured by the insistence on an inherited culture, an unbroken continuity with the values of the past represented by class, race, nation, and language, and the exclusion, marginalization, and/or erasure of many American citizens. For the most part, the drama in the periodicals participated in this division of the nation into the visible and the invisible, perpetuating an imagined and wholly inauthentic construct that enabled crippling class and racial hierarchies.

In the minds of some, one way to secure a singular identity was by establishing a unique and autochthonic literature. One unlikely spokesperson for this function in drama was Theodore Roosevelt in his role as contributing editor to *Outlook* in 1911, the year before he announced his candidacy for president. In an introduction to an essay on the Abbey Theatre and to a new play by Lady Gregory, Roosevelt pointed to the "lesson" Americans were being taught: "The Irish plays are of such importance because they spring from the soil and deal with Irish things, the familiar home things which the writers really knew. They are not English or French; they are Irish. In exactly the same way, any work of the kind done here, which is really worth doing, will be done by Americans who deal with the American life with which they are familiar; and the American who works abroad as a make-believe Englishman or Frenchman or German— -or Irishman—will never add to the sum of first-class achievement" (915).

This is not to suggest that the periodicals presented a united front on this or any other issue. There were ripples and sometimes shouts of discontent and displeasure with ostentation, sanctimoniousness, solipsism, hypocrisy, and false sentiment. Selfish individualism and pretentious posturing were considered to be undemocratic and un-American. The price, the argument could be, is that the end result is the *bourgeoisie*— complacent, even fatuous, unenlightened because narrowly educated, stultified by consumerism, and only marginally progressive. But to have been extremely antagonistic to the hegemonic formation would have been to be anarchic or eccentric, attributes vilified or ridiculed in the periodicals. As for "decadence" or "degeneration," those dark, regressive shadows were consigned to Europe and did not darken the dramatization of American life in the periodicals. If crime and corruption were polluting America, they could be traced back to their immigrant and/or impoverished origins and could be dealt with variously by social reform, progressive legislation, nativist restrictions on immigration, and Christian social intervention.

For the most part the periodicals' aesthetics were equally conservative: the embrace of illusionistic realism, a delight in the sensational and melodramatic, a lingering and persistent romanticism, linear and descriptive narrative, logical syntax, consistency of generic expectations, a normative tone, and recognizable themes dominated the pages. With the notable exception of the *Forum*, inherited culture was valued and the disruptive yawps of abstraction, sharp juxtaposition, sexual energy, religious doubt, and ambiguity rarely openly disturbed the serene bourgeois façade of these periodicals before 1918. The social reality of a lively and vigorous popular theatre was not mirrored by the dramatic texts published in the periodicals though the readers were expected to be literate in the ways of theatre and drama. Despite their occasional ameliorative rhetoric, the voyeuristic depictions of popular theatre in periodicals were complicit with what I am calling the drama of social distance and difference, that is, plays that set up clear social hierarchies, ethnic categories, and racial distinctions. One of the cultural contexts was the positioning of vaudeville as belonging to immigrants and lower classes; the "legitimate" stage, by contrast, accrued higher social value.

"The American Burlesque" by Laurence Hutton in *Harper's Monthly* (1890) gives a detailed history of the art claiming Aristophanes as "The Father of the Burlesque Play" and citing John Brougham as America's

Aristophanes (60). For Hutton, Brougham's *Pocahontas; or, The Gentle Savage* (1855) and *Columbus El Filibustero!* (1857) are classics because "their wit is never coarse, they ridicule nothing which is not a fit subject for ridicule, they outrage no serious sentiment, they hurt no feelings, they offend no portion of the community, they shock no modesty, they never blaspheme" and, finally, because they were written with the crowning comic conceit of earnestness (64). Since then, however, as far as Hutton is concerned, the American burlesque has lost its dignity having deteriorated with "opéra bouffe and the coming of the English blondes" (73).

"How the Other Half Laughs" by John Corbin in *Harper's Monthly* (1898) focuses on the Italian and Yiddish theatres of the lower Bowery, characterizing the plays produced there as "crude and often absurd enough," yet having an "artistic spirit" "more vital and spontaneous" than the plays of "the most prosperous uptown theatres" (30). Though the people are to be pitied for the harshness of their daily lives, he says, at night they are to be envied. The Teatro Italiano had already closed when he wrote the essay as a retrospective on an art form that was lost to the Americanized tastes of the second generation, but Corbin values the audience participation it had elicited, running "the full gamut of human emotions" (31). By way of contrast, Corbin turns to the still active Yiddish theatre where he finds a marked difference in audience behavior: "The racial instincts of the audience are as plain as the nose on your face—or on theirs." Corbin describes how seats are stolen and how fights break out, commenting "I seldom went to a Jewish theatre that some such row did not take place. At the afternoon performance the disturbance is continual. The babies who cannot be left at home to sleep are amply in evidence. They are not like the polite Italian babies, who are nursed quiet in an instant" (38). The "threat" was political, of course. The growing Yiddish population, part of the second major immigration of Jews between 1880 and 1910, came from Eastern Europe, especially Poland and Russia, and was marked as "lower" than the German Jews, professional people who had been assimilated. The ugliest anecdote concerns Corbin's efforts to meet the performers in the company of an American scene-shifter who spoke Yiddish and who openly mocked the "Yids" to their faces. Of this "Rabelaisian opprobrium," Corbin writes: "It was not nice, but it was very funny, and it gratified my Saxon pride to feel that this derelict of our people had through all these years maintained his racial pride in the face of immigrating people. It is almost compensation for our lack of the sympathies and the assimilative powers that make up an artistic people" (43).

Corbin's opinion would have carried weight with his readers; he had been chief drama critic for the *New York Times* between 1902 and 1924 and then became an editorialist for the same paper. Nor was his an isolated vitriolic opinion. Mark Hodin describes the "judeophobic" commentaries that explicitly set up a racialized commercial stage as a threat to the "literary" and cultural elite (224). In his study of the Jew on the American stage, Harley Erdman contextualizes Corbin's attitude within the rise of "racialist or eugenicist sociology" that increased in prominence in the first decades of the twentieth century, pointing to "the widespread application of Darwin to a variety of social issues and the appearance of such influential tracts as Prescott F. Hall's *Immigration and Its Effects Upon the United States* (1906), Alfred P. Schultz's *Race or Mongrel* (1908), and Madison Grant's *The Passing of the Great Race* (1916). Rooted in the nineteenth century's increasing interest in race as a defining way of understanding nature and civilization, these works traced an increasingly vociferous argument for racial regulation and separation" (123–24).

In *The Making of American Audiences: From Stage to Television, 1750–1990*, Richard Butsch notes that "by the 1880s much of variety had transformed from concert saloon to vaudeville," that the "entertainment was changing from something akin to minstrel turns to something more like drama," and that "this newly respectable entertainment" had become "big business" (108). Part of the impulse to praise vaudeville arose, according to Butsch, from a class division; the sympathetic portraits of rambunctious and engaged working-class audiences were contrasted with the inattentive and tasteless affluent audiences of the "legitimate" theatres (121). The imposition of rules of decorum and the efforts to attract women and a higher class of clientele still did not offset the dominant conception that vaudeville was racy, vulgar, and rowdy and, of course, depended on audience interaction for its liveliness. Even so, the attitudes toward vaudeville were shifting. In "The Vaudeville Theatre" in *Scribner's* (1899), a description of the enormous commercial success of the vaudeville stage, Edwin Milton Royle, an actor, observes that we should be grateful for the decent, family entertainment it provides the nation: "At present it would seem that the moral tone of a theatre is in the inverse ratio of the price of admission. The higher the price, the lower the tone. It is certain that plays are tolerated and even acclaimed on the New York stage which would have been removed with tongs half a dozen years ago" (486). He praises the scrupulous censorship that has removed offensive language, quoting the notice to performers: " 'Such words as Liar, Slob, Son-of-a-Gun, Sucker, Damn and all such other words unfit for the ears of ladies and children, also any reference to questionable streets, resorts, localities, and bar-rooms, are prohibited under fine of instant discharge.' " In short, "the vaudeville theatres may be said to have established the commercial value of decency" (487). For Royle, the ultimate value of vaudeville is that it is modern and "very American" in its wide, populist appeal "to the American of all grades and kinds who wants a great deal for his money. The vaudeville theatre," he concludes, "belongs to the era of the department store and the short story" (495).

Despite Royle's appreciation, the social differentiation established in his and the other essays is underscored by the accompanying illustrations that depict either the broad "types" on stage (Henry Dixey as a country girl in Hutton's essay and the flirtatious "Singing Soubrettes" in Royle's) or the rough faces of the audience. Two of Lucius Hitchcock's line drawings for Corbin's essay are cases in point. "The pathetic in the parterre" (43) and "The audiences shout and whistle their appreciation" (35) illustrate the crowded conditions, the low social status, the indecorous behavior, the paucity of women, and the presence of babies—all of which would keep a sedate middle-class audience out of such gatherings (see figure 2.3). It is quite clear that the audiences for popular theatre were not the readers of the periodicals. Of this kind of differential marking of cultural offerings, Mark Hodin observes that advocates of legitimate theatre articulated "the value of literary practice in explicitly social terms" and that "such promotions drew by locating cultural legitimacy in unmarked identity, promising to restore for the dominant classes a threatened social order by confirming the dominion of 'white' authority in an 'ethnic' commercial landscape" (212).

All of these essays on popular theatre share in a kind of cultural voyeurism in that readers safely enter vicariously into an unfamiliar social and cultural space, a place where alternate behaviors prevail and where the socially marginalized characters are ethnologically strange, even exotic. The unfamiliar is not exactly tamed and domesticated in these essays, but it is ordered, shaped, and contextualized into a comprehensible form for the

THE PATHETIC IN THE PARTERRE.

Figure 2.3   Lucius Hitchcock for John Corbin's "How the Other Half Laughs" (*Harper's* 1898)

readers who were unlikely to venture into such a theatre or, if they did, would have been well prepared for the experience. The periodical essay relieves anxiety about a potentially alarming form of popular entertainment and about the potentially disruptive members of the audience. The essays help readers make the transition into a changing cultural landscape, reassuring them that temporary participation would not violate their tenacious hold on respectability and that the culture of "the other half" will remain separate from the dominant culture. Thus, both social distance and difference are insisted upon and is maintained in the drama; when the lower classes do make their infrequent appearances in the plays, usually as shiftless laborers or ignorant servants, the distance is equally marked.

This strategy of framing the lower classes and immigrants as part of a cultural landscape, as "urban color," of insisting on the superficial "spectacle" rather than multidimensional reality, reassured the middle class that there would be no potential infection from or real interaction with their inferiors, only one-way involvement that they controlled. Some instances in William Dean Howells's novel, *A Hazard of*

New Fortunes (1890), exemplify this habit of mind. Mrs. March reflects on traveling by the elevated in New York: "that the night transit was even more interesting than the day, and that the fleeting intimacy you formed with people in second-and-third-floor interiors, while all the usual street life went on underneath, had a domestic intensity mixed with a perfect repose that was the last effect of good society with all its security and exclusiveness." Her husband agrees: "He said it was better than the theater, of which it reminded him . . . . What suggestion! What drama! What infinite interest!" (66). Later, Mr. March finds the "picturesque" variety of "these poor animals" to be "unfailingly entertaining" at the same time he notes "the numerical subordination of the dominant race" (158–59). Sabine Haenni connects the "pictures" produced accidentally by the elevated train to the "intraurban tourist industry [which] quickly capitalized on the pictorial potential of the new means of transportation. By 1904 'Rubberneck' automobiles, staffed with a 'Megaphone Man' who provided commentary on the urban landscape, were taking curious spectators on tours through the city" (501). By turning some citizens into protected, mobile voyeurs and others into static, scrutinized objects, new forms of transportation foreclosed genuine intimacy and understanding; social problems were transformed into aesthetic adventures, and immigrants became only typed fictional characters contained in a dramatic text, not real fellow citizens in need.

The mastery of spoken English was another marker of class division. For instance, May Isabel Fisk pillories a rural, lower-class woman in *Mis' Deborah Has a Visitor* (*Harper's* 1903). In this monologue, the woman's speech, her ignorance of what is actually going on, and her topics of discussion are held up for mockery and are understood to be inextricably connected. If a person could not speak properly, the poor mastery of language indicated other cultural incompetencies; only those in command of standard English were credited with intelligence. For instance, Mis' Deborah, firmly accepting Mr. Phipps's insistence that he is "strictly temperance," describes his bout with "nooroligy" as being helped greatly by midnight gulps from "a black bottle," one of many he keeps in a trunk (156). Her social position is as clearly marked in her description of a friend's efforts to improve her child: "Mis' Sims' learnin her little girl sech stylish manners. She learns them to her out of a book— something called sociable etyquette" (158). It is clear that Mis Deborah always be contained by her insurmountable limitations.

Helen Green Van Campen's nine plays for *McClure's* in 1913 are also good examples of the drama of containment, of marking social difference and distance. Eight focus on Flossie, a New York hotel telephone operator, Elmer, the head coat-boy, and Evangeline, a show girl. Under the rubrics "The Woes of Two Workers" and "Life on Broadway," the satiric character sketches have nothing to do with the very real woes of working people in 1913 and everything to do with maintaining an unsympathetic, derisive stance toward the striving class whose material desires and social aspirations (unlike those of the validated reader) are ridiculed. Flossie and friends are dramatized as social-climbing, gold-digging, fast-talking, slang-slinging hustlers. Clearly the reader is understood to be familiar with the "types" but to be in a different and superior class, a hard-working and responsible class with superior values and goals. Though some historians have drawn attention to the ease with which it was possible for immigrants and lower classes to integrate into an "amorphous" middle class by learning manners, correct speech, and codes of civility, the plays in periodicals do not allow any slippage between language and class or any ease of social transition (Archer and Blau 310). The lines are firmly drawn and attempts to rise are dramatized as patently ridiculous, assuring the reader that no "low" person will penetrate the decorous sanctity of the middle class.

Much of the humor derives from the workers' jumble of slang and pretentious speech. Flossie: "Another illusion faded, Elmer, but leave it pass. I'm so used to bein' hectored by Fate that I don't care no more" (80). Evangeline: "Toe-rings ain't half so modish as jeweled circlets with your dog or your fiancé's picture for the ankle anyway. An' when I get in one of my Egyptian moods, I wear sandals, dearie, an 'cultivate a deep an' thoughtful expression" (217). Flossie: "It was wrote by a great genius, 'The sweetest noise on earth, a woman's tongue, a string which has no discord.' An' he says: 'That gink'd enjoy the openin' of the Chinese parliament!' " (227). Flossie: " 'Farewell to thee, you blonde deceiver, an' to the Sapphic follies of my wasted years,' he says. An' though maw hollered outa the window as he tore up the street, he never looked back. His folks is Dutch, yunno" (203). The workers' vulgar attempts to refer to higher culture are not only the objects of mockery but also the markers of the readers' superior education; a reference to "Sapphic follies," for instance, is humorous only in its fullest context. To the speaker, as in all farce, it is a serious concern. The mockery of speech and desire works in concert with Van Campen's clear sense that these "workers" do not work; they are lazy, petulant, and resentful of demands on their time. Their speech marks their class and the limits of their abilities; they can only laughably ape, not become, autonomous individuals. As Kenneth Cmiel explains, "One did not speak in a certain way because one belonged to a particular socioeconomic class. One found a place in the social order by one's cultural attainments" (200).

Van Campen makes it clear that these coarse imitators lack the intelligence, integrity, and moral fiber necessary to successfully strive upward and that they will never occupy the same cultural space as the readers who can be secure in their social distinction, difference, and distance. If there were any doubt, the illustrations underscore the complete hopelessness of her characters to sustain dignity let alone imitate or achieve a higher class status. For example, Wallace Morgan's two-page illustration for *The Disillusions of Flossie* shows the disaster that strikes the tacky apartment back yard, complete with laundry hanging from every fire escape, which Flossie describes as "a reg'lar fairy scene, with Jap lanterns an' three palms an'a table with ice-cream an' claret cup. Oh, how we slaved, gettin' the effect artistic." As Flossie is "toyin' nervously with the janitor's wife's best glass," "the eighth floor's line of wet wash broke an' lit on us" (80). The sketch shows her hapless male guest flailing under the wash, the whole a deplorable scene of social pretension brought comically low (see figure 2.4).

The clear, sharp separation of laborer from employer is also the essential component of the comedy in John Kendrick Bangs's *A Chafing-Dish Party* in *Harper's* in 1896. Bangs's piece is an extremely trivial tempest in a teapot over a club gathering to try out Welsh rarebit in a new chafing dish. The play begins with the housewife complaining about decorators who didn't keep their word and finish the dining-room on time, forcing her to use the (inappropriate) parlor instead. First the husband, who has been sent to buy the dish, reports that the salesman confused the cooking utensil with a "shaving-dish," then the efforts to make dinner are impeded by the hapless maid, Jennie, who tells her mistress "I've always served beer with them rabbits, ma'am" (161). The rarebit fails because Jennie reports, in tears, that the cook said "there wasn't no bread in the house, and I forgot to tell you, ma'am; but there's chocolate cake" (165). When they dig out the cheese, it has hardened into a disk which the householder, annoyed with Jennie, suggests that she be made to eat. The

Figure 2.4   Wallace Morgan for Helen Green Van Campen's *"Life on Broadway":*
The Disillusions of Flossie (*McClure's* 1913)

party ends with the oppressed group congratulating themselves for passing
this "test of character" (166).

At the other end of the social spectrum is George Hibbard's *A Matter
of Opinion*, a dialogue for a middle-class courting couple. All the material
in the play—letters, newspapers, telegrams, and books—is read by the
actors who are never without a text. The author explains in a note: "It has
been the intention of the writer to make a play for amateurs, the 'parts' in
which it will not be necessary to learn, as each character has, in all situations, something in hand on which the words may be written and from
which they may easily be read" (231). With this device, the reader
becomes a player who is reading but, more important, the reader also is
being shaped in acceptable social behaviors, particularly decorous speech,
by virtue of the enactment. Here is another instance where Michael
Taussig's *Mimesis and Alterity* usefully illuminates the "two-layered"
process, "a copying or imitation, and a palpable sensuous, connection
between the very body of the perceiver and the perceived. . . . On this line
of reasoning, contact and copy merge to become virtually identical" (21).

The activity of reading aloud transfers the characters' behaviors to the readers, now reinscribed as embodiments of the cultural norm and demonstrably competent as readers and speakers of correct English.

This sense of decorum marks another aspect of the drama; though certainly there is sustained implicit racism, there is little overt or explicit racist discourse. Derogatory references in the plays under consideration are infrequent: "Jap" in *The Progress of Mrs. Alexander*, "squaw" in Royle's *The Squaw-Man*, and from Zoë Akins's *The Magical City*:

> "For he's too big a man to act
> Like some drunk dago.
> He's not a nigger with a razor
> Ready to slash a girl
> That's done with him." (510)

Matthew Schneirov in *The Dream of a New Social Order: Popular Magazines in America 1893–1914* makes a distinction between the cultural work done by the older "genteel" magazines—*Harper's Monthly, Century, Scribner's,* and *Atlantic Monthly*—and the newer popular magazines—*Cosmopolitan, Munsey's,* and *McClure's*. He describes an evolutionary shift from the older magazines, "fearful of immigration, working-class unrest, and the emergence of a mass society," to the "business and journalistic perspective of the new popular magazines, which presented themselves as "vital and timely," positing a "new social order," a dream of an "American Utopia" the foundations of which would be cemented in "material abundance and technological mastery" (2–3). Popular magazines, he argues, "were central in the development of the new social order of corporate capitalism." These magazines, he continues, were "the first dominant discursive medium of mass culture in American history" because they were the "only medium that reached a national audience on a regular basis and, second, they did not claim to represent a particular, political party, or interest group, ideology or constituency. As a result, when an article or story or illustration appeared in one of the popular magazines, this fact conferred on it a kind of substantiality, acceptability, or weightiness" (4). Schneirov sharply demarcates the difference between what he calls "family house magazines," which looked to the past as a "source of reassurance, a repository of timeless and permanent virtues," and the popular magazines that looked to a future promising the possibilities of social justice, regenerative energy, material abundance, and public order (257). For him, the periodicals are representative of a polyvocal nation and a nation directly confronting its problems, not hiding in a national imaginary.

Dramatic literature does not figure in Schneirov's study nor did it have much presence in two of the three magazines he analyzes; *McClure's* published sixteen plays between 1901 and 1916, but *Cosmopolitan* only two and none in *Munsey's*. Nonetheless the question that needs to be answered is: did the drama participate in doing the cultural work Schneirov claims for these popular magazines? *McClure's Magazine* (1893–1928) was one of the trio of successful ten-cent monthlies of the mid-1990s, the others being *Munsey's* and *Cosmopolitan*. Initially *McClure's* gained a large readership because of the popularity of Ida M. Tarbell's serial lives of Napoleon and Lincoln and an impressive roster of fiction writers such as Kipling, Hardy, Crane, O. Henry, and Doyle. But in January 1903, with the publication of Lincoln Steffens's "The Shame of Illinois," the first installment in a series later published as *The Shame of the Cities*, the third part of Ida Tarbell's history of Standard Oil, and Ray Stannard Baker's attack on the United Mine Workers in "The Right to Work," the magazine embraced reform and, as a fortuitous consequence, boosted its circulation and advertising revenue. The investigative crusade ended in 1911 and the magazine shifted its attention to Montessori's educational system and the war, during which circulation rose to one half a million, the highest point during its history.

McClure's published two editorial statements of intent, the first in the first issue of June 1893 and the second in January 1903, as the magazine shifted into its investigative mode. In the first, the magazine announced itself to be "modern," by which was meant that it would bring "the edge of the future" to its readers in a series of articles and interviews on a wide range of scientific and business matters (94). The second editorial spoke to the "coincidence" that three articles on "capitalists, workingmen, politicians, citizens—all breaking the law, or letting it be broken"—are published in the same issue. *McClure's* contention was that the "public" was being squeezed by capital on the one side and labor on the other, thus marking its readers as neither big moneyed businessmen nor as workers but rather as the paying public having to carry the burden of both increased costs and increased wages while getting none of the benefits (333). Frank Mott says nothing about drama in *McClure's*, nor does Harold Wilson in his history of the magazine, but five of the seven plays published between 1900 and 1916 clearly share the magazine's mission: Elizabeth Phelps's *Within the Gates* (1901), Margaret Cameron's *Committee on Matrimony* (1903), Mary Raymond Shipman Andrews's *A West Point Regulation* (1904), Arnold Bennett's *What the Public Wants* (1910), and Charles Hanson Towne's *The Aliens* (1916).

Elizabeth Stuart Phelps (1844–1911), the granddaughter of an operator of the underground railroad, understood herself to be using the magazine to promote her causes. In "A Novelist's Views of Novel-Writing," she set forth her beliefs in "the life everlasting," "the enfranchisement and elevation of my own sex," and the abolition of liquor, a horror as morally objectionable as slavery, all of which are dramatized in *Within the Gates*, a play about the power of religious faith triumphing over evolutionary thought, which I discuss in another chapter (78).

Arnold Bennett (1867–1931) reviewed extensively for English periodicals such as *Bookman* and *Cornhill* and was a ubiquitous presence in many American periodicals between 1910 and 1914. One obvious reason was his visit to American in 1911 where, as he traveled to most major cities in the East and Midwest, he was acclaimed and publicized as no visiting writer had been since Charles Dickens. The tour created an American audience for his book *Your United States (Those United States* in England), published in 1912. Bennett had two plays in *McClure's: What the Public Wants*, serialized over three months in 1910, and *The Honeymoon* in 1911. *The Honeymoon* is a conventional "courtship" play lacking much in the way of social critique, but *What the Public Wants* (1910) exposes and attacks a multitude of ills from press monopolies to dubious press practices to the commercialism of theatre to social climbing and the buying of British peerages. Though it is set in England, the depiction of corruption alerts the American reader to the corrupting power and deceitful practices of the press. That the corrective proves to be a woman with plans to run articles on women's suffrage directly reinscribes the dominant cultural desideratum that women should be moral guardians, not only in the home but also increasingly in the public arena.

In his history of *McClure's*, Harold Wilson notes that after 1905 an increasing amount of fiction came from the staff; this also may account for the appearance of the play *The Aliens* (May 1916) by Charles Hanson Towne, who was in fact the magazine's managing editor from May 1915 to February 1920. *The Aliens* is a short play satirizing the vulgar attempts of a "nouveau-riche contractor" to buy high culture "several years after the present war" (12). Specifically, the contractor has joined the ranks of wealthy Americans looting a war-ravaged Europe and has purchased "The Mona Lisa" and Rembrandt's "Man with Helmet." He boasts to his guests: "Those European countries couldn't afford to keep anything like these here paintings after the War was over. That's where us rich Americans won out! . . . I hear Carnegie got ten of o' the best—Madonnas, though, mostly. . . . Never cared for them much myself. Morgan got a lot, too, and Vincent Astor seemed to grab all the Eyetalian school. I tell you, America will be the sight-seein' place hereafter" (12). His wife's insensitivity to world events is signaled by her occupation: "Knittin' for the Chinese. Ain't it awful how Japan is treatin' them poor benighted creatures? Seems to me, though, we're always knittin' for some forlorn nation" (13). To this point *The Aliens* appears to be little more than a wry commentary on the uneducated acquisitiveness of wealthy Americans, the kind of barbaric display of conspicuous consumption Thorstein Veblen had analyzed in *The Theory of the Leisure Class* (1899). The thrust of the play is underscored by the accompanying cartoon by May Wilson Preston of a pompous and overweight group in evening attire, one of whom is so indifferent to the paintings and/or drunk that he is asleep on a sofa. In this value system, in which cultural power is asserted by mere acquisition, the real or intrinsic worth of a work of art is distorted and commodified.

But the play shifts mode halfway through when a young couple, sensitive to the beauty of the paintings, stays behind to be alone with them. At this moment, the paintings come alive and in unrhymed free verse (a mark of high culture) tell of their yearning for the "reverent" Old World museum goers who can "wonder" and of their pain in being "unloved, unhonored" (76). The couple, about to set off on a European honeymoon, promise to restore the paintings to "those who love you, but were too poor to keep you, at the Louvre and the Kaiser Freidrich Museum in Berlin" (76). The play clearly aligns its readers with the young couple against the social climbing vulgar rich, portraying a middle class sensitive to the distinctions between a merely monetary worth and a higher aesthetic value. However, it also implies that America has no high culture of its own and so reinscribes a Europhilic stance. The dramatic device of prosopopeia, the endowing of things with voice and consciousness, shifts the emphasis from the fetishization of objects in a culture of consumption and returns to these pictures their authentic uniqueness and individuality that had been stripped from them by their boorish owners. In conversing with the young couple, the paintings, in effect, transcend their American demotion to "thing" and, in being recognized by the couple for their real worth, are returned to their rightful place as works of art with complex aesthetic and historical heritages.

One of the guiding tenets of *McClure's* was that it valued essays and stories characterized by realistic portraiture, "personality," and the clear delineation of characters—all with an eye to emotional effect. To this end the magazine published a lavishly illustrated "Human Documents" series as well as "Real Conversations," a new style of interview intended to be verbatim conversations between authors with conflicting points of view (the first being between William Dean Howells and H. H. Boyesen) and an "At Home" series. According to Wilson, "The pattern of *McClure's* political exposures was to discover in every community a natural leadership, one man or group representing the shadow government and one the moral order. This was a dialectical struggle between opposites where the good leader represented the forces coming to terms with the technological revolution" (237–38). The young couple in *The Aliens* presumably embodied the virtues of the moral order *McClure's* validated and anticipated a more enlightened "modern" culture to come, facilitated by the magazine's edifying material.

Though hardly operating on the same high plane, *The Committee on Matrimony* by Margaret Cameron (1903) follows the debate pattern so valued by *McClure's* and models the way in which a couple could safely discuss and resolve dangerous "modern" ideas. A young couple debates the pros and cons of their possible marriage, testing two "modern" approaches held by their friends. The modern male view argues that married men are victims of untoward circumstances; the modern female view, from "the ultra-anti-masculine wing of the woman movement," opposes marriage on principle (663). The young suitor mocks the rhetoric of the "modern" woman, saying that "love between a man and a woman is, of itself, an insurmountable subjective obstacle, evanescent in its very nature, and paralyzing to the conservation of soul energy; and that only when these subjective distortions are cast aside, and the higher potentialities of the spirit are educed, can the submerged mentality become transcendentally greater in scientific idealism, and the ego, vibrating to a dominant note in the thought-atmosphere, become a finited spirit, potentially whole"

(664). The couple abandons the "modern" ideas and embraces the necessary status quo on which class consolidation, national cohesion, and racial purity are preserved. This dramatized argument followed by resolve to accept convention participates in *McClure's* valuation of "dialectical struggle," a struggle exemplified in Lincoln Steffens's incomplete work on "Ethics and Evolution" in which he argued for the "Science of Morals." Wrong conduct was defined as that which hindered evolutionary process and bad conduct as that which hindered survival. Individualism could only lead to the extinguishing of the race. *McClure's* editorial group concurred and "the role of environmental control was thus accentuated without contradicting the need for men to embrace custom at the societal level" (Wilson, H. S., *McClure's Magazine and the Muckrackers* 284–87).

The second important issue raised by Schneirov concerns making distinctions among the reader as a backward-looking, fearful, and genteel conservationist of a sharply divided status quo, the reader as capitalist consumer and the reader as a dreamer of the new social order, a progressive looking to the future. In making his claims, Schneirov rejects previous studies that focused on popular magazines as "vehicles for a hegemonic culture" (6). Specifically, he resists Richard Ohmann's Gramscian-based contention that mass circulation magazines were an essential part of molding a consumer culture, itself the consequence of the development of national advertising, which, in turn, was a response to the need of businesses to reach a national market of consumers. It is difficult, however, to resist Ohmann's analysis when, for example, a page in *Everybody's Magazine*, a popular periodical of the kind Schneirov has in mind, addresses the public as follows: "Now when you, Mr. and Mrs. Reader, go on a purchasing expedition and see the exact article you want at the price you want to pay, isn't the fact that it is made in America an added reason for buying it . . . you would rather trade with your friends than strangers, wouldn't you?" (December 1914, 4). With one simple exhortation the reader becomes a patriotic consumer.

Though the plays in periodicals are less overtly implicated in consumerism beyond the obvious fact that most of the readers were bourgeois and presumably were engaged in the getting and spending activities of middle-class life, three plays in particular, John Kendrick Bangs's *The Bicyclers* (1895) and *The Golfiacs* (1897) in *Harper's* and W. G. Van Tassel Sutphen's *First Aid to the Injured* also in *Harper's* (1896), stand out for their direct participation in two of the most dominant consumer fads of the late nineteenth century: bicycle riding and golfing. The development of the modern "safety" bicycle in 1884, the addition of pneumatic tires and a coaster brake in 1889, rapidly falling manufacturing and distribution costs, advances in dress reform and social freedom for women, Roosevelt's call for "the strenuous life," increased leisure time, and the expansion of cities all culminated in the 1890s, which became known as the "decade of the bicycle." Periodicals were filled with advertisements, short stories, and essays pro (riding assured healthier Anglo-Saxon mothers) and con (riding simulated masturbation). In *The Adman in the Parlor: Magazines and the Gendering of Consumer Culture, 1880s to 1910s*, Ellen Gruber Garvey demonstrates the ways in which "fiction that appeared to serve no commercial purpose," in fact, was embedded with descriptions of products in a social context and associated with "romance, happiness, freedom, social acceptance, and socially approved behavior" (107).

Bangs's slender farce, *The Bicyclers*, one of six he wrote for *Harper's Monthly* between 1894 and 1897 with the same cast of characters, is overtly marked by product placement. Though Bangs makes fun of novices trying to master the wheel, the play is little more than an extended advertisement for the accessories required for bicycle riding: pneumatic tires, tool-chest, cyclometer, lamp, ammonia gun to deter dogs, short trousers, and Pond's Extract, all items that figured prominently in magazine ads. After the invention of the safety bicycle in 1888, manufacturers were prominent advertisers. In May 1896 alone, the *Century* carried twenty-one pages of ads for bicycles and paraphernalia.

Similarly, *The Golfiacs* celebrates the golf craze, which, like the bicycle craze, engaged both men and women. The virtues of golf are extolled by the women because it gets their husbands "out-of-doors, and that's what we need these days" and because they can be healthy too: "It's so exhilarating walking and climbing over the country" (151). More important, however, is the plot line in which a long-haired musician, wholly ignorant of the game, is taught to play, swear, and drink Scotch and soda like the rest of the men. Any man who doesn't play golf is dismissed as "an ass" (155), and the play ends happily when the indoctrinated musician, who not only becomes converted but also proves he is not a high-brow snob by playing "Bluebells of Scotland," is admitted into the "inner circle of the golfiacs" (159). The message is clear: golf is good for men and women; it is commendable to be obsessed with the game; and real men don't play Chopin, they play golf, a game requiring lots of equipment, membership in a club, and the desire to drink hard liquor.

Sutphen's play, *First Aid to the Injured*, later published in a collection of stories on golf, *The Nineteenth Hole*, also casts characters as consumers. In this little farce, the game of golf temporarily comes between a courting couple, Miss Cheviot and Mr. Hazard, part of a group of the young leisure class with appropriate names (Driver, Brassie, Niblet, etc.) whose lives are totally absorbed by the game. The dialogue, with some allowance for the romance, is for the cognoscente: "You might say to Mr. Hazard that I expect to make the course in eighty-two or under, and that I shall use a straight-faced driver. The bulger 'PULLS' the ball" (966). Attired in full golfing regalia and discussing varieties of clubs, expensive dogs, and private stock whiskey, the characters, who do pair off by play's end, demonstrate the social desirability of the game (they find suitable athletic spouses) and are extensions of the many advertisements for golf equipment that filled the magazines' pages. Thus are courtship, class, and consumerism mutually reinforced.

On one hand, because I accept Brodhead's contention that literary genres "formed mutually supportive parts of a concerted textual program," even if that program is characterized by a tension between the desire to be singularly and exceptionally "American" and the equally compelling urge to remain part of the "Larger England," I cannot support Schneirov's assertion that the popular magazines he champions "did not claim to represent a particular subculture, political party, or interest group" (4). On the other hand, I think Schneirov is correct in arguing that contemporary critics must consider carefully the diversity of opinions expressed to the nation in the mass communication revolution facilitated by the popular monthly magazines. But, as I will continue to argue, despite significant different agendas, the periodicals in general and the plays in particular were engaged mutually in the imaginative production of a middle-class American citizenry in its own cultural zone, marked by social distance and difference as necessarily distinct from "The Other Half" and on which the "national imaginary" of the "fictive ethnicity" so urgently depended for its Anglo-Saxon identity, its network of closed social relations, and its expansionist rationale.

3. Women as American Citizens ❧

I nvited by the *Arena* in 1897 for a retrospective on fifty years of women's progress, "our half-century of struggle," and to prognosticate about the future, Susan B. Anthony documented a wide range of women's advances in areas ranging from education to professionalization to legal status (901). In her estimation, it remained only to win complete national suffrage to realize the full "capacity and power of women for the uplifting of humanity," for the "perfect comradeship, the ideal union between the sexes, that shall result in the highest development of the race" (908). Though Anthony's new women were the subject of such periodical essays as Mary Gay Humphreys's "Women Bachelors in New York" and "The New York Working-Girl," they figured infrequently in the plays in periodicals. With the exception of women in *Arena* and *Forum*, the female characters in most plays about women had more in common with what Barbara Welter called the early nineteenth-century "cult of true womanhood," Dana Gibson's haughty aristocratic "girl," or the well-bred "American girl" promoted by *The Ladies' Home Journal* during 1900. This difference should be understood as the primary dramatized tension between advocates of the "New Woman" and traditionalists insisting on the necessity of maintaining the "Angel in the House." At stake for both sides was the nation's future: for the progressive women, full civic participation was essential for national growth, whereas for their conservative opponents, nothing less than the preservation of the "superior" race was at stake. In neither instance were minority, immigrant, or ethnic women much at issue; the primacy and centrality of Anglo-Saxon middle-class concerns were undisputed in the drama. The markers of being an "American" woman were largely marital (getting the right man) and material (acquiring the right goods).

Half of the thirty-one plays about women examined in this chapter were written by women and, with the exception of Laurence Alma Tadema (the well-known painter's daughter), all the women are American. Of the men, Arnold Bennett, John Galsworthy, and Max O'Rell represent an overseas perspective. In "Do Women Possess Any Dramatic Vitality?" from *Poet-Lore* (1895), the anonymous author argues that "in America, the best dramatic work done so far has been done by women. I refer to that of Emma Lazarus in 'The Dance of Death,' Miss Wilkins in 'Giles Corey,' Mrs. Rives Chanler in 'Athelwold,' and Miss Monroe in 'Valeria' " (516). Of these, both *Giles Corey* and *Athelwold* were published in *Harper's Monthly*. Women wrote plays prolifically; Frances Bzowski's checklist covering 1900–1930 includes 12,000 plays written by several thousand American women. Felicia Londré covers the expansion of women's careers from 1890 to 1929, marking the ways they became visible in the many magazine articles devoted to their successes. In Sherry Engle's review of the "irruption of women dramatists" between 1890 and 1920, she calculates that fifty-one playwrights had two or more productions and that eighteen became prominent with five or more Broadway productions (31). None of these, however, were published in the periodicals under consideration. She footnotes the thirty-three playwrights who had two or more productions in New York during this time span but, of these, only Zoë Akins, Marguerite Merington, Josephine Preston Peabody, and Amélie Rives were published in the periodicals under consideration here (46). This suggests that the American women whose plays were published in periodicals were not writing for the professional theatre and had little or no expectation of more than a parlor performance. I would argue that in the main the plays were meant to be read and understood as literary contributions, not as scripts for theatrical production, and that the primary attraction of most of the plays was not a call to citizenship through suffrage and participation in social reform but the allure of a moving "story," the modeling of decorum, deportment, discourse, and, in the case of illustrated plays, dress.

Three important studies of turn-of-the-century readers, Kate Flint's *The Woman Reader 1837–1914*, Peter Stoneley's *Consumerism and American Girl's Literature, 1860–1940*, and Jennifer Phegley's *Educating the Proper Woman Reader*, focus particularly on the construction of the female reader and her engagement with materials specifically designed for her "improvement" under strict paternalistic surveillance, her participation in communities of taste, the reinforcement of middle-class behavior and values, her formation both as a consumer and a product to be consumed, and her standing as a patriot. Though my study assumes a "general" reader, both male and female, I recognize that periodicals did participate in gendering certain subjects, selecting either those specifically aiming at or appealing to men or women. The plays about women certainly would have been of primary concern to female readers who would see themselves dramatized as being at the center of the middle class, positioned as significant agents of social control as well as vital participants in securing the racial and class "health" of the nation. This may have been a convenient literary fiction given that, in fact, women were circumscribed as domestic and social beings lacking the full civic agency of men.

As Dana Nelson in *National Manhood* and Linda Kerber in *No Constitutional Right to Be Ladies* have argued, the gendered images that structured nationalist rhetoric reinscribed women in the domestic sphere, making properly gendered configurations central to a strong nation. This insistence was predicated on naked fears openly expressed in the periodicals. For example, in "The Survival of the American Type," the endurance of the Anglo-Saxon ("the pith of the tree of liberty" and "the cohesive force of the republic") was depicted as essential to prevent the nation being overtaken by "vermin," animals, foreign socialists, and anarchists (Denison 23). Women were essential to the reproduction of "the American type" and women were essential to the social coherence by which the nation was secured.

I want to frame the discussion of dramatized women with two plays, one early, one late, both of which set up dialogues on citizenship between two generations of women, immediately noting that the comprehensive range of topics in these two plays is quite anomalous. Though I will argue that all the plays are instrumental in modeling the ideal American woman, these two, *A Woman's Luncheon* and *The Progress of Mrs. Alexander*, are unique in their scope. I begin with *A Woman's Luncheon* (1895), which was published in the *Atlantic Monthly* in the same year as "The Survival of the American Type." The only play of all those in this study to have been published anonymously, ironically, it is also the most supportive of the New Woman. *The Atlantic Monthly's* archival files reveal that the author was Ellen Warner Olncy Kirk (1842–1928), who published many novels, from *Love in Idleness* (1876) to *Marcia* (1907), and eight fully credited short stories and essays in *The*

Atlantic Monthly between 1892 and 1898 as well as two stories in *Lippincott's Magazine* (1900 and 1902). That she was the second wife of John Foster Kirk, a contributor to *The Atlantic Monthly* and editor of *Lippincott's Magazine*, may account both for her presence and for the anomaly of her anonymity, given that *The Atlantic Monthly* customarily did not publish plays.

The play itself is similar in style and spirit to those of Howells, James, and Wharton in that it is a conversation among ten women of various upper-middle-class types including a New Woman, a Ph.D., an heiress, a clever young writer, and a club woman. Despite their differences, all of the women are at ease with the rituals of polite behavior, civility, and decorum. Each scene is a course in a lavish meal, from grapefruit to *fraise glacées*, during which the women discuss American women in general and the New Woman in particular. The debate follows a genera-tional divide; the older women argue for the virtues of tradition, the younger "modern" women praise the new patriotism, freedoms, accom-plishments, and literary enthusiasms; the older women cherish Austen and Cranford, the younger ones are excited by Ibsen's plays and Sarah Grand's 1893 novel, *The Heavenly Twins*. The younger American women are dramatized as energetic, politically engaged, serious, and essential to the cultural superiority of America; the clever writer observes, "Oh, we love to go to Europe still; only formerly we used to go for ideas, stimulus, occupation; now we go for intellectual rest" (195).

Teresa, the New Woman, insists that the engaged American woman is central to American reform: "There are so many important questions to be agitated." Suffrage is the most important: "Of course, first and fore-most everything which concerns the full enfranchisement of woman: but besides, the questions of water filtration, street-cleaning, school boards, nominations for mayor and city council" (195). She also positions the new American woman on the global stage: "The American woman has discovered herself; she is finding her relations to her surroundings, to the events of the past, present, and future. She no longer ignores the great events of the world. She is interested in public affairs, in good administra-tion of government, in purity of politics. Our young girls, instead of being taken up with balls and germans, are absorbed in cleansing and uplifting the world" (196).

The creation of moral distance from what might be called an "American aristocracy" and the simultaneous assumption of the duties of discrimination by a new professional meritocracy was a fairly recent phenomenon coextensive with the burgeoning commercial expansion of the magazines. It should not be surprising to find that the perpetuation of morality, progressive reform, and the preservation of culture by the middle class would be key themes and concerns in the periodicals that served them. One of the most strident and prolific voices in establishing the rights and responsibilities of a middle class over both the upper and lower classes was Robert Grant, author of several series modeling correct behavior and attitudes. In a series of ten essays under the rubric "The Art of Living" for *Scribner's* in 1895 and in four "Search-light Letters" in 1899, Grant measured "effete" (European) civilization against "free-born" Americanism and found it wanting in democratic spirit. At the same time, Grant, who would later be remembered for his role in the Sacco-Vanzetti case of 1927 as one of the state-appointed "Hangmen in Frock Coats," railed that "the pioneer strain of blood has been diluted by hordes of immigrants of the scum of the earth" (586). Locating the ideal American in Anglo-Saxon stock, Grant, in "The Conduct of Life," part of "The Art of Living" series, availed himself of the authority of Emerson's original and laid the responsibility for "the great educational and artistic enterprizes" squarely on the shoulders of the "large minority," that is the professional, middle-class man. Charging that the "shallow worldlings," the "four hundred" of New York aristocracy, those who ought to represent the "most highly evolved civilization," had abandoned their civic mission for French immorality and "splendid inane social fripperies," Grant insisted that America's hope lay with "our clergymen, our lawyers, our doctors, our architects, our merchants, our teachers, some of our editors, our bankers, our scientists, our scholars, and our philanthropists" (588–90). None of these sober professional types, presumably the readers or those married to the readers of periodicals, are ridiculed in the plays, and only a light hand of mockery falls on women's frivolousness and garrulousness. Too much is at stake for the nation for the periodicals to risk substantive criticism of the class that had to be the foundation for the future.

When middle-class women are censured or mocked, it tends to be for the minor, "feminine" failings of talkativeness or self-absorption; in these instances the plays work as comic correctives for behavior. For instance, in *At the Door: A Little Comedy* by Tudor Jenks in *Century* (1899), Mrs. X and Mrs. Y, both claiming to have domestic duties to attend to, gossip idly with each other, complain about their servants, and moan about their suffering as "the drudges of the world" (858). Similarly, Marguerite Merington's *A Gainsborough Lady* in *Scribner's* (1902) features a couple who at last are able to speak to each other after 100 years of silence. As the stage directions note, "The gentleman is constantly on the point of saying something, but never once does the lady give him a chance" (65). Twenty-one of the twenty-two comic monologues May Isabel Fisk wrote for *Harper's* between 1903 and 1914, and later published in collections as *The Talking Women* (1907) and *The Eternal Feminine* (1911), dramatize women as self-absorbed, silly, and indifferent to the inconveniences to which they put others. *Buying Theater Tickets* in *Harper's Monthly* (1914) is the running drivel of a dithering woman holding up the ticket line and, after endlessly changing her mind about where she wants to sit, walking away without making a purchase. Most of Fisk's women are simply ridiculous and annoying, but *Her Tailor-Made Gown* in *Harper's* (1904) is a much harsher indictment of a self-absorbed woman and is an interesting example of how class was used as an incentive for correction. The monologue, being delivered to her tailor, shows the speaker to be blind to the needs of her sick child, whom she nearly poisons because she is distracted by the doctor's good looks, and completely unaware of the fact that working people get no vacation when she babbles on about her month in the country. A succession of such incidents makes it quite clear that this woman places her own needs and interests, all of which are petty, above consideration for others. The same sort of bad behavior is demonstrated in *A Woman in a Shoe-Shop* (1903), *Bill from the Milliner* (1903) and others in the series. And though ridicule might be reason enough for any reader guilty of such behavior to change, Fisk saves the clincher for last. *Her Tailor-Made Gown* ends with a description of a walk the speaker took with her husband while she was wearing a large hat with a tall plume, making her seem taller than her husband: "when we were going to church, and, walking up the avenue, one of those horrid little urchins came along and called out, 'Get on to her nibs with her Fauntleroy!' " (652). The clear message is underscored by the accompanying illustration of a grinning street scamp and the annoyed couple: the worst thing that can happen to you if you are conceited and preposterous is not that you might injure your child or offend a shopkeeper but that a member of the lowest street class will mock you in public and, worse, be right to do so (see figure 3.1).

I wore it one Sunday morning

Figure 3.1   Florence Scovel Shinn for May Isabel Fisk's *Her Tailor-Made Gown* (*Harper's* 1904)

Another play critical of women and leveling a more serious charge, Annie Nathan Meyer's *The Scientific Mother*, appeared in the *Bookman* (1897). Meyer's authorship would have carried weight. Meyer (1867–1951) was an outspoken opponent of women's suffrage and, later, the founder of Barnard College (1889). The play attacks a "club woman" who is so taken up with modern theories of child raising and an endless cycle of club going that she ignores her own child. The women's club movement, which flourished between 1880 and 1920, like the debate over women on bicycles and dress reform, was a very divisive issue. From a conservative perspective, clubs took women out of the home but from a progressive point of view, they were educational and socially responsible. Meyer's position on the debate is clear: mothers belong at home. In the play, Mrs. Oman Page, who has just come from a lecture on the duties of motherhood and is about to rush off to her Child Study Club and from there to a birthday party for the children of the Slum Street kinder-garten, assures the skeptical Mrs. Ole Vashion that "never before in the history of civilization has motherhood claimed such an important position. A new light has streamed in upon the subject, and it is the sacred duty of every mother to spread abroad the right knowledge of motherhood as a science." Brushing aside pleas for attention from her toddler, the scientific mother announces that she is going to be address-ing the Mother's Congress with a speech entitled " 'The Necessity of Living with Our Children' " (382).

The conservative stand Meyer takes in the play anticipates her most notable attack on women active in public life, "Women's Assumption of Sex Superiority" in *North American Review* (1904), in which she writes of her "dread" of women voters, questions the notion that "the majority of women may be counted on as a force that would make for political right-eousness," and blames club women for abandoning "the daily uncom-plaining attention to household details that make for comfort and a restful home atmosphere" (103–07). Ultimately at issue for Meyer are a host of national ills. The question, she asks, is "what could the sex bring to the service of the state to offset the degeneration of public life, to offset the indifference, the sloth, the moral cowardice, the greed, the dishonesty that are seriously menacing the moral life of our Republic?" (104).

For the most part, however, middle-class women in the plays are rarely ridiculed but, instead, serve as models of decorum and propriety, the domestic analogue to their husband's responsible professionalism. One such model is Mrs. Campbell in Howells's *The Unexpected Guests* (1893) who tells a series of white lies to protect her guests from embar-rassment at arriving late and uninvited at a dinner party. Though Howells mines the escalating situation for its humor, he clearly also approves of the impulse to spare the feelings of others; of her diplomatic lying, the men agree "it *is* a feminine virtue" (224). The most extreme example of such a virtuous woman is "She" in Max O'Rell's *The Pleasures of Poverty (A Wife's Pleading)* in *The North American Review* (1899). "He" is an ambitious painter who wants to be rich but "She" is very content being poor: "the rich don't know the pleasures they miss, the sweetest pleasures of poverty. Their gifts cost them no sacrifice. They don't possess their wealth, it is their wealth that possesses them" (287). "She" continues in this mode, reminiscing about the happiness of their impecunious past despite her husband's jocular retorts, until he stops the discussion with his final observation that his greatest pleasure in connection with his days of poverty is that he is poor no longer.

Taken at face value, *The Pleasures of Poverty* seems to be a valuation of the wife's simple piety and contentedness set against her husband's materialism and cynicism. Yet because the husband has clearly expressed his annoyance with her repeated interruptions of his work and because his arguments throughout for material comforts are presented as commendable, the wife's position ultimately appears naive. The unresolved conflict between two virtues is understandable only if Max O'Rell's sharply gendered bifurcation of roles is known, as it would have been to any constant reader of *The North American Review*.

Max O'Rell was the pseudonym of Léon Paul Blouet (1848–1903), known as the "Mark Twain of France," who was the author of the enormously popular *John Bull and His Island* (1886) which went into twenty editions in the English version and was followed by several variations on the theme. Prior to the appearance of *The Pleasures of Poverty* in 1899, O'Rell had published extensively in *The North American Review*, a serious political journal to which he contributed the only levity. But for one article in the *Arena*, O'Rell's thirteen pieces were published exclusively in *The North American Review*. Therefore, by the time they read the play, readers would have been quite familiar with the sardonic tone and testy posture of an aggrieved misogynistic curmudgeon. Most particularly they would have been familiar with his very conservative attitude toward women who, as far as he was concerned, belonged at home reproducing and mothering. He was quite incensed by the American New Woman.

One of his most aggressive assaults on the "New Woman" who was "transforming this great land of liberty into a land of petty, fussy tyranny" was launched in "Petticoat Government" (1896), which opens with "I loathe the domination of woman" (101–02). "The Anglo-Saxon 'new woman' is the most ridiculous production of modern times and destined to be the most ghastly failure of the century," he fulminated (102). To dramatize his point, he contrasts an "old style" woman with her "bright eyes" and "rosy, plump" mouth with the "restless, bumptious" New Woman who is thin, sallow-complected, and wrinkled (103). With this template in mind, the reader who accepted O'Rell's dictates easily could reconcile the unresolved conflicts in *The Pleasures of Poverty*; it is as correct for the wife to be content with impoverished domesticity as it is admirable that the husband craves professional success and material advantages. That "Petticoat Government" is followed by responses from two rightly annoyed women who point out O'Rell's failures in reasoning (to say nothing of his peevishness because he can't drink in temperance towns) might redress the balance of the argument about the New Woman, but it does nothing to mitigate the play's portrayal of a happy wife embracing simplicity.

The image of the happy wife was part of the larger cultural project of sentimental domesticity of which many of the plays by and about women were a prominent articulation. The plays were instrumental in defining the middle class against the lower vulgar classes as well as claiming the gendered authority of women to be stable moral forces in the home and in the community. The genteel woman, in perfect possession of her values, could move across class lines free from contamination, secure in her identity and purpose as a charitable "angel" in and out of the house, untempted by suffrage, free from the need to work, an agent of social harmony. In particular this kind of woman was understood to be responsible for influencing the moral life of men.

Newell Dunbar's *Das Ewigweibliche: The Ever Womanly* in the *Arena* (1904) takes its title and epigraph from the well-known phrase from the closing lines of Goethe's *Faust:* "Das Ewigweibliche / Zeiht uns hinan" (180). Readers familiar with *Faust* would have approached the play anticipating that the woman in question would be significant. Specifically, as Harold Jantz explains, the "Eternal-Womanly" represents love, grace, the power of inspiration, motherhood, the feminine principle in religion as she "draws the heroic soul upward to a higher sphere of existence" (803–04). Dunbar, an editor of the works of Goethe and Heine in the 1890s, was also the author of *Phillips Brooks: Bishop of Massachusetts* (1891), a biography of the clergyman known for writing the hymn "O Little Town of Bethlehem." Dunbar's other contribution to *The Arena* was a translation of Gorki's "The Billionaire" in 1907. One of only two plays in the *Arena* (the other being Hamlin Garland's *Under the Wheel*), *Das Ewigweibliche*, a "homily in dialogue," argues that compassion is gendered female.

The sentimental insistence that women were the compassionate sex, predicated on the essentialist assumption that "feminine" and domestic virtues could overcome differences of class, race, and ethnicity, should be understood as a literary and political strategy to authorize white, middle-class women to uplift the lower and lesser citizenry and to participate in a carefully circumscribed way in mediating charitable activities. Given editor B. O. Flower's commitment to publishing articles addressing a host of social ills including sweatshops, child labor, and the low age of sexual consent, it is not surprising that he and his contributors, one-fourth of whom were women, were crusaders for reform and the necessary engagement of women in public causes. The final part of the equation was that the crusade was yoked to religion. For instance, as C. C. Regier notes, in an essay in *Forum* in 1892, Jane Addams "had expressed her conviction that in social settlement work lay the hope of a renaissance of Christianity, of a united Christendom bound together by a desire to serve humanity" (41).

In Part I, "the text," two men, Van Rensselaer Gildersleeve, "a young quintuple millionaire (by inheritance)". . . and "good for little useful" is chatting with his friend, the impoverished writer Hollis Bradford, who is engaged to Gildersleeve's sister, Grace (180). The play begins with Bradford's question: "Van, did you ever try to feel, think, and act like a woman?" This leads to a number of memories of college days, all involving cross-dressing men: the rusticated Wat Brant who "saw the Yale football match in petticoats and a picture hat" (181) and Billy Todd, a "manly enough fellow; no suspicion of effeminacy" who dressed up for "petticoat parts in theatricals" and "got *inside* the part. Showed his appreciation of the True and the Good, as well as of the Beautiful" (183). Van recollects appreciatively that "every time he lifted his skirts and showed a slim patent-leather and a bit of open-work silk stocking, the fellows all over the house used to gasp—just the same. That was queer!" (184). Billy's impersonation of a woman is so convincing that he used it to get into a hotel room with a group of girls who were so deceived that they discussed underwear and being "*crazy after men*" (185).

Men in drag were a staple of college life, and pictures of cross-dressed men were featured in stories on college life in the periodicals as part of normal male hijinks. There was no artful intent to conceal the dresser's masculinity and, in fact, evident "maleness" was an essential part of the joke. The light theatrical practices of the time such as Brandon Thomas's *Charley's Aunt* (1892) and the Harvard College Hasting Pudding show also underscored the insistently heterosexual nature of the cross-dressing. In the play itself, this cross-dressing, whatever fundamental anxiety about sexuality and gender identity it may have indicated, was comic, temporary, insistently heterosexual, and inconsequential. It should, however, be read in its wider social context, the construction of homosexual identity, a subject treated at length in Jay Hatheway's *The Gilded Age Construction of Modern American Homophobia*. Hatheway argues that Gilded Age discussions about the homosexual were metaphors for a host of concerns including order, harmony, stability, control, and tradition during a time of "extreme social stress, to legitimately construct a national ideology of middle-class normalcy" (7).

Bradford and Gildersleeve's conversation also turns to the capacity of women writers such as Madame Dudevant, George Eliot, and Sarah Grand to penetrate men's consciousness ("Madame Dudevant must have spent a large part of her life a *man*") but their primary concern is their own capacity to feel what a woman feels. This is put to the test in Part II, "the application," when they leave the club and are confronted by a tramp in desperate need. Gildersleeve's initial response, "Great Scott! Where did *this* come from? There's the sort o' thing the town's got to get rid of" (187). The tramp politely but persistently explains his need for food: "Ain't had nawthin' but a bone a dog left over by the River since yes'd'y maw'n" while the two men playfully and cruelly cast him in a variety of cultural roles: "as an acephalous hexameter with limping feet. Or fill a frame as a Modern Lily of the Field. Or disfigure a book-shelf as a Travesty of man. Or personate In the Last Ditch—The Bottom Step—An Aching Void" (188). Bradford calculates that "we must have just guzzled and burnt up, in a couple of hours, enough to have supported Belisarius here for nearly a month." And the author acidly notes that "*here is a curiosity so rare that the situation is mildly entertaining, and, for once, these gilded youths do not shun poverty*" (188). Bradford realizes that he has had virtually no experience of real poverty: "A subconscious sense of the existence of poor devils, I take it, is the *sauce piquante* of life. But, really, isn't it a little jarring to be brought thus unexpectedly face to face with the Antipodes—a Human Vacuum?" (189). Helpless in the face of acute suffering, the men do not know what to do.

The dispirited tramp mumbles that he knows a kind lady who always helps him out and, at this, Bradford seizes on the bright idea of imagining that a character in a novel he is writing, Alice, is in his place. Bradford plays at being Alice, imagining the "woman's standpoint," which is "goodness, and receptivity, absolute truth, and love" (190) and, in this guise, after some masculine resistance, hears the "inner voice" of his womanliness that proves to be the Golden Rule: "Let me throw my soul open, woman-like. Ah, it comes to me—I feel it—I *know* it. No matter how low—poor, ignorant, unlucky, ill, deformed, insane, *criminal* even—deserving or not deserving, 'worthy object' or not—every human being should be treated as in his place we'd wish to be treated ourselves" (193). Giving the tramp some money, Bradford notes that he had only been making a character study which is still imperfect because he relied "more on reason than on intuition or feeling." Nonetheless, he decides that "there's a germ in me that might be developed into the Feminine Soul. I suspect, when that feminine soul within or without a man sets before his masculine apprehension the Truth, by the sheer impossibility of refuting it, the masculine mind—if its owner wishes to retain his self-respect—is compelled to absorb the lesson. I seem to see it: Put in man, beside his own, his sister's soul, and from the union and interplay, *plus* his strength, would come a god . . . My study began professionally, but upon my word I believe it's touched my private capacity. The play's turning out serious and real" (194–95). The confirming gesture is that Bradford removes his gloves "courteously" and "clasps the ragamuffin's chill and blackened paw." Gildersleeve, "*touched through the one rift in his worldliness*," offers himself as a partner in philanthropy: "may the Ever-womanly win!" (195).

Part III, "the benediction," introduces Grace who, returning from the theatre, is compelled to stop at the sight of her brother and lover with the tramp: "Here's a play more breathless than the one I've just been crying at,—and in real life, too" (196). She is so moved by the spectacle of Bradford's kindness as evidence that he has "conscience and a heart," that she renounces convention, offers to marry him immediately despite her family's objections to his poverty, and pledges herself to Christian mothering alongside Bradford: "*He* sank self, *I* can—*he* blessed, so can I" (197). Apart from the unsettling idea that to be charitable is to "sink," in all this, the tramp proves not to be the ultimate concern. The play is less about directly addressing the needs of the poor or rectifying the conditions that cause poverty than it is about reforming well-educated upper- and middle-class men upon whom society depends for leadership. In the end, Grace has seen to it that Bradford has increased his moral capital and bolstered a Christian economy of charity, but, to achieve this end, he has had to imitate the aptly named Grace. The question has to be does he "become" Grace or merely remain in a state of imitation? I want to reinvoke Michael Taussig's *Mimesis and Alterity* at this point. Taussig, in arguing for the transformative power of imitation, says that "the ability to mime, and mime well . . . is the capacity to Other" (19). Dunbar certainly suggests that Bradford's assumption of "womanliness" is genuine and that he becomes authentically "feminine"; in this instance the mimetic act and the model are undifferentiated.

The idea, even the belief, in the transformative power of mimesis undergirds many of the plays about courtship and marriage in the periodicals. Marriage, especially concerns about its "decline" in the face of divorce, free thought, and the modern revolt against the institution, was a subject extensively and intensively investigated in all the periodicals in essays, fiction, and plays. In "Fiction's Inadvertent Love Song" in *Selling Culture: Magazines, Markets, and Class at the Turn of the Century*, Richard Ohmann analyzes the plethora of "courtship fiction" that filled the pages of *Cosmopolitan, Ladies' Home Journal, Munsey's Magazine*, and *McClure's Magazine*, describing the complex layering of cultural work that was aligned with a specific class destiny. Though he states that he is reluctant to offer a paradigm, Ohmann does discern a number of shared characteristics, all of which point to the reconciliation of the spirited individual to accepted social institutions: "most courtship stories take the negotiating of class in the public sphere as beyond the need of representation" (314); the heroine will always make the "right choice" (315); the couple will appear to be "modern" and breezy in their verbal exchanges but fundamentally traditional when the role playing of courting is settled (317); and, ultimately, though the heroine may be a New Woman, her true independence will be realized only in a conventional and socially sanctioned marriage (308).

Plays, as well as stories, modeled such "correct" behavior during courtship. Some are quite simple, one-dimensional dramatizations of one aspect of the negotiations. Elizabeth and Anne Gleason's *Signal Service*, in jingling rhyme in *New England Magazine* (1892), stresses the desirability of honesty and openness; had the couple not been direct with each other, they would have missed the opportunity to marry. This is particularly important for the woman, Miss Paragon, who is taken by Mr. Evermore Napping's appearance at the ball where she must do the work of securing a mate because he would be more comfortable at home where, in fact, the domesticated man belongs. His suitability as a spouse also is clearly spelled out before she begins her maneuvers: he was at college with her brother, he has aristocratic looks, and he was on crew. Miss Paragon's flirtatious behavior, therefore, is socially sanctioned and encouraged as a necessity for securing an appropriate spouse.

Miss Paragon represents the type of woman most prevalent in the American plays in this study, the "Beautiful Charmer" as Martha Banta calls her in *Imaging American Women: Idea and Ideals in Cultural History*. Banta contends that between 1890 and 1920, three variations of the American Girl were evolving, the other two being the "New England Woman" and the "Outdoors Pal." Though there are instances of overlapping characteristics, the three mainly were quite distinct: "the Charmer charms, the New England Woman thinks, and the Outdoors Girl cavorts" (46). The young women dramatized in the American plays of courtship all fit the conventional model of Charmer; they may toy with new ideas but they always willingly capitulate to the male will and the social norm. They are skilled in pleasing men, manage their delicate egos with consummate tact, and secure them as husbands.

Several of William Dean Howells's plays for *Harper's* dramatize the woman's efforts to control the courtship process. *A Previous Engagement* (1895) is case in point. Phillippa, in an effort to elicit all the details of a young man's previous love life before she agrees to marry him, behaves in a way her uncle finds "peculiar" but which her aunt understands perfectly: "*I* don't think she's a fool. I think she knows very well what she's about . . . . You wouldn't understand, and you're so silly about the girl that you would take it the wrong way. You never can understand that women can't go about things as men do, and you think if they use a little finesse with themselves, they are doing something criminal and false" (37). Phillippa, in effect, throws herself at the man, tells him the truth about herself, then pulls back, gives him a kiss, and sets him free, leaving him in "awe." His only response is to tell her the truth, at which point she capitulates; thus, their engagement begins from a position of mutual honesty and respect all because of her artful if unconventional contrivances. *Indian Giver: Comedy* (1897) concerns a woman's complicated maneuvers to win back an earlier love whom she has "given" to another woman, behavior her mother explains to the confused young man as "wholly incomprehensible . . . . Before she could realize your loss, Lillian had to give you to someone else." Puzzled, he asks: "If you wanted anything, would you put it out of your power, in order to realize your desire for it?" She replies, "No, but Lillian would . . . . Such innocence as yours is *criminal*" (248). The young woman in *Parting Friends* (1910) tries so hard to be "correct" and not kiss her beau in public that she misses her chance for his proposal. In *Self-Sacrifice: A Farce-Tragedy* (1911), Isobel Ramsey tries to drive away the man she loves because she believes him to be engaged to another woman. Trying to disgust him by acting like a New Woman, she attempts to smoke and drink cocktails, chats in a vulgar fashion about "passion" in novels, and suggest that she has been in the company of crude men. The man, once he understands her reasons and reveals his dedication to her, loves her even more and acknowledges her superiority to him in "moral grandeur" (757).

Tudor Jenks's *Parried* in *Century* (1899) is another case in point. The play sets up what appears to be a babbling young woman futilely pursued by an ardent admirer who, because of her constant domination of the conversation, cannot complete his declaration of love to her. At the play's end her maneuvering is revealed as skillful and tactful when she tells her chosen suitor that she deliberately babbled to protect the rejected man from embarrassment. The play's epigraph, "L'homme propose, mais la femme dispose," flatteringly positions the reader as both well-read and worldly (318). The epigraph is a parody of Thomas Kempis's *De Imitatione Christi* (I. xix) in which God disposes. Putting the epigraph in French only plays at sophistication because it safely secularizes the saying and puts the reader into a complicit relationship with the artful young woman who is definitely not a flirt. Propriety, decorum, and tact in the hands of a controlling woman are established as social desiderata.

The same kind of artful maneuvering is at the center of Arnold Bennett's *The Honeymoon* in *McClure's* (1911). At issue is whether or not a young aviator, Cedric, will cut his honeymoon short in order to compete with a German flyer in a contest. The woman, Flora, argues that what she brings to the marriage is "the gift of heaven cultivated by the labour of a lifetime" (699) and she expects a "sacrifice" from him (703). When the German breaks his leg and the competition is delayed, the aviator covers up the fact and seemingly makes the required sacrifice. Flora discovers the truth but, because she wants to marry him, turns his deceit into a virtue: "Last night you hesitated to sacrifice your aëroplane to me. But this morning you tell the most frightful lies on the chance of getting hold of me . . . . You forfeit your own self-respect. Cedric, that is what I like. It's just that shows how much in earnest you are. Your deeds are far superior to your arguments" (706). And, with this rationalization, she throws herself into his arms.

Annie Eliot's *As Strangers: A Comedietta in One Act* in *Scribner's* (1896) is an extended depiction of a frivolous young woman picking a fight with her fiancé because he turns up a little late. Eliot had published a similar "comedietta," *From Four to Six*, in *Scribner's* in 1899, so presumably the readers knew what to expect. In *As Strangers*, the young man teases his intended, declaring that his ideal woman should be her opposite, that is, "deeply intellectual, with a natural distaste for pettiness—a soul that looks abroad upon life with a gaze that sees no trivialities" (202). Of course, in the end, he claims her, thereby validating her impetuous childish behavior. The desired outcome is never in doubt; at the start of the play, the young woman considers the only alternative, a life of political and intellectual engagement, which she decidedly rejects: "I'm tired of the Civic Club—I've been a voter nearly a year now—and I never heard of the 'Religio Medici,' and I dare say it is some horrid, new advanced thing, anyway" (189). In both cases, the reader is presented with manipulative young women who are quite capable of managing their courtships but who have little inclination or capacity for much else. The light, uncritical tone of the plays, of course, sanctions the behavior as desirable and the marriages at the end demonstrate that the prize goes to such women, women who reject the "modern" path that would take them beyond the home and whose charming ignorance renders them incapable of sustaining a meaningful intellectual or civic life, a life not much valued in the play anyway.

Other plays do more complicated cultural work, embedding class issues within the courtship frame. For instance, George Hibbard's *A Matter of Opinion* in *Scribner's* (1900) dramatizes the many moves a courting couple makes from the beginning, in which Amy is writing a description of breaking off her engagement, to the conclusion, when Amy is reunited with Lawrence. Though the couple disagrees throughout the play, they never lose their tempers and the perfect decorum of middle-class life is emphasized as the necessary soothing oil for the desired end, matrimony. Several issues are raised to test their values. A factory strike prompts Amy's irritation: "Isn't it intolerable that the respectable members of a community should be obliged to suffer from mere mob rule? Isn't that *tyranny*, and the worst form of *tyranny*—the tyranny of ignorance?" (239). Under discussion is also the malign influence of one

Mrs. Ida B. Manly, a woman given to public service who is descried as "that horrid woman with two divorced husbands" (240). Amy hears from her brother that his betrothed, Minerva Owlish, has left him: "it's all this cursed nonsense that she's learned at Barnard and afterwards at Girton. She says she has work to do, and a 'vocation' and must not sacrifice her 'career' " (241). Throughout the play, Amy is working at sewing as if to visually underscore her domestic virtues. Her reward, of course, is Lawrence. The personal in this case is clearly political; the "correct" response to the strike is echoed by the equally "correct" responses to women's leadership in civic affairs and participation in higher education. The reader receives only one message from this play: the social welfare and propagation of class privileges and gendered distinctions take priority over all other issues, issues that prove to have been little more than topics for discussion to signal the socially normative opinions of the couple.

For Ohmann, ultimately the cultural work of "courtship fiction" and the periodicals was the instantiation of what he terms the "PMC," the professional middle class, and the establishment of mass culture, a "tight linkage of social identity with the purchase and use of commodities, including cultural products." It could be argued that the work of the periodicals was as much about selling products as it was about selling class, the two were so inextricably linked. In fact, Ohmann argues that consumption did and continues to cloud "clear thought" and "sensible politics"; "commodification is a strong ally of hegemony" (362). A good example is Howells's *Parting Friends*, in which the taste and class of the courting couple mark them as privileged: "they are seated on one of the most restricted sofas in one of the remotest embrasures of the music-room on the Anglo-Teutonic-Batavian triple turbine wireless 30,000-ton Ritz restaurant steamer" (670). Another instance is Van Tassel Sutphen's *A House of Cards* in which a separated couple is reunited because her father is coming to visit them and the young wife has returned to what had been their shared home to set up a temporary false front. The place, now decorated "*en garçon*," has been denuded of books and pictures and filled with golf-clubs, fencing-foils, cigar-boxes, and a picture of a "modern" woman, "Carita of the Hyperion and the reigning mode along with squash-ball and motor-cars" (902). As the couple set up the house in preparation for the father's visit, they replace the bachelor goods with the cultural icons unequivocally marking their status as a prosperous, "sophisticated" bourgeois couple: statues of the Winged Victory and Hermes, a Corot painting, and "Au Clair de la Lune" as well as the appropriate reading matter, *Les Miserables* (which they confess to each other they find boring). She pulls out her sewing basket and he takes out his pipe. Now the place has all the attributes of married propriety. When the father arrives, he informs them that he is in town to make a purchase—"a superb Izaak Walton princeps"—and praises the womanly, domestic atmosphere of the room. Before he leaves he insists on seeing the "shrine" the young husband had made to the wife, her bridal photograph. The wife protests but when the curtain is drawn the bridal picture is in place and, after the father leaves, the couple are clearly reunited in old-fashioned domestic fidelity shored up by the correct cultural commodities.

Clearly one social institution that regulated class solidarity and promoted racial stability was marriage. It should come as no surprise that the plays in the periodicals all dramatize the desirability of marriage and, specifically, marriage within one's own class and race. Many of Howells's plays, for instance, are focused on the lives of prosperous couples, usually with no indication of employment or source of income, their only worry being how to pull off a dinner party smoothly as in the case of *The Unexpected Guests*. The commitment by the middle and upper classes to their own is largely a given; any departures from the social norm produce either tragedy (Royle's *The Squaw-Man*) or farce (Bangs's *A Proposal Under Difficulties*). Some plays are cautionary in their aims. Laurence Alma Tadema's *An Undivined Tragedy* (*Harper's* 1894) is a mother's narration to her daughter about her matrimonial mistake, namely marrying an idea, a dream, rather than a real man. The mother recounts her courtship by Sir Jasper, a handsome but stone-cold stoic who did not need or want her, and her deep love for a laborer, Piers, a man with an infant daughter, with whom she experienced meaningful rapport. They meet secretly, and she realizes that the true face of the fair knight of her youthful imagination is Piers's because he is a "natural" man with intuitive intelligence, not the dry bookishness of her husband. One day "our last weapon, self-command, beaten at one blow from our grasp by the divine monster whose strength had outgrown the bulwarks of our consciences, who, nourished in the darkest depths of our hearts, now burst from its prison and stood in naked radiance before our failing eyes" but, thinking of her parents not her wedding vows, she pushes Piers away : "If we do this, if we buy these joys—oh, Piers, think of it!—the price is deadly sin; we might die cursing each other" (626). Sir Jasper witnesses this and, soon after, Piers disappears. Three years later, Sir Jasper brings her a little girl. The daughter, that child who has always believed herself to be her mother's and Sir Jasper's daughter, is horrified by the revelation but the mother reassures her: "Not mine, but his! Weep not, thou ten times dearer than my own!—thou child of my love, in whose dear eyes I still possess the light of those that are gone!" (629). The play ends with the mother's speculation that Sir Jasper had driven Piers to his death and that the adoption was an act of atonement, but she seems untroubled by that possibility especially given that he is now dead. In sum, *An Undivined Tragedy* warns against marriage based on girlish fantasy but, because the mother "gets the girl," rewards marital chastity within that same marriage. Even though the "natural" man is preferable to the scholar and even though the aristocratic scholar may be a murderer, the sanctity of marriage outweighs all other considerations.

John Galsworthy's *Hall-Marked: A Satiric Trifle* in *The Atlantic Monthly* (1914) also depends on the social sanctity of marriage but for comic effect. The joke turns on the question vexing the community: is the dashing newcomer, "Herself," married to her companion, Mr. Challenger? Everything about Herself is socially attractive, but the conventional middle-class people won't accept her until they have absolute proof of her marriage. On the other hand, the working-class chauffeur is unconcerned: "I can't afford to take notice of whether there's the trifle of a ring between 'em, as the sayin' is" (848). Lady Ella, representing the upper class, is also unconcerned, arguing that married or not, Herself is still a wonderful addition. Only the middle-class character is horrified that the ring should be considered only a "trifle." In the end, of course, Herself is revealed to have left her ring in the bathroom and finally comprehends the odd behavior of her neighbors. In "Some Platitudes Concerning Drama" for the *Atlantic Monthly* (1909), Galsworthy had made his case that all worthwhile drama needed to be "moral" and that the serious dramatist had three options, one of which was to remain detached from his characters in order to allow the public to make the judgment. Slight though it is, *Hall-Marked* presumably asks the reader to evaluate the moral codes of the represented classes in the play and, in the end, to join with Galsworthy in affirming the middle-class moral code of matrimony while safely delighting in the slightly salacious innuendos.

An example of the way in which the inevitable necessity of class hierarchies is an operative assumption for marriage is one of John Kendrick Bangs's slight farces, *A Proposal Under Difficulties* (1895), one of a series with the same cast of characters he wrote for *Harper's Monthly*. In this instance, Robert, a suitor for the hand of Dorothy, is practicing his proposal in her fashionable drawing room when he is overheard by the maid, Jennie, who takes this as directed at her. Coyly she accepts: "I has been engaged to Mr. Hicks, the coach gentleman, sir, but . . . I has no doubt as how you'll be doin' the square thing by Hicks, for, as I was a-sayin', I has been engaged like to him, an' he has some rights; but I think as how, if I puts it to him right like, and tells him what a nice gentleman you are, it'll be all right, sir" (152). Much later, with an angry Hicks threatening to beat up his reluctant rival, Jennie explains to her mistress that Robert "got down on his knees to her on that Proosian rug" and "recited some pottery" (157). Whatever Jennie's feelings for her coachman, she believes herself obliged to defer to class superiority: "It ain't for the likes o' me to say no to the likes o' him" (158). All is resolved when Jennie assures her mistress that Robert must be telling the truth about the confusion because, unlike "all the other gentlemen I've said yes to," he did not kiss her (159).

Everything in the play points to Jennie's unsuitability for Robert even had he been interested: her poor command of English, her limited education, her parade of suitors, her choice of current suitor, the bellicose Hicks, and her matter-of-fact attitude to being kissed by other "gentlemen." All of this Bangs presents to his readers as the subject of "farce." If there were any doubt, the illustrations support the play's class distinctions. Jennie in her maid's uniform is shown frantically waving her feather duster while her mistress, elegant in a white gown, tea cup poised gracefully on her lap, converses with her two rival suitors, trim gentlemen in morning frocks decorated with boutonnieres. Hicks, by contrast, is allowed no such dignity; in the final illustration, he is depicted as a husky man, his uniform jacket off and his sleeves rolled up, scowling and ready for a brawl. As if to underscore the point, Hicks is depicted in miniature and the upper-class characters are in a full-page illustration (see figure 3.2).

Margaret Cameron's *The Committee on Matrimony* in *McClure's* (1903) is also a good example of Ohmann's contentions. Set in a "richly furnished, if somewhat conventional, drawing room," the play follows an argument between a young couple about the advisability of their

Figure 3.2 Edward Penfield for John Frederick Bangs's *A Proposal under Difficulties* (*Harper's* 1895)

impending marriage. The play opens with an unresolved debate about Kipling (which immediately marks the couple as having educated, middle-class taste) and moves quickly to the idea of having a committee of friends decide on their suitability: "we're in no position to judge whether our marriage would be best for us—best for humanity" (661).

Neither of them, however, is happy with the other's choice of judge. He rejects her choice because she "belongs to the ultra-anti-masculine wing of the woman movement, and opposes marriage on principle" (663). She objects to his choice because he is "too modern. He seems to regard married men as victims of untoward circumstances, and he *congratulates* engaged girls!" (663). After parodying the theoretical rhetoric of the woman's movement, the exasperated young man simply delivers an ultimatum: "You know what my circumstances are, financially and socially, and what your position as my wife would be. You say that you love me. If you love me, you'll marry me" to which the tearful young woman, fearful of losing him, accedes (664).

A West Point Regulation by Mary Shipman Andrews, also in *McClure's* (1904), follows a similar pattern. The social standing and suitability of the couple is a given: she is the daughter of a West Point officer and he is a lieutenant. She is being pursued both by a rambunctious and socially clumsy cadet (he gobbles his cakes at tea time) and by the Lieutenant who is known as "The Stony Charmer" because he is impervious to love. After some comic business with the spurned cadet, he proves to be the facilitator of the inevitable match between the woman and the socially appropriate suitor, the Lieutenant whose military bachelorhood needs to be domesticated.

Two plays follow the courtship model but with twists to produce socially "correct" if less than happy endings. Margaret Sutton Briscoe's *An I.O.U* in *Scribner's* (1893) dramatizes the unspoken and unrequited love of a middle-aged guardian for his young ward. The conversations, set in his drab lawyer's office, span a year. In the first act, the lawyer gently rebuffs her school-girlish declaration of love, accepting an I.O.U. for her kisses. When she returns, a year later, having reached the age of maturity and consent, and he wants to declare his love for her, he teasingly produces the I.O.U. Now, however, she is love with a young man who the lawyer realizes is the suitable match; leaving his own feelings unstated, he consents to her marriage to her suitor who can offer her "an honorable name, an eager devotion, and the pride of strength and youth" (313). The play serves as a double warning: to the young female reader about moderating her infatuation and to the older male reader about the correctness of reticence. It also suggests the kind of sacrifice that is necessary to maintain the status quo: the lawyer's love for the young woman must be understood to be deep and real in order to make the point that the desired social condition is defined by what is given up to achieve it.

George Duncan's *A Proposal* in *Harper's Monthly* (1904) explores the same theme from a woman's point of view. Similarly constructed as a drawing room conversation between an elegant "He" and "She" (the illustrations depict them in evening dress), the play is a verbal fencing match. He comes to tell her of a lie he told another woman, namely that he loves She, a lie he told to enable a convenient breakup. Now He tells She that once he did really love her but he never declared this love because what mattered to him was that he *could* love, the *who* did not matter because it was like a dream. Against his thoughtless banter, She's real feeling for him is made evident. Having destroyed her long-held dream of passionate love, He then proposes marriage, pointing to the obvious social advantages: *He*: "But, really, it would be a good sort of match. We are both rich, belong to the same set, the families would like it, and all that sort of thing, and—but you have thought about it, haven't you?" *She* (*wearily*): "Yes, I suppose so" (801). After He leaves, She lights one of his cigarettes but then collapses, weeping. The personal desire is overridden by her capitulation to the social correctness and inevitability of the loveless match. Their lack of specific names suggests that such behavior is endemic to the upper class but, presumably, not to the middle-class readers.

Aside from the issue of class distinction and the close connection with consumption, there are also two other important cultural issues to consider concerning plays about courtship and marriage. The first is "race suicide" as the panic about the dwindling Anglo-Saxon demographic dominance was called; the second is the related matter of miscegenation. It is important to stress, as Alexander Saxton does in *The Rise and Fall of the White Republic*, that the insistence on white supremacy was an essential element in legitimating the class coalitions that dominated late-nineteenth-century America. Undergirded by the new science of eugenics, which warned against the consequences of breeding from inferior stock, nativists seized upon the idea to legitimate immigration restriction and insure American purity. Three prominent examples of the expression of this virulent anxiety in the periodicals will serve to set the stage: Francis Amasa Walker's "Immigration and Degradation" in *Forum* (1891); William Z. Ripley's "Races in the United States" in the *Atlantic Monthly* (1908) in which he reiterated assertions he had made earlier in *The Races of Europe: A Sociological Study* (1899); and Madison Grant's "Race, Nationality and Language" in the *Geographical Review* (1916), the first part of his book, *The Passing of the Great Race* (1919). Walker, the president of M.I.T., opened the floodgate of eugenicist arguments, which became ubiquitous in the periodicals. Walker, troubled by the decline in the "vitality of our native American stock" (634)— by which he meant descendants of the original Europeans settlers "(leaving the Africans out of account)" (637)— charges that the continuous immigration constitutes a "shock" to the native element (640) and is responsible for civic rupture: "For the first time in our history the people of the free States became divided into classes. The classes were natives and foreigners" (641). Heightening the alarm, Walker announces that the climax of this "monstrous"influx was reached between 1880 and 1890 and that the "vast hordes," the "stagnant pool," represent "the utterest failures of civilization, the worst defeats in the struggle for existence, the lowest degradation of human nature" (642). So, by his account, unless the United States ceased its "indiscriminate hospitality," "these Huns, and Poles, and Bohemians, and Russian Jews, and South Italians will continue to come, and to come by millions," bringing with them the diseases, physical infirmities, and criminal impulses that sap the "reproductive vigor" of Americans (644). Ripley, a prominent economist, struck much the same discordant note on the "wave," the "horde," the "mongrel" from the "political sinks of Europe" (747). Charging that "these foreign-born men" "covet an American-born wife" (750), Ripley invokes theories of breeding stock to argue for the necessity of preserving racial purity, to warn against "abnormal intermixture" (755), and to predict that the domestic Anglo-Saxon stock is committing "race suicide" (756) and will pass as did the "American Indian and the buffalo" (758). In 1903 the formation of American Breeders Association marked the beginning of an official movement to control stock, a movement that accelerated when human geneticists took over in 1906 and set up a eugenics section.

Madison Grant, whom historian John Higham called "the most important nativist in recent American history," extended Walker's and Ripley's arguments with his own "scientific" reiteration of French and German racial polemics, adding that moral, intellectual, and spiritual attributes were as persistent as physical characteristics and were also transmitted unchanged generationally (155). An enormously influential nativist polemic, *The Passing of the Great Race, or the Racial Basis of European History* went through several editions, was translated into several languages, and was used during the 1920s congressional hearings on immigration restriction. His apocalyptic thesis was that the superior "Nordic" race was courting its own destruction because of war, alcoholism, and disease and, in America, intermixture with inferior, immigrant stock, which resulted in reversion from "higher" to "lower" type. This "voluntary race suicide" was causing the passing of the "great race." The solution was an increase in the "superior" classes and the sterilization of the "unfit." In general, Grant's ideas were well-received in the scholarly journals but also in the popular periodicals such as *Nation* and the *Literary Digest*, and he continued to be a major force behind immigration restriction, publishing in *Forum* and *North American Review* into the mid-1920s.

Walker, Ripley, and Grant were but three prominent voices raised in anxious, fear-mongering protest over immigration. As Gail Bederman points out in *Manliness & Civilization*, Theodore Roosevelt's presidential policies were shaped by "considerations of manhood, race and 'civilization' " (196). Bederman stresses that though the birthrate controversy certainly was part of the issue, there was a broader and deeper context for race suicide, namely fears about "effeminacy, overcivilization, and racial decadence" (200). She credits Roosevelt with introducing the term "race suicide" into popular usage when a letter he wrote to Bessie Van Vorst, praising her exposé on the hard conditions facing women factory workers in *Everybody's Magazine*, was reprinted as the preface to her book, *The Woman Who Toils: Being the Experience of Two Ladies as Factory Girls* (1903) (202). Another important voice on the side of this eugenic position was that of William James, who concurred with Roosevelt, " 'The race should never cease to breed for every one is sensitive to its superiority' " (Watts 85). Clearly the stakes for the nation could not be higher, and it was the duty of every American citizen of "superior" stock to propagate within marriage.

The need to redress "race suicide," however, was up against another strong social force, and the courtship plays should also be understood in the context of what Howard Chudacoff has called the "Age of the Bachelor." In his study of the vital "subculture" of bachelors and masculinity from 1880 to 1930, Chudacoff observes that bachelors "had become a serious social problem" by the late nineteenth century (4). The statistics bear out his argument: in 1890, 41.7 percent of men over fifteen were single, 67 percent of men between fifteen and thirty-five were single, and the nation's marriage rate, the number of marriages per 100,000 population, dropped from 98 in 1870 to 91 in 1890 (Chudacoff 48). The polite periodicals, like the ones publishing courtship plays and stories, had strong competition from the popular magazines read by men, especially *The National Police Gazette*, which catered to men across class lines and specifically targeted single men with luridly illustrated stories on sports, sex, and crime extolling the pleasures of single life. Distributed to boarding houses, barber shops, fire halls, and saloons, *The National Police Gazette* was one of the most influential and widely read magazines at century's end; Chudacoff estimates that by the 1890s its regular subscriptions exceeded 150,000 with some special issues at 400,000 (187). Given that the magazine was readily available in public places frequented by men, I want to suggest that the courtship plays and stories in the more genteel publications were written to address the "problem" of proliferating bachelors. Single women reading the plays could be reassured that a good match was possible, and male readers, single or married, would find no acceptable alternative to married life; marriage was dramatized explicitly as the normative social state and implicitly as necessary to revitalize an American gene pool threatened by degenerate, dark immigrants. Finally, the men in the plays are "gentlemen" trained in drawing-room manners and decorum; there are no hyper-masculine, Rooseveltian, aggressive, swaggering physical types. Nor is sex or reproduction ever directly addressed as the real object of courtship; the veil of romance is drawn over the pragmatics of redressing "race suicide."

As I noted earlier, the second important cultural issue was miscegenation, and one safe way to include the alarming subject in the drama was to relegate it to the past. Edwin Milton Royle's *The Squaw-Man: An Idyll of the Ranch* in *Cosmopolitan* (1904) is a case in point. *Cosmopolitan*, founded in 1886 as a "family magazine," gained distinction after 1889 when John Brisben Walker purchased it and employed writers such as Theodore Dreiser, Edith Wharton, Jack London, and Annie Besant. Mott notes that by 1900 *Cosmopolitan* had a circulation just shy of half a million and, with a hundred pages of advertising per issue, was a desirable commodity. In 1905 *Cosmopolitan* was sold to William Randolph Hearst who added investigative journalism to the mix and brought the circulation up to one million by 1914. Under Hearst,

Cosmopolitan was more sensational than before and heavily staffed with journalists. For instance, his drama critic for a decade, Alan Dale, had worked on Hearst's New York papers and lavishly illustrated his *Cosmopolitan* theatre articles with photographs (Mott, *History 1885–1905* 489–92). Hearst's journalistic leanings may account for the appearance of *The Squaw Man*, one of only two plays to be published in *Cosmopolitan* (the other being a farce by Howells in 1892).

The Squaw Man, one of the most successful plays of its day, opened at the Star Theatre in Buffalo in April 1905, moved to Wallack's Theatre for a long run in October 1905, and was produced in London at the Lyric Theatre as *The White Man* in January 1908 (Quinn, *From the Civil War* 390). At the end of March 1910, it had run for 2,000 performances and went on to many revivals including a musical treatment in 1927 (Hall 202–06). It also had a long life in several film versions, the first being in 1914 directed by Cecil B. DeMille. Though essays and stories about the west figured regularly in the periodicals, Royle's is the only play about Indians and the American west. It is possible that the popularity of Buffalo Bill's Wild West shows, which were seen by tens of thousands, and his insistence that "his exhibition was not a show at all, but 'reality itself' " displaced the viability of the script for a published play (Reddin 61). It may also be that because the Indian had already been consigned to history, the physical immediacy of a stage Indian would seem archaic. On the other hand, Don Wilmeth lists ninety-four Indian plays between 1890 and 1918 in a tentative checklist of the phenomenon. I can only speculate that the same reasons for avoiding African Americans in the periodical drama obtained for Indians: polite American readers did not want to be grunting in their parlors if and when they read the plays aloud nor did they wish to replay any sordid historical event from America's troubled history.

By the end of the nineteenth century, Indians as a "question" or as a "problem" for white Americans had been answered and solved by relentless military intervention and, for most periodicals, the Indian was a "picturesque" figure from an increasingly remote past. The recent horrors of Indian resistance such as Sitting Bull at Little Big Horn were memories and, with the Dawes Act of 1887 and the 1907 admission of Oklahoma to the union, the Indian presence seemed to recede. As Brian Dippie observes, "the Vanishing American, in short, represented a perfect fusion of the nostalgic with the progressive impulse" because it proved the inevitable decline of inferior races (xii). Indeed, most of the articles in periodicals stressed the extinction of the full-blooded Indian and focused on issues of assimilation and the inevitable and necessary Anglo-Saxon cultural dominance, both reassuring stances for the readers. For instance, in the *Arena* (1896), B. O. Flower described Simon Pokagon, chief of the Pottawatomie tribe, as "an interesting representative of a vanishing race" and George Bird Grinnell in the *Atlantic Monthly* (1899) reassured his readers that "the wild Indian" is extinct and those that remain are no more than children unable to assume white men's ways. Attention is paid to mixed-blood Indians who accept the inevitable march and superiority of "civilized" ways. In a survey of attitudes toward Indians and Blacks in American periodicals, Charles Wilson observes that the insistence on Anglo-Saxon superiority was the driving force behind the denigration of both races as infantile, uncivilized, and primitive. Though the African was understood to be submissive and educable, the pure-bred Indian, proud and resistant, clearly was doomed to extinction.

Despite such dire prognoses, the Indian survived into the twentieth century still shrouded in late-nineteenth-century assumptions. In "The Last of the Red Race" in *Cosmopolitan* (1902), William Draper portrays "little copper-brown babies" as "an anachronism" (244). Such aboriginal children, he argues, understand the "scalping knife" by "instinct" (245) whereas the Indian who will survive and thrive is the "amalgamated" individual whose gains in "advantages" more than outweigh what he loses in "racial entity" (Draper 246). Thomas Millard voices similar views in "The Passing of the American Indian" in *Forum* (1903). Like Draper, he notes the loss of the "picturesque" figure but heralds the Indians' "absorption by the white race," which is "inevitable." The few autonomous "minor" tribes left "must be classed among the melancholy human relics left over from a barbaric age" (466). "Full-blooded Indians" are largely "backward" and don't appreciate and accept the beneficent improvements readily embraced by the "American Indian." The line is clearly drawn: on one hand there is the doomed "full-blooded Indian," and, on the other, there is the culturally, politically, and racially "American Indian" of mixed blood who will be assimilated and, over time, "improved." But neither type had a place in the plays in periodicals, and the illusion of a nearly "pure" white nation was maintained in the safe cultural zone provided by the magazines.

Whatever the explanation for the anomalous appearance of this play, Royle assumes his readers' familiarity with the conventional depictions and tropes of the west. The concept of Manifest Destiny suffused the periodicals, which were dedicated to promulgating Anglo-Saxon institutions, Protestant Christianity, and U.S. civilization. Also, the characters would have been familiar. The "cow puncher" and "cowboy" had been given a good deal of exposure and some measure of respectability in Buffalo Bill's Wild West shows, which had been traveling throughout the United States since 1883. As Richard Slotkin points out, displaying Indians in the Wild West show demonstrated the superiority of the Americans, repeatedly reenacted the defeat of the Indians, and reinscribed the national epic that blended myth, history, and legitimized force (*Regeneration through Violence*). Even the squaw man was, as Brian Dippie explains, "a ubiquitous presence in western history," briefly taking on "a certain romantic aura" as a bridge over the racial gulf. By 1904, though, miscegenation could only breed tragedy; "one of the partners either terminated it in obedience to the inexorable law of color consciousness, or made the ultimate sacrifice, surrendering up life itself" (260–61).

The play dramatizes the impossibility and inadvisability of assimilation and is part of a genealogy of a lengthy American literary tradition of first ennobling and then dispensing with "Indians." Women, in particular, were marked for exclusion and magazine readers would have been familiar with this trope from mass market fiction. For example, the first dime novel, Ann Stephens's *Malaeska: The Indian Wife of the White Hunter* (1860), a melodramatic story of miscegenation, which had been serialized in 1839 in *The Ladies's Companion*, depicts the maternal devotion and endless suffering produced by an "unnatural marriage" (163). It ends not only with Malaeska's death but also with the suicide of her half-breed son who cannot bear the revelation of his mixed blood. The focus on Indian women in such narratives in particular goes to the creation of a national narrative that Dana Nelson diagnoses as "Inindination," the process by which white men secured their "white/national male identity" (62).

In the final version of Royle's play, there are four acts, the first set in England. The earlier version, written as a sketch for the Lambs' Club and published in *Cosmopolitan* in 1904, is one act only, set outside a cow puncher's cabin on the Greene River. The plot concerns the attempts of a London solicitor, Petrie, to bring Jim Carston, now in line for an earldom, back to England. Petrie, a "conventional English gentleman in the conventional English riding-habit," would "appeal to the cowboy's sense of the ridiculous" (413). Carston, on the other hand, makes a claim to being "plain people," refuses to be addressed by his title, and insists that he cannot return to England because the mother of his son, Hal, is an Indian, Nat-u-ritch ("pretty little girl"), and "there isn't any place in England for Nat-u-ritch"; "even here I am a 'squaw-man'—that means socially ostracized. You see we have social distinctions even out here" (415–16). The term "squaw man" was derived from four members of the five principal "civilized tribes"–Cherokees, Choctaws, Chicasaws, and Seminoles—which passed laws admitting the intermarried whites or "squaw men" to tribal membership. According to Eugene Jones, the first fully developed "squaw man" in American drama was Abel Doe in Louisa Medina's *Nick of the Woods* (1838). Furthermore, Carston explains, "I would not desert a dog who has been faithful to me" and knows that even though she belongs to an "inferior race," Nat-u-ritch would kill herself if he left her (415).

Petrie, reluctantly agrees, consigning Carston to "a living death" and shifts his attention to the boy, insisting that he be allowed to return to England to claim his "manifest destiny" and clinching his plea with the final thrust, "England expects every man to do his duty" (416). Carston accepts the imperative but worries about the effect on his wife because "she is almost as much of a child as Hal" (416) He explains the situation to her: "Nat-u-ritch, big chief come for little Hal. Pretty soon make Hal heap big chief. Tougewayno teguin! Good friend! Long trail, heap big mountains, Washington. [To Petrie] Washington means a lot to them. Pretty soon, some day Hal heap wickiup, heap cattle, heap ponies—pretty soon heap big chief." Nat-u-ritch's responds by putting her hand on his arm: "love, trust, submission, terror, despair—it means all these and more" and, stricken, she "drifts out into the night" (417). Moments later, a gun shot is heard and the cowboys enter carrying the dead woman, "poor little mother" (418). Carston, of course, is now free to return to England and take up the title of earl untainted by an Indian wife but also as a better man for the job because of his heightened masculinity acquired in the west. The problematics of Hal's mixed blood, however, are never addressed, though presumably, they are overridden by his gender, by his westernized Americanization, and by the assurance of an English upbringing, a double cultural heritage that will place him securely under the aegis of the "Larger England."

Of the production, Quinn writes, "Royle determined to put the real Indian on the stage and he cast for the character of Baco White, the interpreter, a Ute Indian, through whom he secured an exact phonetic reproduction of the Ute dialect for the squaw Nat-u-ritch and her father, Tab-i-wana, the Peace Chief of the tribe" (*From the Civil War* 124). Quinn says nothing of who represented Nat-u-ritch and the Chief. The printed version in *Cosmopolitan* is markedly different. The only Indian in the play is Nat-u-ritch and, but for a greeting of "how" and an impassioned cry of "no" when her small son is taken from her, she is silent. As Roger Hall observes, "It shows us the Indian who has been a savior, a protector, a nurse, and a lover to the white man, but who has outlived her usefulness and must step aside so that he may be happy" (204). Passive, supine, wifely, motherly, silent, and self-sacrificial, Nat-u-ritch's ultimate displacement draws attention to the power relations inherent in the social and racial hierarchies: English aristocracy/ American "plain folk"/ Native American woman. Because of such ambiguities, Don Wilmeth suggests that *The Squaw-Man*, like William C. DeMille's *Strongheart* (1905), represents a shifting attitude toward Indians by American dramatists: "the plays written in 1905 suggest that dramatists are beginning to portray Indians as real people and as part of a real societal problem, and yet there is definite hesitancy to embrace them as a meaningful part of the white man's society" (*Noble* 60).

One could point to the five accompanying photographs illustrating the play as an index of such "hesitancy" or of Dana Nelson's "Inindination." The editorial note lists the actors who "kindly imper-sonated the characters": Nat-u-ritch is portrayed neither by a Ute Indian nor even by a woman but by a white man, Edward S. Ables. The three images of the "Indian woman" show her bent over her child in terror in a state of "universal motherhood" (413); grasping piteously on Carston's arm in an attitude of "love, trust, submission, terror, despair" (415); and, in the final tableau, lying dead at the feet of six men with the cap-tion "poor little mother!" (418). Now that she is conveniently dead, her work of procreation done, the woman can be the safe subject of pity as a *mother* and not the threatening agent of miscegenation as an *Indian*. That there is no other woman in the play suggests that America really belongs to westernized men (see figure 3.3).

I began this chapter with an examination of *A Woman's Luncheon* (1895) in which the New Women and the old discussed the many ways

"LOVE, TRUST, SUBMISSION, TERROR, DESPAIR—IT MEANT ALL THESE AND MORE."

"POOR LITTLE MOTHER!"

Figure 3.3 Two photographs for Edwin Milton Royle's *The Squaw-Man* (*Cosmopolitan* 1904)

in which they participated socially and civically in American life, the young being full citizens in ways not comprehensible to the older generation. I want to conclude with a very unlikely protagonist and representative of modern America in Louise Rogers Stanwood's *The Progress of Mrs. Alexander* in *New England Magazine* (1911), the only play of all those under consideration in this study to directly address specifically the formation of an individual's national identity. Significantly, because the protagonist is a middle-aged woman, not the ingénue of the courtship plays, the play suggests that people are capable of change and that women young and old can participate meaningfully as citizens. The protagonist, Mrs. Alexander, goes through a series of sharply satirized social climbing transformations and geographical relocations until she comes to her senses and reclaims her Midwestern, middle-class American identity. This enthusiastic embrace of possibilities, however, is constrained by the nationalist polemics of Kipling's "Larger America," which emerges as the play's ideological foundation. A "farce comedy" in three acts, the play was written for George Pierce Baker's "English '97" class at Radcliffe and, having won the Fall Competition of the Harvard Dramatic Club, was presented by that organization in Cambridge and Boston in December 1910.

In the first act, set in Breezeboro, "a small city of the Middle West," and in a "very pretty, very pink, prosperous and up to date" room, Mrs. Alexander, anxious to impress a fashionable woman who has "all the insolence of a true New Yorker," trots out not one but two secretaries (a man and a woman) and a "Jap" servant and, with her husband's newly acquired railroad riches, determines to "go East and conquer." Insisting that her name now be hyphenated, she tells her husband, Mr. Smith, that he should "attend to the business end, while I do the—the *climbing*" (540). It is worth noting, given that the play is about what it means to be a good American, that Mr. Smith's business creed of "Grasp, Grab, Graft and Grit!—and I might add Gumption"—is never ridiculed or critiqued as his wife's social pretensions are (539). In this play, capitalist ambition is a sign of authentic and productive Americanism, but social climbing is a mark of inauthentic and effete Europhilia. In fact, Mr. Smith is an exception in plays in periodicals in that he is one of only a few middle-class men identified with a job; most male characters float idly as if disconnected from the realities of work, the plays sustaining the illusion of a cocooned material life maintained by servants but not by earned or even inherited capital.

Act II finds Mrs. Alexander-Smith in Newport in a gold room dominated by a pretentious portrait of her in ermine and a tiara. Now marked by care and "the arrogance of wealth," she has lost interest in her old concern, the Woman Suffrage League of Michigan, and is focused on her dinner guest, Prince Sarski, to whom she plans to feed out-of-season strawberries and hummingbirds' eggs (542). Deaf to the secretaries' reminders that many Americans are going hungry and thirsty, she calls for a fountain of champagne. This Veblenesque barbaric display of conspicuous consumption leads her into deception when she decides to continue socializing with the Prince even though her husband has exposed him as a fraud. Furthermore, she toys with immorality when she decides it is a good thing to be believed an adulteress and be gossiped about. As she explains to her dismayed husband, "There'll be scandal talked about us, and I shall be utterly in the fashion!" (549).

Still not satisfied, she sets her sights on Beacon Hill, the setting for Act III. This elegant room is correctly but predictably furnished with a bust of Dante, two Copley portraits, the works of Henry James, the *Atlantic Monthly*, and a butler, all of which stake her claim to high culture and, by default, a higher class. Mrs. Alexander is troubled that she actually bought the "ancestors," so much so that she confesses her foolishness to her husband, but she determines to carry out her plan to entertain the Cameo Club, a prominent women's club wasting its time on squirrel rescue and fountain design. Finally unable to contain her mirth at their folly, Mrs. Alexander tells the truth and admits to her deceit. Prince Sarski, however, has managed to get one of the gullible Europhilic Bostonians to agree to marry him. Ultimately, Mrs. Alexander understands that "the people who know—the really right people,—would think better of a real Smith than a make-believe Alexander" (662). In the end, she returns to Breezeboro, renounces her false identity, a fraudulent, effete Europhile staging the effect in Boston, for her true identity as a genuine down-to-earth American living in the Midwest.

All this would be a fairly transparent morality lesson about the folly of social climbing reminiscent of earlier American satiric comedies such as Anna Cora Mowatt's *Fashion* (1845) were it not for the prominence of a poem by Kipling on which the play turns. The importance of being American and what being American means are set up at the beginning of the second act when Florence, Mrs. Alexander's female secretary reads part of Kipling's poem, "An American," to her male counterpart, Charles. Florence, "a distinctly modern type," has an Eastern education and the good taste her employer lacks (531). Charles, a serious, self-conscious Harvard man with "a very gentle manner, a touch of superiority," is a journalist only playing the part of a secretary to get his story and win Florence (534). The couple is united in their desire to save Mrs. Alexander from her social climbing though they have differing perspectives on everything. Florence will allow Charles to be "Secretary of the Department of the East! I'm the West. I'm a Suffragist, Republican, expansionist, progressive, a Rooseveltite—I suppose he is a Democrat and Anti-everything!" (535). Throughout the play Florence's vital modernity is played against Charles's stuffy Bostonian speech and attitudes; the play has a double purpose, to demonstrate that both Mrs. Alexander and Charles need to be reformed.

Though reclaiming Mrs. Alexander is their mutual objective, when Florence reads Kipling's poem, "An American," to Charles, their cultural territorial differences are laid out. This hymn to the American Spirit written in 1894 predates Kipling's "The White Man's Burden" (1899). That poem, in which Kipling urged the United States to assume its "responsibilities" in the Philippines is, as John Carlos Rowe observes, "often considered a sort of historical marker for the infection of public discourse in the United States with the jingoism of conservative public discourse" (124). By 1911, the date of the play, U.S. imperialism was a geopolitical fact and its military intervention understood as part of the larger global struggle by rational Europeans to control "savagery." The extension of American power was a new variation of Britain's *imperium* and, as the British had been effective colonizers, so too would the Americans. In other words, that Mrs. Alexander will be returned to sanity is a given; Anglo-Saxon supremacy is a settled issue because it was a global necessity. What is not settled is what *kind* of American Mrs. Alexander is going to be: a productive, down-to-earth American citizen or a useless, stuffy Europhile? That question is answered by the way in which the Kipling poem, "An American," is interpreted in the play.

"An American," written in 1894, was published in a collection, *The Seven Seas*, in 1896 during Kipling's sojourn in America from 1892 to 1896. Of Kipling's interest in America's relations with Britain and the Empire, Peter Keating writes that Kipling believed that "if the achievements of the Empire were to be maintained, it was of vital importance that the American people should regard the imperial mission not only with sympathetic understanding but with sufficient enthusiasm to participate in its expansion. To Kipling's mind the imperial cause was no longer British; it was Anglo-Saxon" (95). Certainly that message had not been lost on William Dean Howells who reviewed *The Seven Seas* for *McClure's* (1897) and who put the entire text of "An American" in the review that he entitled "The Laureate of the Larger England." Claiming Kipling as "some sort of American," one who has "given us a kind of authority to do so by diving our actual average better than any American," Howells predicts the expiration of the English empire ("it has happened so with all empires") but, significantly, contends that "it is very material that what is good in English feeling and English thinking should still inherit the earth" (455). The conflation of English language and English imperialism is transferred to the American "spirit," which proves that English patriotism is "not love of the little England" but of the "great England whose far-strewn empire feels its mystic unity in every latitude and longitude of the globe" (453).

In staking the claim for the perpetuating of the "Larger England" and the recentering of global politics in America, that is "at home in the heart of every man," Howells makes only a passing reference to the actual occasion for the poem, "a well-known moment of civic trouble," a railroad strike taking place in Chicago (453). Keating notes that an earlier title for the essay was "As it Strikes a Contemporary" (95). The reader of *The Progress of Mrs. Alexander* would be conscious that Mrs. Alexander's husband made his wealth from railroads and mines because the millions he makes on a deal allows them to go to Newport. Given that Henry Adams had recently observed that his generation was "mortgaged to the railways," Stanwood's choice of a business for Mr. Smith, therefore, seems deliberately to take a stand for big enterprise (940). The choice of railroad wealth in particular is significant because the muckraking journalists had been attacking railroad corruption in a variety of periodicals including *American Magazine*, which agitated for public safety measures; *McClure's*, which ran Ray Stannard Baker's exposés of abuses; *Colliers*, which published several articles; and *Twentieth Century Magazine*, in which Charles Vrooman discussed corruption privately and publicly owned railroads.

The poem, an address by The American Spirit, opens with a promise of the ultimate control of an unruly force:

> If the Led Striker call it a strike,
> Or the papers call it a war,
> They know not what I am like,
> Nor what he is, my Avatar. (210)

As Keating explains, the poem sets up a conflict between The American Spirit, "the traditional, humane, wise, law-abiding" principle and its Avatar, "the brash, loud-mouthed democrat whose 'heart leaps, as a babe's at little things' " (96). The Spirit continues with a vivid description of a wild Celtic force, "unkempt, disreputable, vast," schooled in resistance and, claiming that "mine ancient humour saves him whole" (211), promises that though

> Lo, imperturbable he rules,
> Unkempt, disreputable, vast—
> And, in the teeth of all the schools,
> I—I shall save him at the last! (212)

Florence, however, perversely evades the poem's true subject recasting it for her immediate ends and, despite Charles's protestation that the poem is deeper and more subtle than she allows, insists on a very literal and superficial reading of humor: "I think *that* means the Sense of Humor!" (541). From this, Florence sets up an East/West binary, claiming a sense of humor for the West and locking the East into "Earnest Purpose" and deep, analytical thinking. "Perhaps between us both,— well, there she is between us both, East and West, and we'll see! But I tell you, Mr. Soberside, that one laugh would be worth more than was ever dreamt of in your Puritan philosophy!" (542). In the end, laughter returns Mrs. Alexander to Breezeboro, Michigan, and pulls Charles into Florence's arms. When he awkwardly proposes to Florence that she marry him and become a member of the Cameo club, Mrs. Alexander chides him: "Charles Fuller, don't be such an everlasting Bostonian! Be an *American!*" and Florence joins in with "And *'I shall save him at the last!'* " (663). The play concludes, therefore, by positioning Mrs. Alexander as a mediating figure between the seriousness of the East and the spiritedness of the West and marking the Midwest as the moderate middle ground, a position supported by her husband's railroad business.

It would be wrong to lay too much of a burden on *The Progress of Mrs. Alexander* and to claim some sort of linear historical progress from *A Woman's Luncheon* where I began this discussion because there has not been much "progress." Every instantiation of women in the plays is imaginary, dramatizing an idea of woman necessary for social stability, procreation of Anglo-Saxons, perpetuation of traditional roles, and affirmation of consumerism. Though woman suffrage surfaces infrequently as a topic in the plays, it does not figure prominently enough to qualify as a substantive or primary concern. American citizenship for women, as dramatized in these plays, is determined by women's willingness to participate in the masculine national imaginary, not their own. As Americans, they are framed by the comprehensive institutions of roles, expectations, and traditional values, which contained and defined the middle class, a cultural community rooted in self-interest and antagonistic assumptions about social and racial diversity. The work of these plays about women was to naturalize the deep contradictions between a state of adult independence and the condition of infantilized subjectivity, to perpetuate a cultural norm that stabilized the domestic space, to sustain class identity by cementing affinities and to rationalize the hierarchies upon which the nation could justify exclusionary and bellicose policies.

4. Cultural Displacement ᐇ

One way for a periodical to secure an elite cultural zone was to resort to the traditional "high" cultural forms, genres, and themes that signaled "refinement" and "good taste," a strategy that was suffused with paradox. The move to create absolute hierarchical categories produced an imaginary nation in which mundane and tawdry material concerns could be ignored and transcended for higher ground and in which the legacy of Western art and culture was sustained and naturalized. The emergence of such a cultural hierarchy in America has been thoroughly examined in Lawrence Levine's history of the division into "highbrow" and "lowbrow" or "serious" and "popular," distinctions, which, significantly, were derived from the phrenological terms used in the practice of determining racial types (222). The periodicals and the plays in them certainly were instrumental in promoting and maintaining the boundaries between "high" and "low." For instance, given that for centuries throughout Europe verse was accepted as the "natural" medium for serious drama, it is not surprising that many of the serious plays in periodicals are in verse and that many of the verse plays are serious; claims to "high" culture were made by writing plays in elevated language and/or with a classical, historical, or Biblical theme.

The paradox of this move was that, under cover of verse and/or seriousness and by setting the plays in the past (real or mythic) and/or in a foreign country, the playwrights engaged in what I call "cultural displacement." Cultural displacement is manifested in several ways including the aforementioned settings in a time and place other than contemporary America, a place remote from the genteel middle-class reader's experience. Early assessments of this kind of cultural displacement marked the move as essentially "Romantic." For instance, of Josephine Preston Peabody's *The Wings* (1905), a verse play set in

Northumbria in A.D. 700, George Baker observed that as a Romantic, Peabody characteristically turned away from the present and its demand for realistic treatment and instead turned to the historic past, which allowed her to imitate Shakespeare and Marlowe and to "protest against submerging beauty in photographic fact" (x). I want to suggest that more than the rejection of a mundane realism and a claim to higher aesthetic ground, cultural displacement was the deployment of a flexible, polyvalent strategy that afforded the dramatist four freedoms. First, the writers were able to dramatize suicide, adultery, fallen women, and sexual depravity, all subjects outside the pale of a normative American middle-class context. Second, cultural displacement also widened the arena to include the naturalizing religious miracles, which fell outside the Protestant norm. Third, it authorized romantic racism and monarchism, which ought to have been anathema in a democratic republic. Fourth, it permitted a de-nationalizing and naturalizing project in which the plays of Irish and Anglo-Indian writers were appropriated and reimagined as serving "American," specifically national, needs. That all these happen in verse suggests that poetry was understood to be a "higher" form, a shield of respectability and a proper lens through which sensational or questionable material could be filtered and authorized.

Compared to fiction, poetry was understood to take the reader away from mundane reality into a higher realm where material distractions were replaced by conceptual, especially spiritual, thoughts. After *Peer Gynt* (1867), Ibsen largely had abandoned verse in favor of prose as more appropriate to contemporary issues, hence his later dramatic verse now appears dated, stilted, pretentious, and effete. Nonetheless, the English verse plays of the Romantics and Victorians constituted a small revival, especially in tragedy, and influenced many of the minor figures in the early twentieth century such as Lawrence Binyon, Gordon Bottomley, John Drinkwater, and others. A contemporary spokesperson for such drama was John Galsworthy (1867–1933) who, between *The Silver Box* (1906) and *The Roof* (1929), wrote twenty-one long plays and half a dozen short pieces. In 1909, Galsworthy published "Some Platitudes Concerning Drama" in *The Atlantic Monthly* in which he mapped out the future of drama as following two separate and distinct trajectories: naturalistic or "photographic" realism and poetic prose, "incarnating through its fantasy and symbolism all the deeper aspirations, yearnings, doubts, and mysterious stirrings of the human spirit"

(772). Galsworthy had had great success with his "photographic" dramas of social grievance such as *Strife* (1909), about the struggle between labor and capital, and *Justice* (1910), which led to prison reform in England, but little success with his strained and pretentious poetic efforts. One of the most over-reaching of these, *The Little Dream* (*Scribner's* 1911), clearly invoking Ibsen, dramatizes a young girl's spiritual quest, literalized as an Alpine mountain climb. Seelchen, the Little Soul, is torn between two men, Felsman, the mountaineer, and Lamond, the world, who represent incompatible modes of life. A succession of six formulaic, allegorical, and static *tableaux* lacking either psychological intensity or philosophical drama, *A Little Dream* locates resolution only in ecstatic death. Personifications such as "Things in Books" and "The Form of What Is Made by Work" are as cumbersome as the insights are banal; The Great Horn, for instance, advises Seelchen that the life of man is "a little raft moored, then sailing out into the blue; a tune caught in a hush, then whispering on; a new-born babe, half courage, half sleep" (535). The play was first performed in Manchester in 1911 with music by Wolfgang von Bartels.

Though most of the twenty-seven verse plays in the American periodicals under consideration are serious and conservative, they range from those with simple, jangling rhymes in comic pieces such as Marguerite Merington's *A Gainsborough Lady* (*Scribner's* 1902): "Gad's life now stab my vitals if they ain't / A credit to the author's paint" (65); Elizabeth and Anne Gleason's *Signal Service* (*New England Magazine* 1892): "Heigho, another tedious hour remains / In which I must forego the use of brains" (101); to the more complex Shakespearean iambic pentameter of Barrett Wendell's *Ralegh in Guiana* (*Scribner's* 1897); and the "modern" free verse of Zoë Akins's *The Magical City* (*Forum* 1916). Two plays by Laurence Alma Tadema, *Love and Death* (*Harper's* 1894) and *The Silent Voice* (*Harper's* 1896) and three plays by Howells (*Father and Mother: A Mystery, The Mother*, and *After the Wedding* for *Harper's* in 1900, 1902, 1906 respectively) are representative of dramas of tragic sensibility, lachrymose sentimentality, and heightened language. Rather than repudiate the past and distrust elite traditions, these writers mined their European legacy for cultural capital. Such work can be linked to the post–Civil War drive for improvement and propriety, which was manifested in literary monthlies, etiquette books, household guides, and self-help manuals. Furthermore, the culture of sentiment insisted on the valuation of emotion as an essential component of taste and refinement in the post-bellum period. Significantly for the turn-of-the-century traditionalists dedicated to "uplift," the desire to transcend mundane social matters to a private spiritual or aesthetic plane authorized readerly identification with a small circle of "civilized" and "cultured" people, the proprietors of good taste and delicate sensibility.

The daughter of the famous decorative painter Sir Lawrence, Laurence Alma Tadema's name conferred high cultural value for the magazine. In her *Love and Death*, a short dialogue between a "maid" and the man who once spurned her, he reveals that he is dead and that his troubled soul has been given one night to return home, "to the heart which lies most empty for the lack of thee," and to apologize before it can rest (152). As he goes off to look for God, the maid vows to join him by renouncing "the young lambs that bleat around me and the birds give twitter" and by drowning herself before dawn. Obviously, the suicide of a young woman in a modern American domestic setting would not be acceptable subject matter but, set in another time and place, the death is historicized, distanced, and romanticized. *The Silent Voice* dramatizes a similar story. Set in sixteenth-century England, the play brings together two former lovers who have been long separated. Once Nancy Sorell, though she is a now duchess with a child, is but a "shell," until this evening when, reminiscing with her old flame, the true love she rejected for loveless wealth and status rekindles her passion. They cannot be together, of course, and, as he leaves to face certain death in battle, she tells him that she now "dies a second death" (409). There could be no adultery in a proper periodical, but there could be a morality play set in the past about the ill consequences of marrying for money.

Three linked blank verse plays by William Dean Howells dramatize the inevitability of domestic life, separation, reproduction, and death as well as the "natural" condition of separate and gendered spheres. The off-stage subject of all three, *Father and Mother: A Mystery, The Mother*, and *After the Wedding*, is the wholly passive daughter who, in order of the plays' publication dates (1900, 1902, 1906), dies, is born, and marries. The gloomy, dark illustrations for the plays show a supine young woman weakened or dead and the adults also as weak and semi-recumbent; life's rounds are almost too much to bear, though the father offers consolation in Wordsworth's reassuring words that heaven is our home, adding:

> We have had our glimpse of life beyond the veil:
> As every one who sorrows somehow has.
> The world is not so hollow as it was.
> There still is meaning in the universe. (874)

One way to understand the somber trilogy is to locate it in a traumatic biographical context, Howells's daughter Winifred having died in March 1889 at twenty-six after a misdiagnosis. From a literary standpoint, Thomas Bailey Aldrich, Howells's successor to the *Atlantic Monthly's* editorship (1881–1890), writing in 1904, observed that the play was "a strangely touching and imaginative piece of work, not unlike in effect to some of Maeterlinck's psychical dramas. . . . The gloom of Poe and the spirituality of Hawthorne touch cold finger-tips in those three or four pages" (47). From a cultural perspective, the plays insist on the primacy of parenthood, the inevitable division between spouses when they become parents, and the remorseless pain of marital anxiety. All this is presented as a necessary part of what the mother calls "this strange unity" of marriage, a condition that isolates them from each other as they attend to the child (873). The couple's submission to biological imperatives is shrouded in deeply conservative sentiment and insistence that there is satisfaction in acceding to the culturally coded moral good. The reader is positioned as sympathetic and invested in participating in the emotional norm. Finally all is dramatized as "civilized" behavior, a tastefully restrained and contemplative response to great grief as befits middle-class Americans (no "foreign" wailing or "lower class" hysterics). Reconciliation and capitulation are modeled as cultural desiderata as tightly here as are the courtship behaviors in Howells's lighter social plays.

At the other end of the spectrum are the plays that engage in cultural displacement, plays that draw on myth, history, and the Bible and which allow the playwright to indulge in titillating subject matter under the rubric of "high art" and "high purpose": Olive Tilford Dargan's *The Woods of Ida*, Edith Wharton's *Pomegranate Seed*, Amélie Rives's *Athelwold*, Robert Gilbert Welsh's *Jezebel*, Arthur Symons's *Cleopatra in Judea*, Josephine Preston Peabody's *The Wings*, and Zoë Akins's *The Magical City*. That these plays are also melodramatic speaks to Peter Brooks's contention that the form is appropriate to a period of rapid change, in which "the traditional patterns of moral order no longer provide the necessary social glue," and which strives "to 'prove' the existence of a moral universe" (20). I want to stress that, much like looking at erotic classical painting, the reading of such plays also permitted the female reader in particular to occupy two cultural sites simultaneously, the unimpeachably high, public site of verse and classical matter dependent on her being educated and the illicit private, sensual site of appetite, the forbidden knowledge presumably outside her experience and couched as a moral lesson.

Olive Tilford Dargan's *The Woods of Ida: A Masque* (*Century* 1907), set forty years before the fall of Troy, has all the hallmarks of Dargan's Radcliffe education. Dargan (1869–1968) would become famous for her autobiographical short stories about life in the mountains of North Carolina, *Highland Annals*, but this stilted, academic play belongs to her early career as a writer of verse drama published in *Semiramis, and Other Plays* (1904), *Lords and Lovers and other Dramas* (1906), and *The Mortal Gods and Other Dramas* (1912). *The Woods* is illustrated with three paintings by Sigismond de Ivanowski, who was also early in his career and who would become well-known for his illustrations of *Ben-Hur, Lorna Doone, The Scarlet Letter*, and others. Every indication, then, is that this play is being positioned as a "high" culture artifact by *Century*. The plot is an elaborated retelling of the Anchises story. Having sworn undying fidelity to the nymph Thesta, Anchises is stricken by the radiant beauty of Venus and spirited away to a bower. The reader of the play, faced with an *interruptus*, would have had to complete the action, which, presumably, was outside her lived reality but not her imagination or even her sublimated desire for an erotic experience. After the abandoned nymph calls for revenge from above, Zeus obliges by striking Anchises blind. Venus, now pregnant with Aeneas, leaves him, and Thesta, passing herself as "Fidea," pledges to stay with him as his guide, promising that "Troy shall stand while Trojans reck thy nod" (604). It is possible that Dargan was inspired by Sir William Blake Richmond's widely exhibited painting, "Venus and Anchises," in turn based on Shelley's "Epipsychidion," both of which depict the transforming power of love that turned night into day and side-step the issue of sexual congress.

Readers were required to bring similar interpretive capabilities to Edith Wharton's *Pomegranate Seed*, which appeared in *Scribner's* in 1912. By this time she had been writing poetry and short stories frequently for *Atlantic*

Monthly and *Century* as well as *Scribner's*, and had established herself as a novelist with *The House of Mirth*, serialized in *Scribner's* in 1905. Of the forty-six poems she published in periodicals, only *Pomegranate Seed* is written as a play. In this reimagined version of the classical myth, Persephone refuses her mother's pleas to return to an earth she finds too cruel too endure; having eaten the euphemistic "seed of death," she will remain: "And there I will heal the wounds that thou hast made" (290–91). Of course, the avoidance of blunt revelation about sex protects the author from any charge of immorality. From childhood Wharton was obsessed with the myth of Persephone and reworked it many times in her fiction. Written during what one critic identified as her "Neurasthenic" period (1909–1913), the play rejects a sentimental view of procreative maternalism and harshly advocates the acceptance of woman's inevitable patriarchal captivity: "the fruits of the Earth" seemed "insipid" to Persephone after "she had eaten of the pomegranate seed" (Donovan 43–83).

By the time Amélie Rives's *Athelwold* appeared in *Harper's* (1892), she had achieved scandalous fame as the author of *The Quick or the Dead?* published in *Lippincott's Monthly Magazine* in April 1888. Rives (1863–1945) established herself as a contributor to periodicals with her first short story, "A Brother to Dragons" (*Atlantic Monthly* 1886), a romance that set the pattern for her use of locales and idioms in Elizabethan or Jacobean England and many stories following. But it was *The Quick or the Dead?*—in which a young widow has to chose between staying loyal to the memory of the dead or soon remarrying—that so shocked the periodical readers, producing a storm of parodies and pulpit denunciations after selling over 300,000 copies. As late as 1912 an article appeared in *The Bookman* cited the work as having founded "the semi-erotic genre" in the American novel (Taylor 41).

Rives, therefore, was a known quantity to periodical readers when the play appeared in *Harper's*. *Athelwold* is more in keeping with her historical romances than her forays into modern social realism and was similar to her first play, *Herod and Meriamne* (1888), a blank verse "Elizabethan" drama. Set in Anglo-Saxon times, *Athelwold* has a noble protagonist in the thane and swordsman of King Edgar (959–75), who betrays his master for love and is betrayed in turn by a woman who would rather be queen. Any reader of Shakespeare would have recognized Rives's magpie appropriation of themes and characters, from yon Cassius's lean and hungry look to Juliet's nurse. One critic notes that though the play is partially flawed in that the mood is uneven and in that it suffers from the burden of archaic language, the blank verse "is as good as the author ever wrote"—which is faint praise indeed (Taylor 67). More to the point, the five-act play, lavishly illustrated by M. I. Gow in a pre-Raphaelite style, may have titillated readers with the extended scenes of heated sexual play ("thou'rt a pretty griffin, claws and teeth") (402).

Athelwold seems tame compared to *Jezebel* in *Forum* (1915) by Robert Gilbert Welsh, the drama critic for New York's *Evening Telegram*. The play sensationalizes 2 *Kings* 30–37 in which the dissolute Phoenician, Jezebel, wife of King Ahab of Israel and worshiper of Baal and Astarte, meets her death when she is thrown to the dogs by two eunuchs. Welsh appropriates the bare outline of the Biblical story and certainly upholds the power of the Christian God, but the play devotes the most attention to elaborating Jezebel's many immoral activities. Welsh's aging Jezebel has just flung the previous night's lover to the dogs when she is told of the impending army of the Host of Israel led by Jehu. So hot with desire is she for Loammi, a Christian servant in love with her maid, Mara, that she is indifferent to the threat outside her palace, the site of "carnivals of lust and the abominations of Bel and Astarte" (649). The abominations are dramatized in lascivious detail from the presence of "*gigantic negro slaves nearly nude, and followed by two priests who lash them with leathern thongs*" to Jezebel's description of her planned rape and indoctrination of Mara into the rites of Astarte (650). In her desperation to appeal to Loammi, Jezebel calls upon her demonic deities to transform her into an irresistible young girl. The sacrilegious act accomplished, the hypnotic advances of the scarlet woman almost sway Loammi. Ultimately, though, he refuses her sensual blandishments: "I am of Israel. Hard fare and a meagre life is mine. Wherefore should I come into thine idolatrous land?" (658). Pitching deity against deity, Jezebel calls for Astarte to speak but he calls to a more powerful force: "Then be thou the instrument of the one God. Wipe from the earth, Jezebel, the mother of abominations!" (659). Jaho, the captain of the host, enters as conqueror and orders the "she-wolf of the Phoenicians" to be thrown to the dogs (660). All this has little to do with the Biblical version but for the person of Jezebel as the female embodiment of sensuality and evil.

Similarly, Arthur Symons in *Cleopatra in Judea* (*Forum* 1916) cares less for his source than for his dramatization of an infamous woman,

Cleopatra, another embodiment of female wiles, vanity, and power. The periodical reader might have read Symons's "The Decadent Movement in Literature" in *Harper's* in 1893 but more likely would bring to bear Symons's 1889 analysis of Shakespeare's play in which he claimed that *"Antony and Cleopatra* is the most wonderful, I think, of all Shakespeare's plays, and it is so mainly because the figure of Cleopatra is the most wonderful of Shakespeare's women. And not of Shakespeare's women only, but perhaps the most wonderful of women" (1). In Symons's dramatization of events, he focuses on the wrangling between Herod and Cleopatra, which followed the assassination of Julius Caesar in 44 B.C., Herod's marriage to Mariamne, and his rejection of Cleopatra's offer of a generalship in order to gamble on being awarded kingship by Antony and Octavius. The epigraph for *Cleopatra in Judea* (1916) is from Shakespeare's *Antony and Cleopatra* in which the infuriated Cleopatra, jealous of Octavia, announces "That Herod's head I'll have: but how, when Antony is gone through whom I might command it?" (III iii). However, it is more logical to read Symons's own essay rather than Shakespeare's play as a template for the play accepting Cleopatra as his "Lilith", cruel and voluptuous, passionate, vain, self-conscious, endlessly fascinating even in weakness, incapable of shame, "a woman to the last" (18), in other words, playing out all the themes in his essay.

The play begins with her vilification by a priest warning Herod:

> This queen, this concubine, this idolatress,
> This white tenth plague of Egypt, brother's wife
> And sister-killer, this insatiate leech
> And whore of all the Caesars, this outspewed,
> Unswallowable and deadly weed of God—. (643)

Following the byzantine twists and turns of court intrigue, the play pits a pagan, unfaithful Cleopatra against a Herod who resists her fatal charms and declares himself a believer in God who respects his honorable masculine and marital bonds with Antony and Meriamne. Furious that she has failed and "with this Jew" (658), Cleopatra nevertheless is spared death at this moment because she has stirred jealousy and doubt about his wife in Herod, who sends her back to Antony. Presumably Symons would expect his readers, knowledgeable about Shakespeare, the Bible, and Christian history, to appreciate the layers of irony that suffuse the dramatization of political power games whose conclusion his reader knows.

Ultimately though, the point of both *Jezebel* and *Cleopatra in Judea* is the reassuring triumph of the moral man's Christian authority over the perverse and dangerous woman and the preservation of his sexual purity in the face of decadent temptation. Though neither Jezebel or Cleopatra figure in their studies, Rebecca Stott's *The Fabrication of the Late-Victorian Femme Fatale*, Nina Auerbach's *Woman and the Demon*, and Bram Dijkstra's *Idols of Perversity* all argue that at century's end such threatening and powerful women were the fabrications of middle-class men who saw their world slipping out of their control. In these two plays, the anxiety over women's sexual prowess is compounded by their horrifying Godlessness; both attributes receive a lot of voyeuristic attention in the overheated dramatizations. The temporal and geographical displacement as well as the Biblical and historical sources allow the playwrights a greater sensational range than would a contemporary American middle-class location.

The "fallen woman" was of great interest at the turn-of-the-century and especially during the following progressive era of social reform when the "social evil" and "white slave trading" were tied to anxieties about "race suicide" and immigration. The "fallen woman" was also the subject of two very different verse plays, *The Wings* (1905) and *The Magical City* (1916), similar only in that the women in the end prove to have been misunderstood and are not really "fallen." The authors are able to appropriate an aura of sexuality and sin before the righteous turn to religious sanctity, thus first titillating, then reassuring their readers that the plays are moral and are safe to read. Josephine Preston Peabody (1874–1925), a poet and playwright, was one of William Vaughn Moody's students at Radcliffe College in 1895 and a lecturer on poetry at Wellesley College (1910–1903). By the time *The Wings* was published, Peabody had already published verse in *Atlantic Monthly* and *Scribner's* and in collections (*The Wayfarers* in 1898 and *The Singing Leaves* in 1903) as well as her verse plays, *Fortune and Men's Eyes* (1900) and *Marlowe* (1901). *The Wings* was published in *Harper's Monthly* (May 1905) but was not performed until 1912 when it was produced at the Toy Theatre in Boston. Of this verse play set in Northumbria about A.D. 700 concerning the struggle between a priest and a mistress for power over King AElfric, Arthur Hobson Quinn's judgment is that though the verse has "her usual distinction," the play is interesting chiefly as prelude to her "masterpiece," *The Piper* (1907), which won the Stratford Prize in 1910 and was "a triumphant vindication of the belief that true poetry is the source of the finest drama" (*From the Civil War* 19). Later, when the play was published with five others in a collection in 1927, the editor, George Baker, was effusive about all except *The Wings* about which he was diplomatically silent.

The dramatic struggle is between Cedric, a man so holy he will not look at a woman's face, and Edburga, the king's mistress. Cedric has advised King AElfric to get rid of the mistress in order to take a proper wife, and Edburga has come to his island retreat to exact revenge. When she appears, the Madonna-obsessed Cedric takes her for a vision of the Virgin, but she reacts angrily at his unworldly ignorance and inveighs against his sentimental religiosity by telling him the truth. The daughter of a serf, she was to have married one Betric but was spotted by AElfric who claimed her:

> —What are you, men and monks,
> That you may give us unto such an one
> To bind your lands together? Or to bring
> The sum of twenty spears of more, to follow
> You, in your man-hunt?
> . . . .
> I'll not be given
> To Betric, would that Betric would have me now:—
> I, a free woman and the gladlier free
> I am a creature rooted in the dark,
> But born to sunlight and the noble air.
> I will to give; and will not be given.
> I fear not right nor left, nor east, nor west;
> Nor thee! For that I have is all mine own
> To give or keep. And I am all I have:
> And I am AElfric's,—for a kingly gift.
> . . . .
> Thou wouldst have hurled my one gift of myself
> Into the dust; and call all men to see
> And curse, and spurn me hence: ay, an thou couldst!— (952)

The king enters on the scene, his sword drawn, and tears are shed before all is resolved when Cedric understands and notes the "Likeness . . . Even to Her / Yea, and to Him who did so love the world: —/ Love, the one Likeness." He commands the king to take her as his wife: "Lift her up and set her by thy side: / Wed her . . . Whom thou hast humbled, lift her up.—/ The gift that thou hast taken, hold it high." The play ends with Cedric clutching a wounded seagull to his breast, "Ah Thou!—Have pity on all the broken wings" (956).

Though Zoë Akins's *The Magical City* in *Forum* (1916) also ostensibly deals with a "fallen woman," the moral issue is only a catalyst for a heated and improbably romanticized tragic triangle to explode. One of the earliest plays produced by the Washington Square Players, the "dramatic branch" of the Liberal Club, *The Magical City* was, as Jennifer Bradley observes, characteristic of all Akins's original plays between 1919 and 1930; it used "glamorous settings, flamboyant histrionics, and remarkable coincidence." And, as Alexander Woolcott noted, she liked " 'her woe well dressed' " (Bradley 88). Because the play was written in free verse, it presumably met at least one of the criteria for the Washington Square Players who had formed to produce plays of "artistic merit" and create a higher standard for American theatre, one that could be reached " 'only as the outcome of experiment and initiative'" (Anonymous, "Bertha Von Suttner" 353–54). The play careens from heated, impassioned verse when the lovers (Petronelle, "the golden girl," David, the poet, and Robert, the magnate) are wooing and fighting to the banal and prosaic verse among those outside the magic circle of passion.

After establishing the staggering richness and tasteful beauty of Petronelle's clothes and apartment in Gotham, which are paid for with hush money from the magnate, Akins sets up the doomed triangle: the poet loves the girl who in turn is terrified that the married magnate who, fearful of a scandal, left her, will return to harm her. The poet is described as "like the hero of an ancient—not a modern—legend, to whom Love and Death are Comrades" (516). Pitched high from the start, the verse soars higher as the poet mythologizes their love:

> Petronelle, you
> Are a golden fairy
> Whose enchanted palace
> Is Gotham . . . .
> And here in the Magical City,
> On the vine at its casement windows
> Blooming at dusk,
> Love like a moon-flower blows,

Whiter against the dark
Than lilies in sun-lit gardens,
In the green and quiet country.
Do not be afraid
Of the Magical City,
Petronelle;
From its hovering shadows
Our deeds,
Our loves,
Our dreams,
Burst with the aspect of flowers,
Starry against the night.
Here you belong; here you must stay. (521)

The idyll is shattered when Rudolph, the magnate, arrives. After much quarreling, all agree that Petronelle will choose and when she tells David that she only loved his poems and chooses Rudolph, David shoots his rival, who takes a long time to die. Rather than turn David over to the police and create a scandal, however, the magnate's flunkies pay him to leave the country. He sees the point:

I have killed Caesar
And so I shall have
An island, if I like,
In the blue Aegean Sea.
So it is written in Gotham. (548)

The "golden girl" had planned a career as an actress and really was a good girl because she had come up out of the slums and had only slept with Rudolph once, so she is granted an instant transfiguration. To his dead body she proclaims:

Always and forever,
With my eyes closed,
I can stand beside you—
Like a bride in a church—
Thinking only
Quiet, holy things. (550)

The second strategy I wish to highlight is the use of a specifically religious cultural displacement to "naturalize" religious miracles, to rationalize genocide, and to romanticize royalism. Religious miracles, of course, fell outside the Protestant norm and certainly outside the end-of-the-century American norm, but placed in a European past they could be credible and still attest to a divine power. Robert Garland's *The Double Miracle* (*Forum* 1915) is a strained religious melodrama about a love triangle among three present-day Sicilian peasants, Marianna, Pancrazio (who she loves) and Salvatore (to whom her parents have betrothed her). The play begins in a mountain shrine dedicated to the Madonna, then escalates quickly into "a fair Sicilian fight, a fight with knives" in which Salvatore wounds his rival and threatens to kill Marianna, who calls upon the Madonna for a sign asserting her virtue (521). Salvatore rejects the sign, a strong light emanating from the shrine, believing it to be a light from a ship in the harbor, kills the woman, and turns angrily to the statue of the Virgin, denouncing her: "And you are no different from those older, happier gods, you tawdry thing, your jewels even falser than your creed. [*He fairly shrieks with anger.*] No longer have you any power, for if you had you'd kill me where I stand, and yet you let me live and tell you what I think of you and that Son of yours" (526). As he flings the crucifix at the Madonna, who remains unharmed, Pancrazio shoots him and Salvatore dies, crying out: "A miracle! . . . A miracle! . . . Blessed mother . . . I believe! . . . I believe! . . . I believe, dear God, yes, I believe" (526).

What readers would accept as a credible occurrence in the mountains of Sicily, of course, differs significantly from what they could accept happening in America; it also is unimaginable that an American protagonist in a religious play would appear as Pancrazio does, "a cigarette is between his lips, a crimson carnation above his ear," or that he would grab his love and kiss her on the lips (515). The exotic and primitive picturesqueness Garland takes pains to depict allows him to indulge in some voyeuristic sensational romanticizing and to establish an aura of "authenticity" for the miracles. Also it allows him to "naturalize" the active, interventionist participation of the Madonna in a modern setting.

Margaret Sherwood makes use of the same device of cultural displacement in *Vittoria* (1905), set outside a plague-ridden cathedral town in Italy. The play dramatizes a father's efforts to protect his daughter, Vittoria, from life's harsh realities to such a degree that she has never heard the word "death" and therefore knows no fear. Because he is about to die, the father seeks continued protective isolation for her in a convent. When she reveals to a scholar, Luigi, that she feels something is missing, that she is waiting with sense of mystery, she also reveals that "Of praying I know naught" but that "this might be the voice to speak / The words for which I have waited" (499). Luigi and the girl fall in love, and as they listen to the convent's prayers for the newly dead, Luigi declares passionately, "Love only, lasts forever, eternal, / Unchangeable, triumphant over chance" (501). Luigi and the father now conspire together to keep the truth from her but vow to tell her the first time they see a dead body. The next dead person happens to be Luigi, who falls off a cliff and is found by Vittoria, who thinks he is sleeping. She rebuffs her father's scientific explanation of dust to dust but is taken by the idea he rejects, namely, that there is a life after death. The father staggers off to die in the mountains grieving for the sorrow she must feel, but a joyful Vittoria, arms around Luigi's corpse, throws herself off a cliff:

> . . . . I hunger, dear,
> For this eternity enfolding you.
> A fall from off this cliff, my father said,
> Will fashion me like this. My life leaps up
> Exultingly to meet this joy of death.
> The silences shall not be silent now. (504)

This transcendent romanticization of death could easily be dismissed as only melodramatic excess, but the play is significant in that it anticipates many of the essential themes of Sherwood's later and most notable work, *Coleridge's Imaginative Conception of the Imagination* (1937). Sherwood (1864–1955), who had a Ph.D. from Yale, a LHD from New York University, and was a Professor Emeritus at Wellesley, wrote that "the one distinguishing mark of Romantic literature . . . is freedom of individual imagination to express itself as will" (7). Tracing Coleridge's theories back to Plotinus, Sherwood argues that his monistic belief, his faith in a living unity of the universe that can be intuited by the imagination, "marks a transition from ancient philosophy to an important and greatly influential phase of modern thought" and is the basis for all "our whole stream of mystical nature poetry" (12). Central to her argument is Coleridge's assertion from Book XIII of *Biographia Literaria*, "The primary IMAGINATION I hold to be the living Power and prime Agent of all human Perception, and as a repetition in the finite mind of the eternal act of creation in the infinite I AM" (12). Therefore, one way to interpret *Vittoria* is as Sherwood's attempt to produce a Romantic play based on Coleridgean ideas. The eponymous heroine is in this reading an embodiment of the imaginative power to understand God, to "read the infinite as finding expression in the finite" (that is, Luigi's dead body and her suicide) (20).

A similar simplicity and sentimentality characterize John G. Neihardt's morality play, *Eight Hundred Rubles*, which appeared in the *Forum* (1915). Today, Neihardt's associations with the American west and especially with his most famous work, *Black Elk Speaks* (1932), understandably have eclipsed his earlier work in other genres such as poetic drama, but in 1915 Neihardt would have been well-known as the author of the critically well-received collection of Romantic poems, *A Bundle of Myrrh* (1907), *Man-Song* (1909), and *The Stranger at the Gate* (1912). His readers would have approached him as a lyric poet, not a dramatist. His first poetic drama, the allegorical *Fugitive Glory*, was collected in *Man-Song* (1909). His second verse play, *The Passing of the Lion* (1909), about Alcibiades, was quickly followed by *The Death of Agrippina* (1913), about Roman decadence. His last experiment with verse drama was *Eight Hundred Rubles*, which picks up a major theme of his two early novels, *The Dawn Builder* (1911) and *Life's Lure* (1914). Blair Whitney complains that sentimentality "destroys" the play whose characters are little more than "bloodless abstractions whose actions are completely predictable." He ties the play to the doomed, anachronistic poetic drama movement that was being rendered obsolete by Ibsenian and Shavian prose social-realist plays (60). Of the early modern period, Brenda Murphy observes that though "there were a number of commer- cial productions of verse 'classics,' such as Shakespeare's plays, full commercial production of new verse dramas by American playwrights was almost unheard of when Maxwell Anderson wrote *The White Desert* in 1923" (*The Cambridge History of American Theatre* 331). Though Blair Whitney concedes that verse drama was effectively revitalized by T. S. Eliot, Archibald MacLeish, and Robert Lowell, he points out that Neihardt stopped writing verse drama long before that revitalization and that, unfortunately, Neihardt had modeled his work on William Vaughn Moody rather than trusting his own instinct and ear for the American west. The irony for Whitney is that though Neihardt "revolted against the genteel tradition in his fiction and in his poetry, he was one of its representatives in drama" (56).

Lucile Aly is more generous in her assessment of Neihardt's achievements in verse drama. Of *The Death of Agrippina*, she writes of his lines in iambic pentameter rhymed couplets, "Neihardt was developing the meter he later perfected in the epics; by controlling phrase lengths he kept the lines from falling into heroic couplet monotony, and he took pains to avoid distortion in the rhyme" (60). Harriet Monroe devoted an entire issue of *Poetry Magazine* (May 1913) to *The Death of Agrippina*, which was later published with *Eight Hundred Rubles* as *Two Mothers* in 1921. Of greater interest than the relative merits of Neihardt's poetic verse, however, is the relevance of the next play, *Eight Hundred Rubles*, to the war. According to Aly, the play was based on an Associated Press news story about a Russian peasant woman who killed a soldier for his money, not recognizing him as her long absent son. It was not until later that Neihardt learned that the story was a filler item summarizing a folk tale and not a news dispatch. Whatever the source of the story, his *Forum* readers would have accepted the parable as immediately pertinent.

Another problem solved by the strategy of religious cultural displacement was that of the American Indian. Though the periodicals registered no guilt or remorse over the genocidal past, nonetheless a comforting message of submissive Christianity poured oil on whatever traces of regret might have lingered. This was especially true for the American foundational myths. In 1907, the anniversary of Jamestown's funding in 1607, there was a little flurry of increased interest in Pocahontas. In previous years and in the years following, there were about four pieces a year on her in part due to the fabrication of "American" heroines as foundational figures by poets at mid-century (Banta 492). But in 1907 there were an unprecedented twenty-seven poems, books and chapters on Pocahontas, reviving what had become a tired trope of American historical narrative. The periodicals participated extensively in this myth-revitalizing process. J. C. Leyendecker, of Arrow Collar fame, did a cover for *Collier's* (April 27) depicting John Rolfe bowing to a regal Indian maid; Laura Portor claimed her as "an ideal type" and "our first American girl" for *Ladies' Home Journal* (May), and Helen Pratt had announced the discovery of a new portrait of "the Indian wife of John Rolfe" with her son in *Harper's Weekly* (June). That painting, the so-called Sedgeford Hall Portrait from the late eighteenth century, pleased Pratt because it shows Pocahontas to be "refined" and in a "modification of her tribal dress" with the "handsome" child who grew up to be a man of "eminence" (958). In a long essay on "American Indians in

Elizabethan England," Pocahontas is noted for her "expressed anxiety to visit her husband's Christian county" and, despite Ben Jonson's hints that she occasionally entered "tavern doors," the parish register of Gravesend where she died described her as " 'of Virginia, a lady born' " (Lee 323). The article also observes that her brother, Tamacoco, who was "long tolerated with some impatience in London society," had, "unlike his sister, declined to accept Christianity, and was prone to blaspheme all religious beliefs but his own" (Lee 323). Therefore, in the mythic figure of Pocahontas all the "desirable" qualities for an Indian are evident: "natural" nobility, submission to the superior culture, partial cultural assimilation, some weakness for alcohol, an early death, and, above all, an acceptance of Christianity. The historical importance of the Jamestown anniversary as well as the renewed interest in Pocahontas may account for the presence of the only play published in *Lippincott's Monthly* during this period; in the late 1890s *Lippincott's* began publishing a full novel in every issue.

As Susan Scheckel notes in her examination of Pocahontas on the popular stage, the story of Pocahontas was "one of the most romantic and romanticized episodes of early American history; it was also the single most popular subject of Indian dramas during the nineteenth century" (45). In tracing the genealogy of the romanticizing of Pocahontas, Philip Young cites John Davis's claim to historical fact, *First Settlers of Virginia* (1806) in which the princess first appears "unrobed" to Rolfe (410–12). Young claims that Davis paved the way for a deluge of plays, most lost, including James Nelson Barker's *Indian Princess* (1808), George Washington Parke Custis's *Pocahontas* (1830), Robert Owen's *Pocahontas* (1837), Charlotte Barnes Conner's *The Forest Princess* (1844), and, as the myth was growing weary as a stage trope, John Brougham's burlesque in 1855.

Werner Sollors argues that the accounts of Pocahontas's love for Captain John Smith reassured Americans that they were chosen as preferable to her own people and that her consent to marry him had the imperialistic function of giving the "chosen people of white Americans a new fictional line of noble Indian ancestry" (79). Though the Pocahontas story had been appropriated to address many ideological concerns, from anxieties about miscegenation to sectionalist propaganda, *A Princess of Virginia* by Kate Tucker Goode (1863–1917) in *Lippincott's Monthly* (1907) is most directly complicit in the production of Pocahontas as "the first Christian ever of her nation" (Tilton 93).

The myth of Pocahontas's heroic rescue of John Smith and her subsequent marriage to John Rolfe were well-established when John Chapman received a commission to paint a mural for the rotunda of the Capitol. Chapman's colossal painting, "The Baptism of Pocahontas" (12' x 18'), which opened to public view in November 1830, and which shows a light-skinned Pocahontas in a white European dress kneeling in an attitude resembling that of the Virgin Mary, celebrated the moment at which, as her chronicler Robert Tilton says, she "freely abandoned her Indian beliefs and accepted an alternate cultural identity" (130), "becoming one of 'us,' a member of white Christian society" (119). Historically, Pocahontas married John Rolfe about three years after her baptism and went with him to England where she died. The most circulated (and copied) portrait from that period, Simon Van de Passe's "Matoaks als Rebecka" (1616), had already "Europeanized" Pocahontas in Elizabethan court dress and figures in Goode's play; a gentleman remarks to John Smith that the artist "all aflame with wonder at her sweet, dark face" has captured her "nobleness" (844). But it is Pocahontas's Christianity which is the ultimate subject of Goode's play and which fueled Chapman's mid-century refiguration. Tilton writes, "Chapman's choice of subject also took away any need to portray the activity and heroism for which Pocahontas was known, in favor of an image of a passive, submissive recipient" (130).

In *A Princess of Virginia*, Pocahontas gladly renounces the flattering court for a greater happiness; as she dies in Rolfe's arms at play's end, she assures him that in Christ all needs are met. In her renunciation and acceptance, Rolfe sees the promise of conversion for all Indians: "May all thy people, taught of God, awake / One day with His own likeness; through His word, / Behold with thee, the beauty of the Lord!" (848). Like Chapman, Goode offers Americans an Indian who rejects her own culture by submitting to European values and who rejects her barbarous idolatry by accepting Christianity. In the unlikely event that any 1907 readers of *Lippincott's* were troubled by the treatment of Indians since 1607, they could reassure themselves that if the Indians had embraced Christianity, they would have been rewarded as Pocahontas was with the "beauty of the Lord."

Resorting to submissive Christianity also allowed Witter Bynner to uphold a belief in "inherent" nobility in *The Little King* (*Forum* 1914). The blank verse drama, which apologizes for Royalism, links it with

Christian resignation in its abject young subject. The hero is the young son of Louis XVI and Marie Antoinette who, as they are being beheaded, is imprisoned by brutal and mercenary Citizens in the Paris Temple. A mason is ordered to wall in the child but a Royalist has bribed his wife to substitute another child. Bynner takes pains to contrast the vulgar brutality of the peasant revolutionaries—the wife is "a squat woman of fifty with thick features and a blotched face" (605) and her husband has long black hair and "a swarthy brutish face" (607)—with the little king, "a handsome, gentle boy" (608). When the child defends his mother's goodness and love of her people, the vile man tries to pry his mouth open with a knife to force alcohol down him and commits a number of atrocities while his bloodthirsty wife yearns for more action at the guillotine. The young king demonstrates his Christianity, his nobility, and his love of France—all lessons he has learned from his parents—by refusing the substitution. Sentimental to a fault, the play is more about the emotional impact of the brutalized child rising above his torture than it is a political argument for monarchy; it does, however, romanticize to a remarkable degree Louis XVI and Marie Antoinette, going so far as to compare Louis's forgiveness of his people with the Savior, and to play up the barbaric savagery of the peasants.

The most religious of the general periodicals was *McClure's*, which dedicated its efforts to uplifting the fallen. When *McClure's* was founded it was staffed largely by evangelical Christians, two dozen Knox College alumni suffused with the humanitarian reformist spirit of the Great Revival fired by the central principles of abolition and temperance as well as Sabbath observance, feminism, and anti-Masonism. Sam McClure's editorial policy was informed by his conviction that a slave-holding oligarchy that had operated under the guise of state rights had become a bond-holding aristocracy perpetuating corrupt government under the same guise. Ray Stannard Baker captured both the political and religious nature of *McClure's* writers when he wrote: "The journalist is a true servant of democracy. The best journalist occupies the exact place of the prophets of old; he cries out the truth & calls for reform . . . The news is the way God speaks to men" (Wilson, H. S., *McClure's Magazine and the Muckrackers* 208). One of the most pressing problems that troubled McClure was alcohol.

From its inception, *McClure's* had been an advocate of temperance and prohibition; the many articles dedicated to the dangers of drink participated in an American religious literary tradition hearkening back to Increase Mather's 1673 "Wo to Drunkards." In Lincoln Steffens's series, "The Shame of the Cities," which began in 1903, the saloon-keeper was portrayed the key to a corrupting alliance of gamblers and prostitutes, an association with a long history that is fully documented in Sharon Salinger's history of taverns and drinking. Similar essays included "The Pleasant Saloon-Keeper—Ruler of American Cities" (October 1908), "The Experience and Observations of a New-York Saloon Keeper" (January 1909), and George Kibbe Turner's 1908 series, "A Temperance Campaign," which exposed the way in which a district political machine used the temperance movement in order to increase the graft from local saloons. *McClure's* also published two autobiographical confessions: "The Story of an Alcoholic Slave" (August 1909) and "Confessions of a Moderate Drinker" (February 1910) as well as a physician's analysis, "Evidence against Alcohol" (March 1909).

Given the religious and temperance convictions of the editorial staff, it is no wonder that the first play *McClure's* published was Elizabeth Stuart Phelps's *Within the Gates* (1901), a lengthy modern morality play. Phelps (1844–1911) had been catapulted to early fame with her first novel, *The Gates Ajar* (1868), in which she offered a country reeling from the suffering and loss of the Civil War a comforting depiction of a heaven in which loved ones were reunited with each other and with Christ. She revisited the theme in "Immortality and Agnosticism: 'The Gates Ajar Twenty-Five Years After' " in the *North American Review* (1893) in which she reiterated her double-pronged credo that "modern" thought and its attendant miseries on earth are fragmentary and that happiness and completion await the sufferer after death: "Heaven alone can justify earth" (576). Her reputation established, Phelps reached a wide audience and wrote prolifically: fifty-six books and hundreds of short stories, magazine articles, and poems. Phelps was also interested in social issues, particularly the rights of women. Phelps, whose grandfather had been an operator on the underground railroad, used *McClure's* in 1896 to further "the enfranchisement and elevation of my own sex," proclaiming that "while the abolition of American slavery was numerically first the abolition of the liquor traffic is not morally second" (77–78). In 1871 she published *The Silent Partner*, a novel exposing the horrible working conditions in a mill, conditions compounded by alcoholism. Given her social and spiritual concerns, Phelps exemplifies the emotional Protestantism linked to secular social ideals that underlay the moral dogmatism and elitism of much progressive thought.

Frank Mott reminds us that Protestant church membership increased by three-fourths between 1885 and 1905, "considerably more than the proportional increase of the total population," a growth that had consequences for both the general and denominational periodicals. The topics under consideration and debate included agnosticism, the ethical culture movement, Christian Socialism, New Thought, Christian Science and faith healing, Theosophy, psychical phenomenon and spiritism, and "the Catholic question" (*History 1885–1905* 276). Aside from the denominational periodicals such as the *Jewish Messenger, Catholic World*, and *Living Church*, to name but a few, interdenominational journals such as the *Independent* and *Outlook* addressed themselves to the general Protestant reader.

Sidney E. Mead also reminds us how powerful and pervasive a force Protestantism was at the turn of the century, arguing that between 1870 and 1900 evangelical Protestant Christianity largely dominated American culture and set the mores and standards by which personal and public conduct was judged, standards "exemplified in its ideological amalgamation with 'Americanism' " (95). But that assurance met with two concurrent challenges at century's end: from the social philosophies drawing on Darwinian and Spencerian evolutionary ideas and from the social programs that arose in response to urban expansion, upheavals in labor from farm unrest due to strikes, and the economic depression of 1893. Mead delineates three "outstanding strands" in American Protestant thought during this period: the traditional orthodoxy or biblical authoritarianism of institutionalized Protestantism, romantic liberalism, and scientific modernism. Clearly, Phelps belongs to the second strand of romantic liberalism, "which was rooted in philosophic idealism and appealed in one way or another to intuition." Spawned by Transcendentalism, romantic liberalism affirmed the direct, intuitive existence of God as real and unassailable, immune from the " 'acids of modernity' " (111).

For Phelps those "acids" included evolutionary thought, alcoholism, urban poverty, drug addiction, and their attendant evils. By indicting evolutionary thought as the cause of social problems, Phelps clears the path for the only viable and reasonable solution, religious faith. Serialized from May through July of 1901, *Within the Gates* dramatizes the extended spiritual journey of Dr. Thorne, a stern man of science committed to evolutionary theory. Stuffed with every one of Phelps's spiritual and social concerns and burdened with a cast of hundreds, the allegorical pattern is clear from the start when Mrs. Fayth counsels the anxious Mrs. Thorne. When the doctor dies in a wreck, he begins his long journey shadowed by a veiled woman in red. At the gates of Paradise, he encounters Azrael, the Angel of Death, children once consigned to dirty urban streets now at play as the theme from Beethoven's Seventh Symphony soars, an ex-alcoholic, and William Harvey, discoverer of the circulation of the blood, who pronounces Dr. Thorne to be "sick of soul" (238). The woman in red is revealed to be an evil spirit, the remains of an opium addict he once tried to cure, who explains that she caused the wreck as an act of revenge. Harvey guides Thorne onward and upward, now accompanied by the strains of a Schubert serenade, to his son (recently dead) and his wife (also recently dead). Mrs. Fayth (also recently dead along with a Mrs. True) laughs at Thorne: "Does Dr. Harvey treat you by scien-tif ic ev-olu-tion? That's a man's way. It's a pretty slow one" (246). After more spiritual trials and struggles up a mountain and across a desert, Thorne is rewarded ultimately with a vision of Jesus the Christ and reunion with his saintly wife and child, a reunion that goes to the heart of Phelps's cumbersome drama. This domestic heaven harkens back to her construct in *The Gates Ajar* (1865), which she explained was written in a grief-stricken state in an effort to reach out to the sorrowing women of the Civil War (Fahs 148). Though complete happiness can be attained only in Heaven, the play argues that if one renounces evolutionary science, sanctity and spiritual bliss can be found on earth in the bosom of the rural, temperate, and religious domestic situation, a Protestant Paradise on earth.

The last set of verse plays I want to examine might too quickly be written off as literary icons published by the magazines to accrue cultural status. Though that may have been one intention and consequence, I am far more interested in the use of cultural displacement as a pernicious strategy that enabled a de-nationalizing and naturalizing project of Irish and East Indian culture, appropriated and reimagined as serving "American," specifically national, needs. Though the "Irish question" was widely discussed in American periodicals, the genteel face of drama turned its face away from this political problem at home back to the east and to high cultural icons: three plays by William Butler Yeats (*The Shadowy Waters* and *The Hour-Glass* in *North American Review* 1900 and

1903 and *The Green Helmet* in *Forum* 1911), two by Lady Gregory (*MacDaragh's Wife* in *Outlook* 1911 and *The Bogie Man* in *Forum* 1913) and one by Edward J. O'Brien (*At the Flowing of the Tide* in *Forum* 1914). All of these plays deal with mythic figures or romanticized peasantry, an Ireland of the imagination, and were held up, as I noted earlier, by Theodore Roosevelt as models for what native American writers should produce, namely "things from the soil" ("Irish Players" 915). The periodicals paid extensive tribute to Yeats in particular; scores of articles about him and his work were featured in the "quality" magazines. Yeats's plays are well-known so I want to pay closer attention to Lady Gregory and O'Brien, an American writing in imitation of them.

In a prefatory note, *Outlook* made much of the fact that *MacDaragh's Wife*, just written on the steamship bringing Lady Gregory to America, had not yet been acted or published. In her note to the play, she explains it as a story told to her by sheepshearers, thereby authenticating it as real and from the people. Two "hags" discuss their fear of MacDaragh, the great piper, when he learns of his wife's recent death. Because the townspeople were jealous of her and because he has been wasteful, the townspeople have refused to help with her burial, but MacDaragh calls upon his friends, the sheepshearers who value his music, and they give her the grand send-off she deserves. This is the kind of play that Theodore Roosevelt wanted Americans to be writing, a play written "from the heart," which has a "broad human element," and does not suffer from being "flaccidly 'cosmopolitan' " (915).

Similarly rural and suffused with a "folk" sensibility, *The Bogie Men* dramatizes the meeting of two chimney sweeps who have been set up by their respective mothers to be afraid of and competitive with each other. As they banter nervously, they realize that they have been striving to "fit" themselves to a false expectation of "high quality." They conclude that they need to be free of Ireland and of chimneys; 'It is to the harbors of America we will work our way across the wideness of the sea" (40). Clearly a play that advocates an Americanist economic superiority and posits the implicit ease with which the two men can make the transition would be pleasing to an American audience. Also, the two men are lovable simpletons, not likely to stir up political problems when they do settle in the States.

It would seem that Edward O'Brien responded to Roosevelt's call. In his prefatory note, O'Brien acknowledges his debt to Lady Gregory and

Douglas Hyde for their help and extols art that deals with "the aspiration of the soul" because through it "we shall come at least through the narrowing borders of sorrow to the deep-burning core of beauty which is timeless in its joy" (375). According to Jacquelyn Spangler, O'Brien, who would make his name as the editor of the annual anthology, *Best Short Stories*, from 1915 to 1941, was preoccupied with defining a national culture, a preoccupation "shared by a legion of modern cultural critics who accepted the primacy of national categories as they built boundaries between high art and mass culture" (99). His criteria for the short story are evident in the play: a valuation of "organic" substance and "beautiful" form, an aesthetic Spangler ascribes to Coleridge, and an emphasis on "the psychological and the imagistic over the sequential narrative" (101–02).

O'Brien dramatized a traditional Irish song about Mary Hynes, who waited in vain for a lover to return, and gave it an allegorical, Christian happy ending that he claims as "spiritual truth" (375). On Christmas eve, an old woman is visited by a blind minstrel who is revealed to be the lover who left her many years ago. On his way to her cottage, he met "Him" who led him to the "door of grace" where the poet builds a cross and they both see visions of God, Eternity, each others' "beautiful soul" and hear the sound of trumpets. As they stand "rapt in adoration," they announce the birth of Christ and "fare forth together through the door of light into the land of Happiness" (384–85). Other than the legendary characters, there is nothing "Irish" about the play and O'Brien, like Robert Garland in *The Double Miracle*, which was also published in *Forum*, would seem to be appropriating the temporal and geographical distance to create a more credible location for the miracle than a modern American setting could sustain. As well, the "Irish" can speak a "poetic" language that is "natural" to them: "If you could be seeing the light of my eyes, you would be know the shining flower of the world and the song the holy angels do be singing all times before the golden chair of Mary in the heavens above" (378). Also, O'Brien depends on a Catholic context for the miracle, much as did Robert Garland in *The Double Miracle* and John Neidhardt in *Eight Hundred Rubles*. Finally, O'Brien and Garland treated Ireland as many of the regionalists treated areas of the United States, described by Richard Brodhead as "a setting outside the world of modern development, a zone of backwardness where locally variant folkways still prevail. Its characters as ethnologically colorful, personifications of the different humanity produced in such non-modern cultural settings" (115–16). The appropriation of the Irish plays, therefore, as models for American drama necessitates the regionalizing and the literary colonizing of Ireland. As another form of cultural displacement, it disregards Irish history, culture, politics, and national autonomy, turning the country into a commodity to be mined by American writers for authentic "content."

India posed more of a problem and the cultural displacement process was more convoluted. Unlike the case of Ireland, the case of India was not one of appropriation for the credibility of religious miracles or models of autochthonic nationalism; India had to be transformed into a Christian entity, an extension of America, and an essential component of William Dean Howells' "Larger England." The catalyst for this revision seems to have been Rabindranath Tagore (1861–1941), who had come to the attention of the West when he won the Nobel Prize for Literature in 1913 for *Gitanjali: Song Offerings*, published by England's India Society with an introduction by W. B. Yeats. As the first Asian to win the prize, his prominence had to be explained to a reading public unused to anything but Anglo-European superiority. Clearly Tagore could not be accepted on his own merits; his achievements had to be rationalized within the cultural parameters the American middle class could accept. The periodicals were instrumental in repackaging Tagore for a Western market. Three examples will suffice. The New York *Evening Post* was "pleased" to observe that with the winning of the Nobel Prize " 'the East can contribute to the West something more than a burden for the white man to bear' " and, furthermore, that " 'Tagore's mysticism brings him fairly close to Maeterlinck and the dreamers of the new Celtic school' " (Anonymous, "Another" 1062). *Review of Reviews* published excerpts from Tagore's appreciation of Yeats also noting "that Mr. Tagore admires Walt Whitman very much" (Anonymous, "A *Hindu*" 101). Tagore, *Current Opinion* argued, was a bridge between East and West, between past and present, spiritual and realistic; this was possible because he was "universal," "modern," had himself translated his work into "crystalline English," and, above all, had "but a single theme," as Yeats noted, "the love of God" (Anonymous, "Universal" 50–51). Repeatedly the periodical references to Tagore are as "Anglo-Indian" not Eastern-Indian because, as the *Literary Digest* rationalized, the term is "applied to Mr. Tagore on the ground that his fame is based upon his work in English verse" (Anonymous, "Another" 1062).

More important, perhaps, was the work of positioning Tagore as an alternative to Kipling, the "craze" for whom had been enabled by the rampant piracy of texts that prevailed before the international copyright agreement went into effect in July 1891 and was fed by the serialization of his novels (*The Light That Failed* in *Lippincott's* in 1891, *Naulahaka, a Story of West and East* in *Century* in 1891–1892, *Captain's Courageous* in *McClure's* in 1896, and *Kim* in *McClure's* in 1900–1901) as well as his popular message of militant and imperialist Anglo-Saxon supremacy. The New York *Evening Post* welcomed Tagore as an "antidote" to the "harshness and brutalities of life—combat, material success, the domination of the weak by the strong, and all that we associate with the Kipling gospel of the strenuous life" . . . as well as "the barriers between race and race, which divides the world into permanent inferiors and permanent superiors, into predestined masters and predestined slave, to the obliteration of the common heritage of humanity in men' " (Anonymous, "Another" 1062). One possible reason to insist on Indian pacifism was that India was not content to be positioned as an "antidote" or to submit to imperial domination and, in fact, threatened the illusion of a sustainable English empire and, by extension, American expansionism. A recent notable and well-publicized act of resistance had underlined Indians' disinclination to be abject subjects. At the International Socialist Congress in Stuttgart (August 22, 1907), Madame Bhikaji Cama, a freedom fighter, had unfurled the first national flag of independence whose red, saffron, and green represented strength, victory, and boldness and which, she announced, was "made sacred by the blood of young Indians who sacrificed their lives."

Even before Rabindranath Tagore's *The Post Office* appeared in the *Forum* (March 1914), the magazine's readers had been conditioned to accept Tagore as safely "universal" if not also as "Western" in three pieces, an essay, a poem, and a three-paragraph sketch all in the January 1914 issue. The subtitle to Mary Carolyn Davies's essay, "Rabindranath Tagore: India's Shakespeare and Tasso in Our Time," lays bare her strategy; she appropriates and transforms his "essentially Oriental" work into culturally recognizable and valued Occidental analogues familiar to American readers (141). Anticipating agreement from her readers, she writes, "We would be slow to concede that the Hindus are our equals in matters of culture," but gives Tagore some stature when she makes the argument that his popularity in India makes Tagore the equivalent of

Tasso. Also, "Bengali sounds very much like pure Greek," she assures the reader (140). In fact, Tagore has more "grandeur" than Shakespeare. Most important, however, is his "touch of Divinity" (141), his spiritual dimension; "you are reminded of Shelley, an etherealized Shelley" (142). Further, Tagore's work "has a charm that is almost feminine" (144). Finally, his religious sensibility is democratic and his philosophy is "thoughtfully optimistic" (144). By the end of her essay, Davies has completely culturally dislocated and relocated Tagore, neatly and seamlessly packaged, emasculated and feminized for Christian Americans into the familiar and "high" canonical Western cultural tradition.

Immediately following her essay is a poem by Tagore, "Day's End," translated by Dhan Gopal Mukerji and Mary Carolyn Davies, which is ambiguous enough to be open to any "spiritual" interpolation. The three-stanza narrative describes the voyage of a person, clearly dead, rowing to a peaceful shore; the reader could fill in the religious or denominational specifics but the poem is so vague as to be "universal." The final reassurance comes twenty pages later in a brief encomium. Though Rabindranath is the grandson of a prince, the reader is told that he is "not so isolate as poet, mystic, and philosopher, that he would not fit in quite happily in Nebraska, for example, or in the vicinity of Mount Tom, Massachusetts" (160). Therefore, by the time the reader got to *The Post Office* itself, Tagore was as accessible as a neighbor, as an American, as a democrat, and as Christian as the reader and totally bled dry of any disturbing, unfamiliar, let alone threatening, cultural or religious differences.

Primarily a lyric poet and writer of short stories, Tagore also was a prolific dramatist, though only nine of his forty-one Bengali dramatic works were translated during his lifetime. *The Post Office* (*Dak Ghar* 1912) was translated into English and produced in 1913 at Yeats's urging by the Abbey Theatre players in Dublin and London, where it ran for only three nights, in part because a puzzled audience had expected an Irish comedy and in part because the critics found it to be too dreamy, symbolic, imagistic, static, and allegorical—in short, not commercially viable drama (Lago 117–19). Despite that first negative response, *The Post Office* became hugely popular; Tagore's own sense of the play, that death is "a kind of revelation of the divine," has had a universal appeal (x). In June 1940, on the evening before the fall of Paris to the Nazis, André Gide's translation was read over the radio, and in 1942, in the Warsaw ghetto, a Polish version was performed in Janusz Korczak's orphanage one month before the children were taken to be gassed. Korczak explained why he had chosen *The Post Office* as the last play to be produced: " 'eventually one had to learn to accept serenely the angel of death' " (x).

The plot is simple: a gravely ill child kept indoors on doctor's orders watches the villagers—a girl collecting flowers, a curd-seller, a watchman, and a fakir—from his window, yearning for their freedom. He also keeps watch on the king's post office because he hopes for a letter from the king. When the king learns of the boy's condition, he orders that the door and windows be opened to let in light. The girl brings him flowers and a whispered promise that she has not forgotten him. The child's acceptance of death as a welcome transition into an eternity of peace and light represented, for Tagore, the " 'interpenetration of human life with the cosmic force of the world," an idea clarified when he added a song for the 1939 production: "May the vast universe / Hold me in embrace, / And with an undaunted heart / May I come to know the Great Unknown" (Dutta and Robinson 369–70). When the play was performed in Berlin in 1921, Tagore noted a shift of emphasis; a friend explained to him that the German version "was suggestive of a beautiful fairy tale, whereas the Bengali version emphasized the spiritual" (Dutta and Robinson 159).

The matter of Tagore surfaces in one other periodical, *New England Magazine*, first in an article and again in a play both by Inar Prakas Baunevji [Indu Prakas Banerji]. In "Rabindranath Tagore in India" (1914), Baunevji describes his visit to see the poet in 1911 on his fiftieth birthday at a performance of his latest play, *Raja*, in which Tagore played the grandfather. Baunevji characterized the work as "an allegorical drama, the inner meaning of which is the struggle of the soul in quest of the Oversoul" (25). Six months later, *New England Magazine* published Baunevji's own verse drama, *Gool and Bahar*, which dramatizes the spiritual union in death of two royal Indian children. Based on an historical event, the play retells an incident arising from the British defeat of Nawab Mir Qasim Ali in Monghyr in the middle of the eighteenth century. When the Princess Gul and the Prince Bahar fled the shelled palace and took refuge in a tunnel, they emerged at night to attack the British. The prince, dressed in a tiger skin, was discovered and killed; his sister, dressed as a man, was found dead at her brother's grave. The British honored the two with a daily gun salute.

In the play, Mir Kasem sends his children off to safety, but they return, believing him to be haunting a graveyard and planning to restore him to life. Bahar dresses in a tiger skin, not to attack the British but to frighten off any intruder. British soldiers, hearing Gool's beautiful singing, seek out "the soul so unalloyed" but when they spot the "tiger," fearing it will kill the singer, shoot it (28). Though the superstitious Indian soldier fears the child is a ghost, the British Major sees the "heavenly fair in truth" and pledges acts of contrition" (29). Gool blames herself for her brother's death and dies on his grave. The play concludes with the reassurance that the "Earth wakes with a joyful tremor" and that Gool is asleep, "her rest is deep" (30). Thus was a significant military action in the expansion of the British empire, the massacre and defeat of Monghyr at the hands of the East India Company, turned into a touching tragic familial "accident." Furthermore, any anxiety the reader might have about the aggressive political action is soothed by the play's long view of history: "Reflect how very soon the murky past/Blots out the titles of the earth's potentates" (19). The conciliatory, if not acquiescent, posture might be explained by the fact that Baunevji was doing graduate work at the University of Nebraska in Sociology preparatory to becoming a missionary, plans not realized because he went down with the Lusitania in May 1915. In the play, religion is a blur of non-denominational Christian precepts, spiritual yearning, transcendent romanticizing, and even domestic virtue and any Indian military threat or resistance is erased by the moral about the "corrective" actions of history that disregards upstart "potentates" as minor disturbances in the greater scheme.

The rescripting of Indian nationalism as Western and Christian may seem to be a long way from my point of departure, the sentimental verse dramas of William Dean Howells, but I want to suggest that his dramatization of the inevitability of domestic life as well as the "natural" condition of separate and gendered spheres does very similar work to the ways in which Tagore was naturalized as a Western figure. I began this chapter by setting forth a proposition, that cultural displacement was a flexible, polyvalent strategy that afforded the dramatist four freedoms: the license to dramatize exotic or erotic subjects outside the genteel parameters, to naturalize religious miracles, to authorize romantic racism and monarchism, and to colonize other cultures for specific national ends. That all of these happen in verse and/or heightened language suggests that poetry was understood to be a "higher" form, a shield of respectability, and a proper lens through which sensational or questionable material could be communicated to the reader. I have deliberately inflated attention to verse drama to underscore the ways in which the "highest" form was instrumental in authorizing and legitimizing cultural displacement, which, in turn, enabled, even sanctified and ennobled, appropriation and colonization and yoked them with territorial modes of imperialism. The internal consolidation of the idea of a cohesive middle class as the backbone of the nation was as dependent on external control as it was on internal illusions of community and shared values. Furthermore, if the cultural barriers could be altered, denatured, appropriated, or transformed, and safely secured for the periodical reader, then Americans could move freely into the evacuated space that they had remade as "theirs."

5. Dis/Contented Citizens ✁

To this point, I have been considering how the playwrights employed various strategies to engage with problematic issues, including: the production of a "fictive ethnicity" of Anglo-Saxon purity in a racially divided nation; the construction of the reader-consumer; the consolidation of a "superior" middle class; the erection of barriers predicated on necessary distance and difference; the insistence that women were happier wedded than enfranchised; the cultural displacement of suicide and sex; and the appropriation and transformation of the Other. Though the periodicals worked hard to naturalize these fictions and to produce an image of contentment with the status quo, there were four issues that were too fraught and threatening to paint over with illusions or deflect with strategic artifices: the social evils of industrial slavery, the rise of immigration, the "social evil" of prostitution, and, above all, the war in Europe. With these problems, citizens were openly discontented. Given the generally circulating assumption of ideological hegemony within middle-class culture, which has been current in the histories until quite recently, and though the most direct, reformist opinions were usually expressed in the two progressive periodicals, *Arena* and *Forum*, it is important to stress the open expression of discontented criticism that circulated in the periodicals. Furthermore, the festering ills of a nation, which often were positioned as regional or local, should be understood in their broadest context as inextricable from the growth and expansion of America as an empire. Anxiety about shifting population demographics and the protean definition of national boundaries as the United States annexed land outside the domestic borders and ventured into wars seriously challenged the dominant ideology of American exceptionalism and cast into high relief America's troubled engagement with the rest of the world.

One of the oldest mythic constructs to be tested was the moral supremacy of a Puritan heritage. Though Arthur Miller's *The Crucible* (1953) may be the best known dramatization of the Salem witch trials, Mary E. Wilkins long before him had seen the resonances between a Puritan past and a morally compromised present. Mary E. Wilkins (1852–1930), later Freeman in 1902, known primarily for her novels and short stories about the hardship of life in New England at the end of the nineteenth century, was a ubiquitous presence in *Harper's* and *Century*. By the 1890s, Wilkins had established herself through her short stories for *Harper's*, which were collected as *A Humble Romance* (1887) and *A New England Nun* (1891). John Getz notes that this body of work "had established her as an important American literary figure, one whom the critics had to notice" though the notice she drew was by way of an unwelcome comparison with Hawthorne, which came at a critical juncture in the academic construction of an American literary history (177). As early as 1899 in *The Atlantic Monthly* the connection to Hawthorne had been made; thus, any reader coming to the play would anticipate some literary merit in her writing.

Her six-act tragedy, *Giles Corey, Yeoman*, appeared in *Harper's* in 1892 exactly 200 years after the Salem trials (at which her ancestor had succeeded in getting his grandson hanged as a witch). Peter Westbrook observes that the play is very dependent on Charles W. Upham's *Salem Witchcraft* (1866) but that though Wilkins adhered closely to the historical record, she weakened the effect by devising a love interest for Olive Corey and Paul Bayley and by introducing archaisms into the dialogue (100–01). More dramatically effective was the reversing of the chronological order of the Giles and Martha Corey executions, because the pressing to death of Corey, Donald Anderson argues, "was not only a historical reality but served as an apt metaphor for a culture repressed by perceptual error" (113). He suggests that Wilkins turned to the Salem witch trials because she saw a damaging connection between two deadened societies, the Puritan and the present. He points to the "so-called 'New England decline' [which] had gripped Wilkins's region since the Civil War, if not longer," a decline from which it had not recovered and which was the subject of concern in the periodicals (113–14). In *Giles Corey, Yeoman*, the martyr's steadfastly silent death is heralded as heroically self-sacrificing for the good of the community: "His dumbness will save the colonies from more than thou dreamest of. 'Twill put an end to this dreadful madness" (40). Wilkins, in her introduction to *Pembroke* (1899), noted that the Puritans' wills " 'were developed past the reasonable limits of nature' " and observed "what wonder it is that their descendants inherit this peculiarity, though they may develop it for much less worthy and trivial causes than the exiling of themselves for a question of faith, even the carrying out of personal and petty aims and quarrels' " (Anderson, D. R., " 'Giles Corey' and the Pressing Past" 115). Though Wilkins is usually typed as a "regionalist," suggesting that her subjects are quite contemporary and local, *Giles Corey, Yeoman* signals her concerned engagement with historical ills of the nation at large; hers was but the first of many plays published in periodicals at this time to be openly critical of the nation, past and present. Though the *Arena* (1899–1909) had several editors, the most prominent, B. O. Flower, was the dominant and shaping force who made the magazine "a kind of textbook of the populist movement" (Mott, F., *1885–1905* 407). As Mott explains, Flower's "family background of reformatory zeal, intellectuality, religion, and quackery" are important in understanding the social goals of the magazine (402). Flower took on a variety of subjects avoided by both the *Forum* and the *North American Review* such as poverty, sweatshops, slum clearance, unemployment, prostitution, birth control, women's rights, and child labor but his chief concern was political-economic reform, especially the issues of free silver, agrarian reform, single tax, the antitrust war, primary elections, reform of municipal government, and prohibition of liquor. Of Flower's reformist zeal, Hamlin Garland wrote "His *Arena* was a dignified and fearless forum wherein every discontented citizen could be heard" (*Roadside* 177).

Flower believed in the reformist social purpose of literature, which, of necessity, needed to be didactic. Excoriating the merely beautiful, Flower explained that the *Arena* was dedicated to reform through the "highest function" of literature and art, which was to champion "the world's helpless millions" (628). Flower gave Hamlin Garland his full support and encouraged the young writer whose short story, "A Spring Romance," had been accepted by the prestigious *Century* but whose polemical play, *Under the Wheel*, had been rejected. In a letter to Garland, Flower reminded him that "we are dealing with the great wrongs and evils of the day and the pitiful conditions of society and I do not wish you to feel in writing for the *Arena* at any time the slightest restraint" (*Roadside* 176). Garland's first contributions to the *Arena* were an essay on Ibsen (June 1890) and a play, *Under the Wheel* (July 1890). He continued to contribute essays, poems, and stories to the *Arena* until 1901 but *Under the Wheel* was his only play published in a periodical and it was never produced. Garland's other reformist play, *A Member of the Third House*, based on a celebrated investigation of the lobby by the legislature of Boston, was no more successful; Garland noted that both were "absolutely unsalable by reason of their austere content" (*Roadside* 85). Though B. O. Flower allowed Garland the fullest expression of his political concerns, Garland also wrote prolifically for other magazines; over 100 stories, essays, interviews, and poems appeared in *Harper's Weekly, Century, Outlook, Forum, New England Magazine, Independent, McClure's, Cosmopolitan*, and others.

Under the Wheel: A Modern Play in Six Scenes, notable as one of only two plays published by the *Arena* (the other being Newell Dunbar's *The Ever-Womanly*), opens with a directive epigraph from Turgeneff's novel about generational conflict and the tension between active radicalism and stagnant tradition, *Father and Sons*: "I have fallen under the wheel" (182). Each scene depicts an economic abuse of American laborers in three sites: a mechanic's tenement in the Boston slums, a boomer's den in the Midwest, and a shanty on the prairie. Though the primary issue is the corrupt practice of the "free land" syndicate scam that Garland charged was "the fundamental cause of poverty and must be destroyed first of all," he also rings changes on a host of other modern problems: on women's rights to work and to remain single, on urban blight, on emigration and immigration, on sugar trusts and coal kings regulating prices, and on railway speculation (*Roadside* 64). The play ends with a rallying call to workers to strike in the promise of imminent change as the young Reeves addresses the older, crushed Edwards: "I say you are fallen, but the column has passed on, the battle will yet be won. Courage, you will yet live to see the outposts of the enemy carried, and Linnie will live to see a larger and grander abolition cause, carried to a bloodless Appomattox, the abolition of industrial slavery" (227).

In his retrospective *Roadside Meetings*, Garland explained that he wanted his work to be "Western and truthful," to create characters who had "nothing European about them," and to address his deep sense of America's "weakness": "How could a nation so burdened with negro problems, bitter sectionalism, unassimilated immigration, and financial chaos survive?" (*Roadside* 178–81). As Warren Motley observes, "In his regional social drama *Under the Wheel* (1890), Hamlin Garland sought not simply to expose the related oppressions of immigrants in the east and farmers in the west, but finally to challenge his audience's vision of American society as a whole" (477). The specific challenge in *Under the Wheel*, Brenda Murphy suggests, is "Garland's typical deflation of the Western myth by exposing the evil forces of Capitalism and Nature at work on the Western farmer" (83).

Under the Wheel is an example of what Garland later defined as the "two sublime ideas" entering the drama, namely "truth" and "sympathy" (*Land* 165). Linking himself with James A. Herne as the two writers responding to American actors' desire to address "social trouble," Garland argued for the interdependency of art and politics, insisting that if the "poor sewing girl" was crushed so too would art be crushed. The single tax reform, and the attendant question of monopolies, was the fulcrum on which social solidarity teetered. Though Herbert Spencer's theory of evolution was the scientific foundation on which he built his art, Garland was also influenced by Ibsen, whose *The Doll House* he had seen and which he had heralded as altering the course of American drama: "If we must imitate, let us imitate those who represent truth and not those who uphold convention" (*Roadside* 66). Both "truth" and "sympathy" were expressed in the use of the vernacular, a cult Garland locates in 1888 with the poetry of Hopkinson Smith and Thomas Nelson Page (*Roadside* 106).

Richard Brodhead contends that regional vernacular literature "served as the principal place of literary access in America in the postbellum decades" and that, excepting Henry James and William Dean Howells, "virtually every other writer of this time who succeeded in establishing himself as a writer did so through the regional form" (116). One of the fortuitous consequences of literary regionalism, Brodhead observes, was a "major extension of the literary franchise" by the empowerment of the socially marginalized such as women from small towns and African Americans (118). Turning to Garland, Brodhead argues that "Hamlin Garland, the first farmer to have entered American literature, felt humiliatingly handicapped for authorship by his provincial origins and immersion in manual labor. But in Garland's case a farm worker was enabled to become an author by the regional form, which converted his rural background into a career-funding resource" (117). Whether Brodhead's psychological analysis is correct or not, Garland was committed to yoking literature to politics through the use of dialect and regionalism, which he discussed in *Arena* in "The Future of Fiction" (1893) and "The Land Question and Its Relation to Art and Literature" (1894).

Hamlin Garland does use dialect in *Under the Wheel* (*Arena* 1890): "Faith! an' if this is free Amurriky, what'll be the Amurriky that'll be comin' wid the faall o' waages and the rise o' rint?" but it is quite clear that he does so as regionalist in deep sympathy with and as an advocate for the people (190). As part of his argument for a democratic literature and for "vertism," Garland argued for the necessity of dialect as "the life of language, precisely as the common people of the nation form the sustaining power of its social life and art" (*Idols* 74). Of the coming "colloquial" fiction and drama, he wrote optimistically, "Local color is the royal robe" (*Future* 520). Garland's play is an anomaly in many respects compared to the other plays in this study: it is the only play with a rural setting, it is the only play in which dialect is used uncritically, and it is the only play to speak out for an underclass. These marked distinctions support Nancy's Glazener's argument that *Arena* was a genuine alternative to the other magazines in "The *Atlantic* Group" (189).

One of the problems with dialect literature, however, is that it could serve two very diverse ends. As Michael Elliott explains, "dialect writing was situated at the intersection of scientific ethnography and literary realism because it provided a literary vehicle through which authentic difference could be textualized in tangible and accurate ways" (63). At the same time, however, "the orthographic representation of vernacular English was mired in the older model of inherited, hierarchical racial difference" (64). For Hamlin Garland, the use of dialect served his serious political and Veritist ends and established his authenticity as spokesperson for his characters. Others, like William Dean Howells, used dialect to harden and highlight the lines of social demarcation, distance, and difference, expressing their discontent and anxiety about a changing nation and especially about the rising tides of immigrants.

In Howells's *Bride Roses* for *Harper's* (1893), a florist, Mr. Eichenlaub, speaks in heavily accented German. When the Lady calls his shop a "tropic" because of its warmth, he replies: "Dropic? With icepergs on the wintows?" (424). In promising to send on flowers, he says: "Goodtmorning, matam. I will sendt rhoundt this afternoon" (428). The play is serious and the florist is not meant to be comic; here dialect marks the class distinction between the shopkeeper and his high-class patrons, all of whom speak in correct English. What is more important is that their dialectical differences also correspond with differences in sensibility and sensitivity. In an exchange about the titular roses, the Lady notes their delicate beauty and compares them to snow but the florist is concerned only with their commercial viability: "It is coing to be a very bopular rhoce" (428). Howells, therefore, marks the florist both as not fully assimilated as a speaker of English and as a member of the commercial class and, in so doing, actively contributes to the growing tide of anti-Semitic anxiety. The language of racial difference within the cultural sphere linked with nascent commercialism, Jonathan Freedman argues in *The Temple of Culture*, was part of the production of "the Jew" in late nineteenth century Anglo-American fiction. Only four months later, George Du Maurier's *Trilby*, in which the figure of Svengali was so grotesquely racialized, was serialized in *Harper's Monthly* (January– August 1894) and was a runaway bestseller as a novel in Britain and the United States, making it, as Harley Erdman observes, "consistent with the anxiety of the moment" (99).

In a later play, *The Impossible. A Mystery Play* (1910), Howells again sets up a "foreigner" to make points about class distinctions. In this instance it is a hired servant, Jules, on hand to assist at a private dinner party. Jules, may or may not actually be French, according to the skeptical man of the house: "they all have French names, no matter what their nationality is" (118). Jules speaks "with a heavy Alsatian accent" (119), "Two mezzenger-boys. Dere is no anzwer. I rezeipted for dem" (121). Apart from supplying such comic interruptions, Jules serves a very important function in naturalizing firm class lines. The couple giving the dinner, having lost all their guests to a round of the grippe, decide to feed ten poor men standing in the Bread Line, but when the men enter the apartment building and use the *back* elevator, the wife tells her husband that she refuses to sit down with them: "We must distinguish! We couldn't sit down with people who had come up the back elevator, now, could we? You see yourself we couldn't. It would be impossible" (124). Jules rescues the situation, first observing that "the servants—the gook and the maits" cannot let them eat in the kitchen and, second, "Well, sör, if you will egscuse my sogchesting somet'ing: I could but dem up a nize lonch, and let dem dake it out, and eat it vhere they lige, ton'dt you know—vhere they usually eat—in the street" (125). Thus Jules is not only a comic butt because of his fractured English but is also complicit with his mistress as a rationalizing reinforcer of indisputable and insurmountable class difference and distance.

In other hands, dialect, an essential ingredient of minstrelsy and vaudeville, was the jester's motley. Josephine Daskam Bacon's *The First of October* (1904) assumes that the reader is familiar with and sympathetic to the woes besetting an "up-town" couple, the Tarrants, who, in the process of decorating and moving into a new home, are impeded by incompetent "foreign" workers. The Tarrants's up-to-date good taste is established in the opening scene when they bemoan the fact that they are cursed with ghastly gifts from elderly relatives: a cast of the Winged Victory, an enormous engraving of the Sistine Madonna, a photograph of the Mona Lisa, and an alabaster bust of Wagner. Thus the first function of the play is either to educate the reader about or to include the reader in the joke about suitable home decorations by mocking Europhilic "old-fashioned" taste. The insult to modern American taste is compounded by the greater injuries inflicted on the couple by careless and inept workmen whose ethnic identities are the source of the comedy. The furniture-polisher mangles English: "We do not bolish marple. It does no goot" (724). The painters, "fat-ferocious looking creatures," trail "miles of filthy grayish cloth" and speak with a "Jewish accent" (726–27). Not only are the workers slovenly, but also they are careless, greedy, lazy, and argumentative. The play ends with the exasperated husband addressing the janitor: "And if the maid comes, let her in . . . Lena—a Swedish girl—I don't know her last name; it doesn't matter . . . If she's Lena and cross-eyed a little, she'll do" (733).

The only instance of an intelligent and well-spoken servant in the plays under consideration is in one of Howell's farces, *Evening Dress*, in *Cosmopolitan* in 1892. Little more than a satiric jibe at a married woman who believes herself to be organized but who inadvertently hides her husband's evening clothes from him, the possible social embarrassment is averted because of the maid's quick thinking. The maid, Bella, has to choose between telling the truth and protecting her employers from ridicule; she sides with her employers, explaining "I wasn't going to have that young waitress of Mrs. Baker's and that nasty cook of Mrs. Merrick's laughing at us." That the well-spoken servant would choose to align herself with her employers against other servants would have been reassuring to the reader who might be anxious about the loyalty of servants. However, even this minimal alliance is tempered by the husband's refusal to concede too much to the maid's intervention; when his wife calls her "an angel," he replies, "Well, that isn't quite what they call them" and hustles everyone off to dinner (127).

Though Booth Tarkington (1869–1946) is better known as a novelist, he wrote twenty-one produced plays, of which *Monsieur Beaucaire* (1901) was the first and *Colonel Satan* (1931) the last. *Mr. Antonio*, his eighth play, produced at the Lyceum in November of 1916 and starring Otis Skinner, was published in *Harper's* in two parts in January and February of 1917. His other play to be published in a periodical was *Beauty and the Jacobin* in *Harper's* (1912). Tarkington was also a known figure in the periodicals; between 1915 and 1918 he had published fifteen pieces in several periodicals and had been featured in several portraits. More a popular than a critical success, the production of *Mister Antonio* received a brief notice in *The Nation*, which observed that "what might easily have been a stupid play" was, in fact, engaging: "The gist of the whole matter is that the unlettered Italian, the half-witted Joe, and even Capitano [a donkey], are better qualified to evaluate human conduct than are the self-appointed mentors of a town in which respectability has been carried to the point of indecency—which means hypocrisy" ("F" 330).

In challenging the educated American middle class with the honesty and astuteness of the uneducated immigrant, Tarkington was weighing in on a debate of long standing. To speak "correct" English was understood to be an essential requirement of assimilation and a homogeneous nation and to be yoked to Christian morality. For instance, Jacob Riis's studies of life in New York tenements, *How the Other Half Lives*, first published in *Scribner's* (1889), stressed the threatening fragmentation and alienation that characterized a city too close to Babel. Vaudeville, of course, thrived on dialect impersonation to represent ethnic caricature, which was the central focus of the comedy. In reading about such entertainments from the privileged position of a comfortable, middle-class home, nervous readers could reassure themselves of their own cultural superiority and distance from immigrant and "low" entertainments such as vaudeville productions, productions that were synecdoche for the potential political threat embodied in immigrant restlessness. Of the pernicious function of dialect, Gavin Jones stresses that it forged the "fictions of racial dominance that countered contemporary ethnic threats" (8) and that "the outlandishness of an immigrant dialect cements a demeaning stereotype, thus confirming ethnic otherness and inferiority" (164).

The matter of how English was spoken was but one dimension of the debate over immigration. Between 1810 and 1989, over forty million people immigrated to the United States, a movement that hit its first peak between 1891 and 1920. Of the leading "sender" states (Germany, Italy, Great Britain, and Austria-Hungary), Italy sent over five million. Except for Ireland, from which the largest influx came before the Civil War, European immigrants came in the three decades between 1880 and 1910 (Simon 3–5). David Blight states the figures this way: "Almost 14 million immigrants came to the United States between 1860 and 1900. Another 14.5 million arrived in the period 1900–15, mostly from eastern and southern Europe" (354). In their survey of four major periodicals, *Harper's Monthly, Scribner's Magazine, The Nation,* and *The Atlantic Monthly,* Simon and Alexander determine that, with the notable exception of *The Nation,* the treatment of immigrants in the major periodicals was more negative than positive. Attitudes ranged from virulent nativist arguments for severe restrictions to romanticized but anxious portrayals of adjustment. All of the articles in *Scribner's* were anti-immigrant and pro-restriction. *The Atlantic Monthly,* which vied with the *Saturday Evening Post* for carrying the most articles on immigration, was more often than not negative and alarmist, pointing to genetic inferiority, the threat of job losses, socialist politics, and a host of other evils. By comparison, *Harper's Monthly* had little to say on the subject, mostly sticking to sympathetic interviews and first-person accounts.

Therefore, when Tarkington uses a heavy Italian dialect in *Mr. Antonio,* he anticipates traditional expectations and can subvert them for dramatic effect. The play begins in a New York dive, affording Tarkington the opportunity to exercise both his Germanic and New York "cockney" dialects when a Midwestern type, on a bender and out of cash, is rescued from the threatening urban types by "a great little Dago." The "Dago," Tony, is a classic "stage Italian": "flamboyant," "half shouting," gesticulating wildly, laughing loudly, the epitome of the "picturesque" (190). And his speech is thick: "Deese bizaness-church gentimens, 'e don know well enough; 'e make *bizaness* weet them. 'E don' wan *know* 'e bust loose" (192).

The next act reveals the rescued man to be the pompous and self-righteous mayor of a Midwest town, who prides himself on having cleaned the town out of the bad, the wanton, the loose, and the idle. What the reader discovers, however, is rank hypocrisy in many instances, one of which concerns poor June, the hired girl, who will be turned out because she has been spurned by a deceitful suitor now planning to marry the Mayor's daughter. Complications ensue until Tony is driven to confront the townspeople with a number of hard truths which are so unpleasant that, in the end, he recants and the town is allowed to continue with the hypocritical norm. Tony and June leave as a couple, playing "Onward Christian Soldiers" on the hurdy-gurdy.

On the one hand, then, Tarkington subverts many of the stereotypes by casting Tony as an honest man and true Christian. On the other hand, Tony and June are not assimilated either into the town nor into the nation because Tony makes it quite clear that his stay in the United States is temporary: "dees summer she 'las for de 'urdy-gurd' man; I am goin' back to Sorrent' for be Padrone" (375). Thus both the Italian and the deceived working girl, though more morally upright than the townspeople, leave America. The desirable return of the native was underscored in the touring production: "For three season after the New York opening in September 1916, Otis Skinner toured the country as Mr. Antonio and, while the war was going on, sold Liberty Bonds during curtain calls *in the broken English of the organ-grinder*" (my emphasis; Woodress 205). It would have been clear to the audience that *Tony* not Skinner was appealing for aid and that that aid would enable his return to Italy.

In the end, the play is only a lightweight piece of entertainment with a modest moral thrust. The reader can laugh freely at Tony's mangled English and at the townspeople's hypocrisy but also be assured that Tony won't be moving into their town or their nation. The play sets up the happy fiction that this Italian, endlessly cheerful and optimistic, not only wants to go back home but will and, in this case, take the hired girl, that uncomfortable reminder of sexual double standards, with him. Despite the mitigation of his Christian dimension, Tony's "ethnic otherness" is as firmly in place as is his comic inferiority as a speaker.

The third major social issue to get a lot of attention was prostitution or the "social evil" and, as might be expected, the plays in the *Forum* are the most serious. Though the "genteel" periodicals such as *The Atlantic Monthly, Scribner's,* and *Century* did not publish articles on prostitution, *Forum, Arena, Outlook,* and *McClure's* did, the numbers swelling from only a few articles in the 1890s to over 150 between 1910 and 1914. Of great interest was the "white slave" trade that, as Richard Maltby observes, was part of "a specifically anti-Semitic nativism" and "particularly visible in a series of articles by George Kibbe Turner published in *McClure's*

Magazine during the New York Mayoral election campaign of 1909" (251). The appropriation and displacement of the enslavement of Africans, the focus on the Austrian, Russian, and Hungarian Jews as procurers, and the construction of white women as victims was not balanced by any investigation of the prostitutes's clientele. The plays on prostitution are uniformly melodramatic in Peter Brooks's sense in that they express "basic ethical and psychic truths" in clear language and reenact "the menace of evil and the eventual triumph of morality made operative and evident." And while the political content may vary, be conservative, or revolutionary in its social implications, it is "in all cases radically democratic, striving to make its representations clear and legible to everyone. . . . Melodrama becomes the principal mode for uncovering, demonstrating, and making operative the essential moral universe in a post sacred era" (15). In particular the plays mark the city as a dangerous place for single women. Cecelia Tichi has noted the close correspondence between Brooks's definition of melodrama and muckraking journalism in particular, drawing attention to his location of melodrama's mode as one of "high emotionalism and stark ethical conflict." She concludes that muckraking narratives can best be understood as "civic melodrama" and that "muckraker prose style shows its debt to the stage melodrama" (77–78).

Forum was deeply invested in "social drama," publishing many articles on the subject, especially those concerned about "morality." Three examples will suffice. In "The Modern Social Drama," Clayton Hamilton heralds this new type of play as the most appropriate for the age because it is less religious than the Greek model, "since science has yet induced no dwelling-place for God," and it is less poetic than the Elizabethan model, "since sociological discussion demands the mood of prose." The modern or "problem" play is best because "in this the individual is displayed in conflict with his environment" (267) and because social "outcasts" such as courtesans, bastards, ex-convicts, and those harboring "dangerous" ideas figure as the protagonists (269). "And," he continues, "the question naturally follows: Is a drama that does this moral or immoral?" (270). Hamilton rejects the criterion and argues instead for the "treatment" of the subject, which must past the test of "truthfulness" (271). Sheldon Cheney also argued for the necessity of the truthful play, what he called the "drama of sincerity," that is the plays of Galsworthy, Barrie, and Shaw, as distinct from the "aesthetic drama" of Gordon

Craig and Max Reinhardt (498). And Reginald Kaufmann, author of *The House of Bondage*, invited to "defend the dramatic representation of the seamy side of life," gladly proclaims himself to be "innocent of morality" and a "Philistine" in the art of ethics (664–65), asserting that today the purpose of the "genuine artist" is not to amuse but to "interpret life truly" (669). To interpret life truly means to disturb the complaisantly comfortable reader and to dramatize "pain and poverty, disease, wrong and death" (671).

Despite these calls for wide-ranging coverage of a variety of ills, Clayton Hamilton notes that "our most serious modern dramatists . . . deal almost exclusively with problems of sex" (270). Certainly this is true of most of the plays in *Forum*, the tamest of which is George Middleton's *The Man Masterful* (1909). Staged as a discussion between Edith Sherwood, a self-reliant woman who, though supporting herself, is "not without connections and sympathies more aristocratic than her present surroundings would imply," and Mrs. Williams, "pinched and bloodless" and middle-aged (369), at issue is the philandering adulterer, Mr. Williams. Edith Sherwood is an honest woman and has vowed to proceed with the affair only if Mrs. Williams no longer loves her husband, as he has been insisting to Edith is the case. Surprisingly, Mrs. Williams says that she does not love him and turns the discussion to a more pressing problem, testifying to his "mastery" and the process by which he sapped her vitality and will. She describes his methodical assault on her independence: "He was devoting himself to accomplish one end––with all his absorbing power, one end: to make himself *necessary* to me; to make me see that I was his dependent thing" (378). He has also done this to other women. Edith Sherwood realizes that he has not been honest with her, takes the lesson of the utterly broken woman, and resolves to break off the affair even though she still feels the power of his mastery. In effect, the play takes a woman through the necessary stages of self-awareness and resolve, modeling a course of action for the female reader while maintaining for the male reader the status quo of inescapable masculine magnetism. In the preface to *The Man Masterful* and others collected in *Embers and Other One-Act Plays* (1911), Middleton spoke of his intention to write plays both for professional American actors because this country lacked "the serious one-act drama so common on the Continent" and also for readers because of an increasing demand following the plays' "unexpected publication" in magazines (n. pag.).

Both George Middleton and Witter Bynner were supporters of women's suffrage and had marched with 100 men in the men's section of the first parade on Fifth Avenue on May 6, 191, in which 10,000 women had marched. Bynner (1881–1968) was involved with Equal Suffrage to such a degree that he thought of it as the essence of the democratic ideal and the fundamental basis of his poetry. Bynner is now best known for his translations of Chinese (T'ang) verse and his partnership with Arthur Davison Fiske as perpetrators of the Spectra Hoax. In 1916, fed up with Imagism and Vorticism, the two poets concocted "Spectrism," a new school for experimental poetry under which aegis they parodied literary pretentiousness.

Bynner also had a career as a dramatist; in 1907, shortly after leaving *McClure's Magazine* where he worked as a poetry and fiction editor from 1902 to 1906, he wrote several one-act plays, all of which were performed: *Tiger* (1913), about prostitution; *The Little King* (1914), about the young Dauphin during the French Revolution; *A Night Wind* (1922), set in a Greenwich Village coffee shop; and *Cycle* (1922), an antiwar play. He also wrote *Kit* and *The Mechanic* with Cecil B. DeMille in 1907, *Anygirl* (1917), a musical version of *Everyman* for a woman, and a comic verse play about Mabel Dodge called *Cake* (1926), which his biographer describes as "high camp" (Kraft 55). In his defense of disturbing, truthful drama, Reginald Kauffman singled out Bynner and his "powerful *Tiger*" as the example of the desirable modern dramatist who "ridicules and exposes Civilization and sends you away with a sense that you are in part to blame for 'What's Wrong with the World,' " the evils to which the base, "smug Anglo-Saxon mind" closes its mind (672).

Witter Bynner's blank verse *Tiger* (1913) has two epigraphs, one an editorial rationale for printing the play, the other the unattributed opening stanza from William Blake's "The Tyger." The editorial statement reads: "Painful and almost terrible as this may seem to some readers, it merely focuses, in dramatic form, the abominable realities to which 'civilized' people have so long shut their eyes, publicly and pharisaically; but to which, in tens of thousands of cases, they have given vicious personal and private encouragement" (522). The abominable reality in question is "white slave trade" or, more exactly, kidnapping and forced prostitution of Anglo-Saxon girls and women. Of all the plays published in the periodicals, this is the only one to warrant a prefatory rationale and a follow-up letter from the dramatist presumably because of the sensational subject matter. Because Bynner, an assistant editor at *McClure's* from 1902 to 1906 and the Phi Beta Kappa poet at Harvard in 1911, had lectured throughout the United States between 1911 and 1922, he could have been known to the readers of *Forum* in 1913.

As Mary E. Odem argues in *Delinquent Daughters: Protecting and Policing Adolescent Female Sexuality in the United States, 1885–1920*, the sexuality of single young women, especially urban working girls, was the focus of public anxiety and state interventionist policies in the late nineteenth century. She marks two distinct stages of moral reform and regulation. The first stage began in the mid-1880s, when white purity activists, fueled by gender, class, and racial tensions, raised the age of consent (from as low as seven in Delaware but around ten for most states in 1885 to sixteen or eighteen in most states by 1920). The second stage was when Progressive reformers replaced the model of female victimization with one of female delinquency, during the first two decades of the twentieth century, when increasingly large numbers of women became wage earners in factories. Furthermore, though the white-slave tracts called for the defense of womanhood, they portrayed women as helpless and passive dupes. Ruth Rosen notes that under the scrutiny of eugenic testing, "a surprisingly high percentage of prostitutes were described as feeble-minded" (22), that prostitutes were considered to be both sinners and criminals (27), and that, of course, once a "girl" had "fallen," she was beyond rehabilitation, a " 'fallen dove' " (20). The adoption of the British term "white slavery" tipped the racist hand; the term clearly indicates that only the sexual exploitation of white women was considered a significant social problem. Fueled by anti-Semitic nativism, fears of Anglo-Saxon "suicide" and immigrant overpopulation, and a determined displacement of the realities of sexual abuse of African American slaves, the "white slavery" scare was addressed in the periodicals as a "social evil."

"White slave" narratives were a flourishing genre in the early decades of the twentieth century. The hysteria generated by white-slave tracts that began to circulate around 1909 was preceded by anxiety over the age of consent; between January and November 1895, Helen Gardener wrote five articles on the age of consent problem for B. O. Flower's *Arena*. According to Mark Thomas Connelly in *The Response to Prostitution in the Progressive Era*, between 1909 and 1914 at least twenty-two white-slave narratives had been published (114). Connelly also points to a number of prominent political responses to the issue: the Rockefeller grand jury investigation in New York City in 1910, a U.S. Senate investigation in 1909–1910, and the Mann Act in 1910. The indignation over white slavery was also expressed in a barrage of articles in periodicals: *Arena* featured a discussion of prostitution as a social problem, *Harper's Weekly* had a story on the making of a prostitute, and *Collier's* dealt with the Raines Law hotels, saloons that could sell liquor on Sundays and had enough rooms to qualify as a hotel. In 1909 *McClure's* published a series of articles on white slavery by George Kibbe Turner who was already well-established as with an earlier exposé, "The City of Chicago" (1907) and a short story, "Daughters of the Poor" (1909) (Filler 286–90). Brand Whitlock's "The White Slave" appeared in *Forum* in 1914 and because he had been the mayor of Toledo, Ohio (1906–1913), was serving as the U.S. Minister to Belgium (1914–1919), and had published a biography of Samuel Jones, the radical mayor of Toledo, *Forty Years of It* (1914), his opinions carried a great deal of force. Readers interested in the subject also might well have read Reginald Wright Kaufman's short story, "The Things that Are Caesar's" (1902) and certainly would have read his bestselling denunciation of prostitution, *The House of Bondage* (1910), which was in its fourteenth edition in 1912 and was one of many works that set up Jews, Italians, or East Europeans as dark debauchers of fair American girls.

Therefore, by the time readers read *Tiger* in 1913, they would have been steeped in the tropes of the genre of white-slave narratives though perhaps not ready for the sensational ironic twist at the play's conclusion. The location is a house near Times Square run by "Tiger," so-called for her "hard, lithe brilliance" (522). She is urging a pimp, the Baron, to bring her in a new girl, a virgin, more desirable than the used commodities because "The other kind is common / And some of the clients amuse themselves, / You know, by being fastidious" (524). The future for the new recruit is clear; one of the rapidly hardening young prostitutes tells Tiger how she's "getting wise to the game / Say to a gink, 'Your nose is beautiful,' / 'Your mouth was made to kiss,' or to call his figure / Military" (526). The innocent girl, Margaret, a runaway from a strict father, believes that Tiger is the Baron's aunt, willing to shelter her on the eve of her marriage to the Baron. They give her some drugged tea, preliminary to the impending induction-by-rape, but the drink makes her fight back so they decide to starve her into submission first. Tiger sums up the imminent procedure: "She knows the Baron's waiting. He'll teach her first. Then nothing matters. Eight or ten hours more at most and she'll begin" (542).

But before the Baron can begin the initiation rites, an old and valued client, a stout, prosperous, middle-aged man enters. Tiger decides to let him have the first go at the girl: "He's an old friend, / He knows the game and plays it like a good one. / In fact it's sports like Willy have to have / the dainty morsels" (542). Willy has just finished a round of golf and has made money on a legal case, so, after a good deal of wheedling on his part, Tiger sells him the rights to induct the girl into the "game." When her room is unlocked, "*there is a pause, then, inside the bedroom, a scream of mingled terror and joy from the girl, and a moan from the man.*" Margaret's heart rending cry rings out, "Father! Father, I knew you'd come! Father!" (546). The curtain falls on collective horror.

A year later, Witter Bynner wrote a letter to the editor of the *Forum* praising his courage for printing the play and describing the aftermath: "It has appeared in book form, been barred from sale by the Comstocks of Boston, been played by students before members of the Dartmouth College Faculty and by a professional cast at the Little Theatre in Philadelphia." He also described the many objections to the play. Pointing to the prevalence of "white slavery" in America, Bynner seizes the Christian high ground to respond to his critics: "What I venture to suggest to this group, to the anti-suffragist, to the feudalist generally, is that in my reading of Christ, we are all 'members of one another,' responsible to one another and eventually identified with one another" (633). In the same issue, Gertrude Traubel, daughter of Walt Whitman's chronicler, Horace Traubel, and the editor of his *Walt Whitman in Camden*, spoke out in defense of the play: "So far I have heard two people say that Witter Bynner's *Tiger* was unnecessary. Men, of course,—and young, equally of course." The question she asks, should the male readers be indifferent to the problem, is "*Whose* daughter?" (583). *Tiger*, to my knowledge, is unique in that it was prefaced with a rationale and was followed by a letter from the dramatist and a defense; the fuss suggests the volatility of, to say nothing of the salacious interest in and anxiety over, the white-slavery issue.

Equally sensational, Paula Jakobi's *Chinese Lily* in the *Forum* (1915), set in the laundry of a woman's prison where the tattooed "drunk and disorderlies" are laboring under the watchful eye of a kind but sad matron, is both dramaturgically and thematically interesting. Like *Tiger, Chinese Lily* takes readers into an unfamiliar subculture to which the middle class turns a blind eye and for which it is clearly responsible. Jakobi wrote from experience; she had taken a job as a matron in the Framingham reformatory in order to study prison conditions. A few years later, as an ardent supporter of women's suffrage and one of five hundred women arrested for picketing the White House in 1917, she was sentenced to thirty days in the infamous Occoquan workhouse along with Louise Bryant and other prominent Progressives (Stevens 361).

The play introduces the reader to women such as Annie, who is "colored" and "evil-looking," and Clara, who has "tattooed arms and chest . . . short greasy peroxide hair. A typical 'sailors' delight,' " and significantly makes of them entirely sympathetic and pitiable victims by play's end (550). One actress doubles in two parts as Kate, "a sweet-faced English girl" who is on the eve of her release and Janey, "pale and worn," who is later revealed to be Chinese Lily's missing daughter. The play also dramatizes the plight of a mixed-race woman, Chinese Lily, who is "half Chinese, half Scotch." The focus on a Chinese protagonist points to historical fact. Ruth Rosen in *The Lost Sisterhood*, a study of prostitution in America in the first decades, offers compelling evidence that a large number of Chinese and Japanese women were imported to the United States for sexual purposes (122). Rosen also connects America's entry into the war with the national municipal movement to eradicate prostitution: "In an atmosphere already charged by the fanatic enthusiasm to combat the Social Evil *and* a 'war to end' all wars,' the exigencies of combat prompted quick federal action to ensure a healthy and fit armed services" (33). The reader, therefore, would have been anxious about prostitution not only as a local moral crime but also as a national hygienic crisis threatening the health and, possibly, the very survival of the nation.

Chinese Lily is set in the present with one flashback in the middle enabling the women to review their hard lives as, variously, a child laborer, an abortionist, a prostitute, and an illiterate, all types of women unfamiliar to the average reader. One recalls her first arrest for prostitution: "Oh, yes, I had dandy fun. It is the first time I am run in. They was Harvard students—fine fellows" (556). While one could charge the play with pandering to the readers' voyeuristic interest in criminal behavior, clearly Jakobi wants to close the gap between what the reader is blind to and the realities of social interaction, that crime is not circumscribed by class difference but is, in fact, fed by it. When Chinese Lily tells her story, the play goes to a flashback of three years prior to a luxurious Chinese interior in which Chin Tau, her pimp, is smoking an opium pipe. He informs her that her fourteen-year-old daughter, Janey, is to be given to Count Romanoff, but when he refuses to let Lily go in her daughter's place, she strangles him with his queue.

When the play returns to the present, the prisoners are getting ready for a commissioners' probation review. Stella is contemptuous of the entire proceeding: "Did you know that the commissioners and social workers are comin' here to-day? I was told to hurry up the white dresses. That'll mean that we'll put them on and when they'll be walkin' through the grounds we'll be let out and we'll play ball. Ain't I cute playin' ball?" (564). Again, Jakobi calls the readers' attention to their complicit roles in the punitive system. A newcomer is introduced; she proves to be Janey, who was forced to take to the streets. At this revelation, Chinese Lily abandons hope, questioning the whole point of incarceration: "You don't learn anything. You're just kept busy—busy at the same tiresome thing day after day. If you don't treat every other woman like a brute you're watched to see that you're not breaking any of their blessed rules." And, she concludes, by the time you get out, you're useless, "You're only fit to made use of" (566). In counterpoint to Lily's lament, a joyous Kate is released, the women gathering around to shout encouragement: "*Don't come back, Kate! Don't come back!*" (566). It is worth noting that the mixed-race women will stay behind bars and that the "sweet-faced English girl" is freed.

The question to ask of both of these plays about prostitution is: did they reduce the complexities of urban prostitution to a drastic oversimplification, effective only as sensational, voyeuristic, and sentimental privatized melodrama, or did they substantively work in concert with the reformists' essays of exposé to dramatize serious institutionalized social issues needing the readers' immediate attention? One way to understand the conflicted cultural work done by these plays is to locate them within the larger genre of white-slave tracts that Mark Thomas Connelly characterizes as "self-contradictory": "They clearly embodied many of the human concerns of the progressive era. Yet they also expressed some of the more sinister tendencies of those years: the ethnocentrism and racial fears of the nativists; the emotional excesses;

illogic, inaccuracies, and authoritarianism of the Prohibitionist crusade; and the conspiratorial mentality that often permeated even the most serious reforms" (134).

I want to suggest that the contradictory responses to prostitution and "white slavery" should be understood as symptomatic of a widespread anxiety about political health and national cohesion, an illusory state fast crumbling under the destabilizing pressures of both domestic upheavals and overseas expansionism and which would soon catapult the periodicals into a debate about the war. Among the first signs of a separation from the ingrained cultural Europhilia and Anglophilia was the critical stance taken by some playwrights against monarchy, a position that they had not taken earlier despite support for American democratic principles. Recently critics have assessed the post–Civil War period, from the end of the war to the beginning of World War I, as a time when the nation was so traumatized that it sought to erase painful divisive memories and construct a conciliatory nationalist narrative (that is, to reinvoke Benedict Anderson's term, an "imaginary"). The process began immediately after the war, with William McKinley's defeat of William Jennings Bryan in the 1896 presidential election in a campaign based on the acceptance of the racial apartheid, which by the mid-1890s had taken firm hold in the South. Patrick J. Kelly specifically ascribes the "campaign of memory" to the Republican party, which grabbed the discourse of "stability, nationalism, business propriety and law and order" (206) for McKinley's challenge to Bryan, noting that "the Republican platform for the first time since the end of the Civil War omitted any demand that the federal government use its military power to guarantee black suffrage in the South" (181). McKinley's victory ended the Populist insurgency. which was, in one historian's opinion, "nothing less than the last significant American challenge to industrial capitalism as a system of social, economic and political power" and which created a formula for dominating national politics for more than thirty years (206–07). David Blight in *Race and Reunion* has demonstrated in depth the lengths to which the nation created a "collective" memory of the Civil War in its aftermath and, especially, during the fiftieth anniversary celebrations (1913–1915) by which time, "racism had become a cultural industry, and twisted history a commodity. A segregated society required a segregated historical memory and a national mythology that could blunt or contain the conflict at the root of that segregation. Most American embraced an unblinking celebration of reunion and accepted segregation a natural condition of the races" (391).

A related construct crucial to the preservation of the national myth of union was the shoring up of a virtuous democracy; as America increasingly exerted its imperial prerogative and manifest right to expand overseas, the uncomfortable analogy with aggressive monarchism (and the British empire in particular) needed to be resisted with an insistent validation of unbridled individualism based on a simple binarism of democracy versus monarchy. In *Imagined Communities*, Benedict Anderson contends that imagined realities (nation-states) need to liquidate their conceptual opposites (monarchies): "As late as 1914, dynastic states made up the majority of the membership of the world political system, but . . . many dynasts had for some time been reaching for a 'national' cachet as the old principle of Legitimacy withered silently away . . . . The new imagined communities . . . conjured up by lexicography and print-capitalism always regarded themselves as somehow ancient. In an age in which 'history' itself was still widely conceived in terms of 'great events' and 'great leaders,' pearls strung along a thread of narrative, it was obviously tempting to decipher the community's past in antique dynasties" (109).

Five plays in the periodicals that are specifically anti-monarchist, anti-aristocrat, and pro-republican span the time of the Spanish-American War to World War I. Because none of them are set in America, I contend that they dramatize the growing anxiety about the taint of affiliations with European values and legacies. They are: John Oliver Hobbes's *A Repentance* in the *Critic* (August 1899), Josephine Dodge Daskam's *The Wanderers* in the *Century* (August 1901), Booth Tarkington's *Beauty and the Jacobin* (August and September 1912), Louis N. Parker's *A Minuet* in the *Century* (January 1915), and Sada Cowan's *In the Morgue* in the *Forum* (April 1916).

"John Oliver Hobbes" was the pseudonym of Pearl Mary Teresa Richards Craigie (1867–1906), American by birth, English by marriage, and Catholic by conversion, who was the well-known author of several novels, including *The School for Saints* and *Robert Orange*. Later she turned to drama, achieving some success with plays such as *The Ambassador* and *The Bishop's Move* despite their "uniform deficiencies" (Anonymous, "American" 405). With George Moore, she had also written *The Fool's Hour*, a Wildean social satire on marriage published in *The Yellow Book* (1894). Both Americans and English claimed her as their own; thus she appears in an article on English dramatists in the *Critic* (1909) as an amateurish writer of conventional melodrama and in an appraisal by William Dean Howells as an American novelist caught between realism and romanticism and as "one of the most original examples of our Anglo-American day" though on a "minor scale" (1258). She was recognized by her critics as an intelligent woman: in an interview with William Archer for the *Critic* in 1901, she invokes the "*féministe*" writings of Bourget, Donnay, Prévost, Tolstoy, and D'Annunzio, the poetry of Byron and Shakespeare, and the thought of Herbert Spencer and George Eliot among others. However, "Hobbes" was understood to have missed greatness because she burdened her work with "theory" at the expense of "actuality" (Anonymous, "American" 404). The sense of her "refined melodrama" and "artificial" characters is accurately captured in Howells's description of her intentions: "to lead the horny-footed plebeian generation over the purple-paths of aristocratic closes; and to touch with pathos the merited or unmerited sufferings of well-born or high-placed people" (1259).

John Oliver Hobbes's *A Repentance* in the *Critic* (August 1899), set in Spain in 1835, was produced at the St. James's Theatre (February 1899) and scheduled for productions in France, Germany, Austro-Hungary, and Russia. A note to the play explains Hobbes's political concerns: "In this short drama, the author has introduced some of the strongest types of character produced by the Carlist question in Spain. Similar types were produced in England in Jacobite time, and, farther back, during the Parliamentary wars. Any reader who is interested in a question dealing with European monarchist politics, may be referred to Daudet's great novel, 'Les Rois en Exil' " (691). Essentially a historical domestic melodrama in which a count, believed to be dead, returns to his wife in Bilbao disguised as a friar because he is fleeing from a struggle between Carlists and Christinists, Hobbes's play supports a populist rebellion against the throne. When challenged to take a position, the count imagines what the situation would be had he been born an aristocrat: "Three nurses watch me day and night, and, if I fall, a dozen fat footmen pick me up. I ride, I fence, I dance and sing, I play the fool, I dress myself up, I swagger, I brag, I am a dandy, I am a rake, I am a hero, or, in other words, an aristocrat." He tells the countess that if such an aristocrat joined with the king it would be only because it was a duty and that "the people, who know nothing of all of this, must win in the end." The aristocrat, he contends, "is a very old story to his own party, but he comes like a dancing poodle on a fair-day among these Republicans. If I were an aristocrat I would be neither for Carlos nor Christina, but for the people—the trusting, simple, rich, enthusiastic people!" (697). Later he calls into question the very concept of monarchy: "I am perishing for an idea, a foolish idea. Who made the first King? Ten to one if he were not a Pretender" (699). Despite his reasoned assessment of the political dead end that will come from the warring aristocrats, the countess clings to her ideals and the count finally realizes that she "would rather be weeping now over your dead hero than listening happily to a man of good sense" (699). By play's end, the count capitulates to the countess's pleas, puts on his Carlist uniform, and dies by the Christinist sword in an empty heroic gesture as a chorus of men's voices from outside are heard singing from *Don Giovanni*, the signal from the Carlists who have gathered to fight.

But why would the two Carlist wars of Spain, which raged from 1833 to 1879, and a disputed monarchy be of any interest to the American reader at century's end? One possibility is the American debate over women's rights, which was at the center of the Spanish dispute. When Ferdinand, before his death in 1833, altered the Salic law of succession in favor of his daughter, Isabella II, over his brother, Don Carlos, most of the Basque provinces and Catalonia, fired by a conservative commitment to the traditional values of a collaborative Church and State, rallied behind the Bourbon male claimants against the more liberal constitution and progressive policies represented by the women, Maria Christina, the queen regent, and her daughter Isabella. Because the Carlists finally were defeated in 1879, the Basques lost their leadership and found their culture threatened (and though Carlists defected and rival groups were formed, the pressure against the church by the second republic of 1931–1939 revived the movement that fought for the Nationalist cause in the Spanish Civil War of 1936–1939). Therefore, a gendered, political, religious, and civil struggle that began in 1833 was still very much at issue in Spain at century's end.

There was another more compelling reason for Americans to be concerned about the Spanish succession. The continued resistance of the Carlists was linked in the minds of some to the rise of Socialism in Spain and the threats it posed to the United States. For instance, in *The Saturday Review* an anonymous assessment of the "threatened revolution" warned that there were "ominous signs of widespread economic discontent" in Catalonia and that claimant Don Carlos not only was rebelling against "the admirable queen" but also was advocating an invasive attack on America, which had entered the war with the sole aim of freeing Cuba from Spanish control ("Threatened" 684–85). At a time when the United States was embroiled in labor unrest, just emerging from an economic depression, shadowed by the Civil War, and engaged in justifying its first war of empire, it is hardly surprising that the argument for civic stability would be paramount. On the other hand, to return to the play, it also seems clear that Hobbes, at least, is taking an anti-monarchist, pro-populist position, dramatizing the decadence of an outworn political system in her support of her (albeit capitulative) protagonist. Whatever their position on the wars in and with Spain, readers would have been immersed fully in the issues by August 1899 when Hobbes's play was published: the United States had declared war on Spain on April 24, 1898, destroying the Spanish fleet in the Philippines in May and taking Guam in June. Teddy Roosevelt and the Rough Riders had charged up San Juan Hill in Puerto Rico in July, and in December Spain ceded the Philippines, Puerto Rico, and Guam and approved independence for Cuba whereas the United States annexed Hawaii.

In 1899, after President William McKinley opportunistically annexed the Philippines, a casuality of the Spanish-American War, he disingenuously explained his actions to a delegation of Methodist church leaders as a manifest gift: "the Philippines had dropped into our laps." To authorize the acceptance of this gift, he told them, "I went down on my knees and prayed Almighty God for light and guidance." The divine guidance fortuitously for the nation was four-fold: first, it would be "cowardly and dishonorable" to return the Philippines to Spain; second, it would be "bad business to turn them over to France and Germany— our commercial rivals in the Orient"; third, they could not be left to themselves because "they were unfit for self-government"; and, fourth, "there was nothing left for us to do but to take them all, and to educate the Filipinos, and uplift and civilize and Christianize them, and by God's grace do the very best we could by them, as our fellow-men for whom Christ also died. And then I went to bed, and went to sleep, and slept sound!" (Rusling 22–23). The rationalizing yoking of commerce and religion, of the civilizing mission with moral obligation, of the racial superiority of Americans with manifest destiny, and the instant ease and ratification arising from such righteous beneficence, though reassuring to some, clearly rankled others who understood the dangerous implications of this imperialist mentality.

Dramatizing resistance to privileging one class at the expense of another, Sada Cowan's *In the Morgue* in the *Forum* (April 1916) is located in an unspecified foreign city in the present. Caren, a decrepit mortician, is coldly and mechanically processing the "stiffs," when an overwrought and hysterical young man, Kraig, breaks in to find respite from the world of the living, to be in a place where things can be "level": "Oh, there's joy down here. You can burrow and hide like a rat from it all. The damn carriages don't roll by before your eyes. The women don't . . .! Oh, those women—how I hate them! Their silks, their jewels, their soft white skins. Fed! Clothed! Housed . . . [*clenching his fists*] while Martha starves. Listen what happened. [*He comes close to Caren and speaks with little control*] Yesterday in the park I stood there . . . shivering . . . wondering . . . And all at once a mad hate came into my heart and I felt that I could kill. [*Caren looks alarmed*] And then . . . ha . . . ha . . . ha . . . then . . . the King . . . the King drove by. [*Laughing bitterly, and with a great flourish*] And off came my hat! [*Making fun of himself*] My hat came off my head, Old Man, and I bowed and cringed [*vehemently*] with the hate in my heart. I could have torn the warm furs from his throat and wrapped my fingers in their place" (401).

Caren assures him that the morgue "is the one spot on earth where you get fair play" (401). When a young female suicide is brought in, Caren refuses to cover her body, pointing out that "meat's meat" (405) and insists that "the King himself wouldn't be treated no different than a beggar" (406). But when the body of the King is brought in, Caren wants to cover it with a silk flag. Kraig protests in vain.

Kraig: This is the one place in the world where all are treated fair. Dreams don't count. POWER don't count. There's no rich, no poor . . . .
Caren: Shut up and get that flag.
Kraig: You're going to cover him . . . but she . . . she! Oh! . . . Even death can't level. No . . . not even death. (407)

Some plays specifically invoke the French Revolution to investigate the corruption of monarchy. Booth Tarkington's *Beauty and the Jacobin* (in two parts in *Harper's Monthly*, August and September 1912) clearly uses the suspense factor to engage the reader and assure the sale of the second issue, a device more commonly used with serialized novels in the periodicals. Tarkington also marks the play as "literature" in that the reader is clearly positioned in an epigraph: "*The author makes his appearance, not now 'as a showman before his tent,' nor to entreat his audience to be seated in an orderly manner, but to invite any one who may be listening to come upon the very scene itself of this drama, which has nothing to do with the theatre, and there, invisible, attend what follows*" (390). This is slightly at odds with the fact that the play was later produced at the Comedy Theatre in November of 1912, to say nothing of the fact that it originated as a one-act comedy entitled *Mme. de Marmantel* for the Dramatic Club in November 1896 and featured Tarkington as the Jacobin (Woodress 69).

What follows is a historical melodrama set in France in 1793. The simple, teased-out plot concerns the imminent capture and death by guillotine of three aristocrats, one of whom, the titular beauty, Eloise d'Anville, imagines that she will be spared because she embraced Republicanism and gave her fortune to the People. The first half of the play, published in the August issue, focuses on her troubled relationship with Anne and Louis, who are planning to emigrate using falsified papers and with whom she is in hiding. At this point in the play, Eloise advocates zealous Citizenry as a "woman of the Republic" in contrast to Louis's insistence on inflexible aristocratic values (397). The play is interrupted at the suspenseful moment when Valsin, agent of the National Committee of Public Safety, breaks into their hiding place.

In the second half, published in the September issue, the play contrasts what proves to be the mere self-serving Republicanism of Eloise with the true Republicanism of Valsin, who taunts her with "the complete incompetence" of her class: "You forgot that power, like genius, always comes from underneath, because it is produced only by turmoil. We have had to wring the neck of your feather-head court, because while the court was the Nation, the Nation had its pocket picked" (542). He points out that she went to live with wealthy relatives after turning over her estate, which was about to be confiscated anyway, and that she continued to go to the opera in her jewels. In the course of his lengthy vilification, Valsin reveals that Louis, once his colonel, had humiliated and beaten him and had drummed him out of the corps because his horse had accidentally splashed mud on Louis. Now aligned with Marat and Robespierre, Valsen has the opportunity to take his revenge. The desperate Eloise offers herself to him but he refuses, laughing. When all seems lost, Valsen devises a ploy to let his prisoners think that they have tricked him into letting them escape. At this, he determines that he is "quits" with Louis who has been forced to scuttle away humiliatingly dressed as a woman.

Tarkington's play has less to do with the French Revolution than with creating a Republican who is also an exceptional individual. He is introduced on his arrival as having "easy power" and as being dressed with elegance that is "fatally dangerous in these days of untrousered democracy," attributes which "indicate either insane daring or an importance quite over-whelming" (399). There is no nightmarish scenario of misrule or sensationalism of the tumbrel here; this Jacobin is rational, clear-sighted, even playful with his enemies. Though he is above slaughtering, he is capable of meting out poetic justice. As he says at play's end to his puzzled henchman: "These are bad times, my Dossonville, and neither you nor I will see the last of them. Good Lord! Can't we have a little fun as we go along?" (553).

Josephine Dodge Daskam's *The Wanderers* in the *Century* (August 1901) celebrates in verse a prince's renunciation of his throne, "The dull, cramped state, the tired formality, / False thoughtfulness and feigned remembrances" (583). Answering the call of a gypsy's song, he goes to make "a dearer court" in nature, free of court flatterers, evil plotters, warmongering councilors, and oppressors of the poor (588). Parker's *The Minuet* does similar cultural work. Louis-Napoleon Parker (1852–1944) would have been well-known in theatre circles though not necessarily to readers of American periodicals unless they were dedicated readers of the *Critic*, which reviewed his work between 1890 and 1900. The Englishman had success as a dramatist collaborating with Murray Carson on *Rosemary* (1896), *Pomander Walk* (1911), and *Disraeli* (1911). By the time *Disraeli* premiered in New York in 1914, Parker had also become important as a pageant-master directing civic pageants all over England between 1905 and 1909 (and later producing patriotic pageants in London during the war). His *A Minuet* in the *Century* (January 1915) in rhymed and free verse is set in the gaoler's quarters in the prison of the Conciergerie during "The Terror." A marquis, collecting himself to meet the guillotine by reading Voltaire, is reunited with his wife, a woman he assumed had left him, who has come to die with him. She admits that court life corrupted their once innocent love, which they shared in natural settings: "At court the life we lead makes love a frivolous pastime" and he responds that "we need the shock of death to show us we are human" (375).

The opening page has a facing illustration of a young eighteenth-century couple á la Fragonard in the woods with the caption " 'Ah, me! what happy days were those!' " (371), but the final page is faced with a contemporary illustration of a poor elderly peasant couple stooped with labor entitled "On the outskirts of war" (377). The framing illustrations complement the shifting tone. Everett Shinn, known for his casual insouciance, did the former, and A. B. Frost, known for his moody pastorals, did the latter; the contrastive juxtaposition extends the implicit argument of the play, bringing it into the present. The very clear visual suggestion is that the heedless and decadent behavior of eighteenth-century aristocrats inevitably resulted in the present war and the suffering of humble people.

I suggested that these anti-monarchist plays indicated a growing dis-affection with and distancing from Europe as a reaction to the war, the fourth and most pressing concern to engage America's discontented citizens. War is a fitting way to end this study of plays in periodicals for at least two compelling reasons. The lesser is because the plays are among the most experimental dramaturgically in this group, marking the beginning of the presence of modern drama in mainstream periodicals; the greater is the engagement with truly global politics. Just as modernism in Europe was a response to a radically altered social and political landscape, modernism in America marked a transformation from the essentially conservative social melodramas that had dominated the stage to more exploratory experimentalism. That willingness to experiment and to engage with the subject of expansionist policy was spurred by a new sense of political urgency, which seems to have been peculiar to this moment in American history. Also worth noting is that these plays clearly anticipate the theatrical work to come between 1915 and 1929, work Ronald Wainscott describes as "the violent, the pathetic, the stairic, the outrageous, or the incomprehensible" (2).

Though three major wars—the Civil War, the Spanish–American War, and the Great War—shadow the periodicals between 1890 and 1918 and could be expected to figure prominently in the plays, only the Great War was dramatized. According to Matthew Frye Jacobson in *Barbarian Virtues*, this kind of "public amnesia" was directly implicated in turn-of-the-century empire building and has had serious repercussions. "Current renditions of U.S. history," he argues, "thoroughly expunge the Philippine–American War and related engagements in Cuba, Puerto Rico, and Guam . . ." and, as a consequence, "in expurgating the period of U.S. expansionism that bridges the nineteenth and twentieth centuries, Americans adopt a broken narrative that casts Manifest Destiny and continental expansionism falsely adrift from 'modern' U.S. history, and obscures the extent to which the modern state was built, and modern nationalism generated, in close relation to the imperialist project" (263). The drama chosen for periodicals, though not the essays and fiction, was complicit in the silence. So how does one account for the change?

As Ronald Wainscott dryly observes in his history of American drama between 1914 and 1929, "it is difficult to ignore some 8.5 million to ten million dead combatants and 20 million dead civilians scattered across Europe, as well as two hundred thousand wounded soldiers who returned to the United States" (7). American dramatists engaged with the subject in a variety of ways but according to Wainscott, "although there were some fresh attempts at tragic, violent, and psychologically scathing material, most treatments of the war experience were comic or sentimentally melodramatic until *What Price Glory* shocked its first audience" in 1924 (8). Contrary to some assumptions, he insists, the war was an important and dominant subject on the American stage and he cites at least twenty-eight plays professionally produced in New York alone from the outbreak of war to the American declaration of war on April 6, 1917 (8). And, as the war progressed, the numbers rose.

It is worth noting that the war produced marked divisiveness in the periodicals: "The outbreak of the European War, as it was then called in the hope that the United States might not be drawn into it, brought to America a competition in British and German propaganda," though "the weight was on the side of the Allies" (Mott, F., *1885–1905* 726). I want to conclude my study with the seven plays in periodicals that specifically target the war. Some are decidedly antiwar, others argue for war but only as a hateful necessity: Henry Van Dyke's *The House of Rimmon* in *Scribner's* (August 1908), Floyd Dell's *A Long Time Ago: A Fantasy* in *Forum* (February 1914), Josephine Daskam Bacon's *The Twilight of the Gods* in *Forum* (January 1915), Lester Luther's *Law* in *Forum* (June 1915), Marion Craig Wentworth's *War Brides* in *Century*

(February 1915), Laurence Vail's *The Inconveniences of Being Neutral* in *Forum* (January 1918), and Mary Raymond Shipman Andrews's *The Ditch* in *Scribner's* (April 1918).

In the periodicals, the earliest, Henry Van Dyke's verse play *The House of Rimmon*, in *Scribner's* (August 1908), at first glance seems like a lengthy and romanticized dramatization of 2 *Kings* 5 in which Naaman, a captain for the king of Syria, is cured of leprosy by the prophet Elisha after a captive Israelite speaks to him of her God. Converted by the miracle of being washed clean in the Jordan river, Naaman abandons the worship of the Damascan pagan deity, Rimmon, for the true God. To this Van Dyke added a romance with the servant, several spectacular scenes of pagan worship, a faithless wife, a fool, dozens of courtiers and soldiers, and all the trappings of sensational decadent Orientalism, an imperialist stance that Malini Schueller locates as early as 1790 in American writing. All this could easily be dismissed as overheated Christian zealotry except that much of the play is given to a political plot hatched by Rezon, Rimmon's high priest, to prevent the king from fighting the Assyrians:

> All the nobles, all the rich
> Would purchase peace that they may grow more rich:
> Only the people and the soldiers, led
> By Naaman, would fight for liberty! (131)

In arguing for capitulation to the Assyrians, a courtier counsels the king:

> The days of independent states are past:
> The tide of empire sweeps across the earth;
> Assyria rides it with resistless power
> And thunders on to subjugate the world.
> Oppose her, and we fight with Destiny;
> Submit to her demands, and we shall ride
> With her to victory. Therefore return
> This bloody horn, the symbol of wild war,
> With words of soft refusal, and accept
> The golden yoke, Assyria's gift of peace. (139)

To this Naaman responds:

> For every state that barters liberty
> To win imperial favor, shall be drained

Of her best blood, henceforth, in endless wars
To make the empire greater. Here's the choice:
We fight to-day to keep our country free,
Or else we fight forevermore to help
Assyria bind the world as we are bound.
I am a soldier, and I know the hell
Of war! But I will gladly ride through hell
To save Damascus. (139–40)

What makes the debate over empire significant is the fact that Van Dyke, who in Henry F. May's words was "a popular minister turned popular lecturer (at Princeton) and a prolific author of comforting semi-religious poems and tales," had been an ardent anti-imperialist forced by the weight of German barbarism to alter his stance (77). Van Dyke chronicled his dilemma in "Fighting for Peace," a series of three articles in *Scribner's* in 1917: "Fair Weather and Storm-Signs" (September), "The Werewolf at Large" (October), and "Stand Fast, Ye Free!" (November). Later that year he published them in book form as *Fighting for Peace*, a memoir of the summer of 1913 when Van Dyke had served as President Wilson's American minister to the Netherlands and Luxembourg and had worked to maintain the work begun by the International Peace Conference at the Hague. Originally part of the American anti-imperialist movement, Van Dyke had changed course and conceded the necessity of war: "It is evident that we cannot maintain (world-peace), as the world stands to-day, without fighting for it. And after it is won, it will need protection. It must be Peace with Righteousness and Power" ("Fair" 281). Van Dyke's concession, of course, is a version of Naaman's argument to the Syrian king about the necessity to resist the Assyrians. By appropriating the Biblical story, Van Dyke makes war with the Germans a Christian imperative. As he writes of the "monstrous" German invader: "The Barabbas of war was preferred to the Christ of righteous judgment" ("Fair" 289).

Two recent historians of the ill-fated, influential, but short-lived anti-imperialist movement, Robert Beisner in *Twelve Against Empire* and E. Berkeley Tompkins in *Anti-Imperialism in the United States*, concur on the chronology of the resistance: the debate began in 1890, was at its most strident between 1892 and 1902, and was dead by 1920. The fundamental objection to imperialism was that it violated the basic principles of American republican government and policy of self-rule. Those such as Theodore Roosevelt and Henry Cabot Lodge who advocated further expansion after the Spanish–American War and the acquisition of Hawaii, the Philippines, Samoa, Guam, and Puerto Rico could find justification in the growth of European empires in Asia and Africa (Great Britain, Germany, France, and Russia), the extraordinary growth of industry at home and the need for markets abroad, and the influence of Social Darwinism as support for the impulse to exercise desirable dominance over lesser peoples. To this Tompkins adds "the theoretical closing of the frontier, the missionary impulses of the Protestant churches, and the resurgence of Manifest Destiny" (291). The anti-imperialists, a small but influential group of aging liberals, Free Soilists, Republicans, and "mugwumps" as diverse as Charles Eliot Norton, Carl Schurz, E. L. Godkin, Andrew Carnegie, and William James, though they shared the imperialists' belief in the incapacity and inferiority of the lesser races, also believed that Anglo-Saxon American blood, social or political, needed to remain pure. "The belief in American uniqueness," Beisner observes, "provided the capstone of anti-imperialist idealism" and to become an imperialist power would deflect Americans from the American national mission, a preservationist and isolationist mission that was understood to be as much moral as it was political, economic, and social (223).

On the other hand, aggressive expansionists such as Senator Albert J. Beveridge argued that "the American people had become the trustees 'under God' of world civilization. He has made us the master organizers of the world to establish system where chaos reigns' " (Bailyn et al. 981). It proved impossible to uncouple spiritualism and militarism from self-interest and global salvation when Beveridge spoke for God: " 'It is God's great purpose made manifest in the instincts of the race whose present phase is our personal profit, but whose far-off end is the redemption of the world and the Christianization of the world' " (Bailyn et al. 993). With this insistent rhetorical ploy, thus were the Christian foundations of nationalism and imperialism strengthened by the prowar movement.

Readers of both *The House of Rimmon* and *Fighting for Peace* would have understood them to be parts of the same conversation, the same ongoing debate that had been an essential component of American public life for two decades. From the pages of their magazine, Van Dyke, a well-known poet and one of anti-imperialism's strongest advocates, concedes the inevitability of war, reasons out for his readers the stages of his shifting policy, and offers a way in which America can continue to adhere to its principles while at the same time join with the Allies to police Europe: "Our conscientious objections to certain shameful things, like injustice, and dishonor, and tyranny, and systematic cruelty, are stronger than our conscientious objection to fighting . . . . In effect, the United States is a pacific nation of fighting men" ("Stand" 519).

The men may have been ready for war but many of the women, some pacificists, some isolationists, some internationalists, and some suffragists and club women, were part of the peace movement. The most conventional and realistic of the war plays is Marion Craig Wentworth's *War Brides* (1915), a melodrama about one woman's resistance to the enthusiasm expressed in a news clipping, which serves as the play's epigraph: "The war brides were cheered with enthusiasm and the churches were crowded when the large wedding parties spoke the ceremony in concert" (527). The image above the epigraph sets the tone: it is of an elaborately decorated dagger thrust through the mask of tragedy superimposed upon a gas-blown field. The setting is a peasant's cottage in a war-ridden country ruled by an emperor. Two girls are excited about their impending marriages because the "fatherland' has ordered women to produce children but one, Hedwig, who is pregnant, is horrified at the thought that she is to be "a breeding-machine," to produce "food for the next generation's cannon" (535). As she is confronted by a succession of people of increasing importance threatening her with accusations of treason, the news comes that three young men, including Hedwig's husband, are dead. Hedwig goes before a crowd of women to deliver her ultimatum: "I shall send a message to the emperor. If ten thousand women send one like it, there will be peace and no more war. Then they will hear our tears . . . I tell you now, *don't bear any more children* until they promise you there will be no more war" (543). Arrested, she is about to be taken away to be shot for treason, when she *"gathers the baby things in her hands, crosses the room, pressing a little sock to her lips,"* takes a pistol, flees to the bedroom and shoots herself (544).

A socialist, Marion Craig Wentworth (1872–?) wrote several plays on social issues, including a suffrage play, *The Flower Shop* (1912), but *War Brides* is her best-known work in large measure because Alla Nazimova starred and toured in the play, which opened in New York on January 25, 1915, and was also in the 1916 longer film version. The play was never licensed for production in Britain, and the film also had a troubled reception. According to Claire Tylee, "several cities and states banned the film because of its alleged pacifism, and Selznick had it re-edited to give it an anti-German bias. However, in 1917 it was suppressed for the duration of the war on the official grounds that 'the philosophy of this picture is so easily misunderstood by unthinking people' " (13).

In her introduction to *War Plays by Women*, Tylee notes that *War Brides* "arose from the international women's peace movement inspired by Bertha von Suttner" (1). The Baroness Bertha (Kinsky) von Suttner, the winner of the Nobel Peace Prize in 1905, had been a powerful force in the peace movement most notably for her novel, *Die Waffen Neider! Eine Lebensgeschichte* (*Lay Down Your Arms: the Autobiography of Martha von Tilling*) in 1889, which, according to *The Bookman*, "made nearly as great a sensation on Europe as did *Uncle Tom's Cabin* in this country" (240). Not only was von Suttner the subject of many essays in American periodicals, but also she wrote "International Peace" and "Making the Air Barbarous" for *The Chautauquan*, the foremost adult-education periodical in the country. Even if Wentworth's readers did not know of von Suttner's influence, they certainly would have been familiar with the issues she addressed because Jane Addams, the most prominent American woman's voice for peace, "newer, more aggressive ideals of peace," had published extensively on the issue in the *North American Review* and in the *American Journal of Sociology*, work that was collected as *Newer Ideals of Peace* in 1907. In this work she singled out the writing of Tolstoy and the painting of Verestchagin, Tolstoy for appealing to "the higher imaginative pity, as it is found in the modern, moralized man" and portraying the plight of "the common soldier in its sordidness and meanness and constant sense of perplexity" with "nothing of the glories we have associated with warfare" and Verestchagin for covering "his canvas with thousands of wretched wounded and neglected dead, with the waste, cruelty, and squalor of war, until he forces us to question whether a moral issue can ever be subserved by such brutal methods" (3–4). Addams also had condemned the war in the *Ladies' Home Journal* (February 1914) and had delivered the keynote address at the first convention of the Women's Peace Party in January 1915. A considerable presence on the antiwar front, at its height the Woman's Peace Party had 165 groups with a total membership of 40,000 women (Elshtain 222–24).

The plays in the *Forum* are the most interesting dramaturgically because they are modern in style and sensibility and have the strongest dramatic antiwar stance, as I have recounted earlier. According to Mott, the *Forum* was founded on four basic principles: a commitment to the specialist writer, a belief in the value of the symposium in order that many sides of a debate could be heard, a balance of "light" and serious subjects, and severe editing (*History 1885–1905* 512). Partisan political discussion, dedication to reform movements (prohibition, feminism, divorce, prisons, etc.), and a concern for belles-lettres explain why *Forum* was used in schools and colleges. At the time of the antiwar plays, the editor was Mitchell Kennerley, young and English-born, who emphasized literature and art and turned to England for most of his contributors. He also published young American writers such as Edna St. Vincent Millay, Vachel Lindsay, Sherwood Anderson, John Neihardt, and Witter Bynner. Henry May notes that though many of the periodicals that had once been the "fortresses" of established culture were being displaced by the "Young Intellectuals" of the *Smart Set*, the *New Republic*, the *Masses*, and the *Seven Arts*, Kennerly had transformed an established magazine into one "that acted like a 'little'one," in marked contrast to *Century*, which was still "discussing the spoiling of servants" and publishing a series on "War Horses of Famous Generals" (294–95). Floyd Dell, politically and artistically, was at home in the *Forum* at least in 1914.

Dell, a socialist, progressivist, and bohemian, was at the center of cultural rebellions; in Chicago, he had championed Maurice Browne's work at the Little Theatre and in New York was a member of the Liberal Club that founded a "dramatic branch" in 1914. Both the Washington Square Players and the Provincetown Players had their origins in the Liberal Club, which Mark Fearnow characterizes as "a mildly subversive haven from the perky optimism of the Progressive Era" (352). Dell, who wrote many sketches satirizing the "Villagers" of Greenwich in 1914 and 1915, was on the opening bill of the Provincetown Playhouse in 1916 with *King Arthur's Socks* along with Louise Bryant's *The Game* and Eugene O'Neill's *Bound East for Cardiff*. His antiwar play, *A Long Time Ago: A Fantasy* appeared in the *Forum* in 1914 and was staged by the Provincetown Players in January 1917. The production of what Douglas Clayton describes as "a decidedly lugubrious tragedy that was very likely patterned on Yeats's short tragedies," so infuriated Dell because the director Allan Macdougall put the actors (including the massive Jig Cook) on stilts, that he resigned from the Players for a year (145).

The play, whose title was amplified to *A Long Time Ago: A Tragic Fantasy* when it was published in *King Arthur's Socks and Other Village Plays* (1922), does show a Yeatsian influence. Dell, who had seen *On Bailie's Strand* when it opened at Maurice Browne's Little Theatre, noted in his autobiography that he had been much taken by the speeches. Set in a kingdom recently at war, his "tragic fantasy" begins with a fool twanging on a harp while he is harangued by an old woman who complains of missing the battles and the heroes they produced. The queen of the land falls for a passing prince, gives him her virginity, only to lose him to the next ship sailing off to the next battle. Her love turns to hate, she poisons a passing sailor just to see what death looks like, turns the fool into a hero by kissing him three times, and, when the prince returns, orders the fool/hero to kill him. The queen now claims the fool as her creation, a man who can only fight, and sends him off to lead her soldiers to pillage, slaughter and burn the neighboring kingdom. The old woman's expression of delight closes the play: "The good old days have come back. Ah, the smell of blood!" (276). America's stance soon changed, and in 1917 the Espionage Act was passed to stifle dissent against the U.S. entry into the World War; those charged could face twenty years in prison. The following year, during which war hysteria and intolerance of antiwar sentiment reached its apogee, Floyd Dell, the editor of *The Masses* and *The Liberator*, became caught up in one of the most celebrated prosecutions of radical dissenters when, along with other editors and writers from the *Masses*, he stood trial and ultimately was freed by a hung jury.

The multiple declarations of war that began in the summer of 1914, the appalling loss of lives in the trenches of the Western front, and the realization that the protracted struggle seemed futile, given that there was little advancement and only endless slaughter, triggered an understandable apocalyptic panic and dramatizations of absolute destruction in two plays in *Forum*, *The Twilight of the Gods* and '*Law.*' Josephine Daskam Bacon's *The Twilight of the Gods* (January 1915) has only deities visible in the cast. Scene I, set in a picture-book heaven, features the "Three Persons of the Christian Trinity. God is represented as a severe, yet benignant man, on a throne of sapphire, elderly, with a snowy beard; Christ is a dreamy young Jew with a crown of thorns; the Holy Ghost in the form of a dove" (7). A war is raging below, but the human cries are indistinct against the noise of shrieking shells and screaming horses that is mingled with the "thick odor of blood," until Mary, dripping rubies from a sword thrust though her heart, enters. Human prayers and curses, all using God's name, can be heard clearly, and Mary asks God to answer the prayers, but God makes no distinction among them: "No one seems to me better or worse for that matter. The boy must have his knife, certainly . . ." (9). Again, when a terrible explosion is heard and Christ asks what happened, God cannot make distinctions: "Do you mean that sparrow which has just fallen to the ground, or that city which has been blown up and has dropped into the sea?" (9). Mary mourns the fact of Christ's death, but God explains that there was so much noise, he couldn't hear the dying pray: "They should pray more loudly, or shoot more softly down there" (10). After a bomb explodes an airship, "*broken fragments of human bodies fall into the sea*" as college students' voices sing "Onward Christian soldiers." Christ turns away, weeping, "My God, My God, why hast *thou* forsaken me?" (13).

Scene II introduces a host of pagan deities and the struggle escalates to a cacophonic spectacle worthy of Antonin Artaud: "*The air becomes thick with crowding, shadowy shapes, hideous battered idols, rude and savage symbols, phallic figures, hundred-breasted, bird-headed monsters, outlines of pagodas; Doric pillars, great stone cromlechs and Druid altars. Clouds of old and withered incense rise faintly through the dimness, and the wails and coughs of slaughtered beasts are heard at irregular intervals through all that follows, mingles with the mutter of priests in all tongues, the chant of choirs, the tears and groans of women*" (14–15). More deities—Wotan, Mohammed, Brahma—join the wrangling over who will have the people of earth, demanding that Christ, now weighted down by his cross, give them back. But more bombs go off as the warrior gods call for battle and "*all is lost in the rolling smoke*" (20).

Similarly catastrophic, the most minimalist and "modern" of the plays, Lester Luther's '*Law*' (January 1915) is a drama for voices only; "the stage is entirely black but for a deep violet-red strip of light lying low around the horizon" (776). The voices—of the young and the old—speak of their ceaseless pain and of the ecological nightmare war has wrought:

"*The voice of the young boy*: It never changes—It never changes—It never changes. It's the color of the snow on the battlefield."

"*The voice of a young woman*: The ocean is red and the earth—and all the clear brooks. There is no water anywhere since the rain of blood" (776).

The horror builds as it becomes clear that one of the voices belongs to a resurrected man: "It is easier to die than to live, but to live and die and live again—my God! The thousands who committed suicide with the hope of bringing the war to an end that way, are resurrected too" (777). The red light disappears and two voices, a man's and a woman's as if from above, intone the end of man: "Call me Buddha—Life—Force—Energy—Christ—what you will—I care not. To name me is as a breath. You make too much of words. You have forgotten me." Claiming to be Love incarnate, the two voices declaim: "man is gone forever." The play concludes with *one terrific shriek from the multitudes of Earth*" and the voices end the play with "I am" (779).

By 1918, the United States had entered the war and though the American Expeditionary Force suffered a high rate of casualties during the summer and fall of 1918 it is possible to note a shift in mood and expression away from frenzied critical anxiety to rationalized acceptance, even affirmation of the value of the war. Ronald Wainscott attributes the shift to "the most significant force working against anti-war plays," "the U.S. Congress, which passed the Espionage Act and the Trading with the Enemy Act in 1917 and the Sedition Act of 1918. These forbade any expression of contempt for government, Constitution, flag, or military uniform" (12). One way around the restrictions was to write about the future after an implied Allied victory, the strategy employed by Lawrence Vail and Mary Raymond Shipman Andrews.

Laurence Vail, the self-proclaimed "King of Bohemia," painter, writer, and abusive alcoholic first husband of Peggy Guggenheim, had published two short stories in *Forum*, "Untrammeled" (September 1916) and "Selysette" (August 1917), before his war play, *The Inconveniences of Being Neutral*, appeared in 1918. Though both stories are emotional, sentimental, and evocative, the sensibility of "Untrammeled" anticipates Vail's play in so far as the subject, a poet, feels distanced and unengaged by the war: "He drifts into the railroad station . . . There are soldiers, so many soldiers . . . going to kill and be killed. The populace is wild, buoyant and alive. Women weep and old men weep. His heartstrings tighten, but not through pity. He knows them not. Never has he known them. How could he pity them?" (353). This character ultimately connects to a woman with whom he flees the war "beyond the city . . . beyond the plains . . . beyond the hills" (354). The tone is far sourer and more pessimistic in the antiwar play, which finds nothing romantic about escapism.

Vail's wry satire, *The Inconveniences of Being Neutral* (1918), has a wide geographical and temporal scope, moving from a Southampton Station in 1916 to a laboratory in New York in 2164. The central character is "Pepito Franz Smith," of no distinct nationality. He speaks in a mixture of Russian and Cockney, was born in a balloon over Lake Constance, and maintains that the war is "most inconvenient. I'm neutral; that's what I am. I'm perfectly neutral" (86). He is sent to France, which sends him to Switzerland, where he continues to maintain his neutrality even when confronted by a Chilean and a Turk who cynically insist that he must be something; if he can't be pro-something, he should at least be anti-something. The Chilean, who announces that he has been "pro-German since yesterday," tells him "I know many people who get on very well in society by being anti-Prussian or anti-British" (90–91). Smith stubbornly clings to his perfect neutrality. Exasperated, the Swiss insist that he leave:

Small Swiss: Have you read Wilson's twenty-eighth message?
Smith: Yes, I think it is beautiful. It is the only sensible thing I've read since the
    war broke out.
Small Swiss: I thought you would like it. Personally, I don't understand it. Why
    don't you go to America?" (92)

Finding that there is no place for him in the world, Smith commits suicide and ends up in hell, which is packed to overflowing with Germans but the devil refuses to admit Smith because he is a neutral and suggests he try Heaven. However, Smith has already been refused entry there, too. In the last scene, two professors in the year 2164 are puzzling over a skull. After first assuming that it belonged to an imbecile or criminal, they decide "It's the skull of a neutral who killed himself in the year 1917. It's the skull of the only neutral of that stormy period" (99). The imaginative and playful call to commitment seems frivolous compared to the more urgently earnest war plays, though it is worth noting that Vail's modernist concerns were as much about resisting the literary norm as they were about protesting the war. In 1926, Vail was one of the sixteen signers (with Hart Crane and Kay Boyle) of Eugene Jolas's "Manifesto: The Revolution of the Word" in which the "plain reader" was damned, Blake was invoked repeatedly and Narrative was set forth "not as mere anecdote, but the projection of a metamorphosis of reality" (Ellmann 600–01).

Like *The Inconveniences of Being Neutral, The Ditch* (April 1918) spans time and moves into the future. Mary Raymond Shipman Andrews (1860–1936), who published novels extensively from *Vive L'Empereur* (1902) to *The White Satin Dress* (1930) and short stories in periodicals from 1903 to 1925, published only two plays in periodicals, the other being the comic, social whimsy, *A West Point Regulation* (1904). By the time *The Ditch* appeared, the prolific Andrews had become hugely popular especially for her story, "The Perfect Tribute" (1905), which detailed a fictional meeting between Abraham Lincoln at the deathbed of a veteran of Gettysburg and portrayed Lincoln as a man of peace seeking only a unified nation, not revenge.

The Ditch, which begins in 1918 and ends in 2018, is set in a first-line German trench just after a charge by "the Blankth Regiment, United States Army" in which all but one American soldier survived. Each of the five acts brings a different perspective to the tragedy, though all sanction the sacrifice. The first to speak is the dying, delirious soldier who addresses his mother and invokes Abraham Lincoln's assurance that " 'these dead shall not have died in vain' " (406). The next four acts are set in 2018 with observations first by French children who know that "the Americans were generous and brave. They left their dear land and came and died for us, to keep us free in France from the wicked Germans" (408). They are followed by four American school girls with their teacher, who understand that the sacrifice kept America free; a newly married couple who know that the military action kept America and all of Europe free "from the most savage and barbarous enemy of all time" (412); and an American Army officer and an English cabinet minister, who review the history and observe that "there will never be another war" because it left the fabric of civilization "clean" (413). By play's end, the Englishman observes that "the race has emerged from an epoch of intellect to an epoch of spirituality—which comprehends and extends intellect" (414). Though far from an optimistic play, *The Ditch* projects a time when there will be a two positive effects: the cleansing, which implicitly mobilizes ethnic and racial prejudices, and the realized finality of conflict under the rubric of progressive evolution.

Finally, though it falls just outside the time frame of this study, John Galsworthy's *The Sun* for *Scribner's* (May 1919) is worth noting for the way in which it too creates closure, even what might be described as a "happy ending," putting the war in the past and allowing the present to look to the future. Jim and Daise wait apprehensively for the arrival of a returning soldier, Jack, clearly Jim's rival. Jim stakes his "right" to her affections: "Aren't I in the fightin'—earned all I could get?" (513) while the girl worries that she should have waited the three years for her first love to return from war. Jim, planning to kill Jack, hides to watch the reunion. Jack enters singing and laughing: "I said when I got out of it I'd laugh. Like as the sun itself I used to think of you" (515). Jim springs forward, ready to fight to the death with Jack who refuses: "It's no use, soldier. I can't do it. I said I'd laugh to-day, and laugh I will. I've come through all that, an' all the stink of it; I've come through sorrer. Never again! Cheer-o, mate. The sun's shinin'!" (516).

Of course, the sun did not shine, the world was not cleansed, and the war was far from over. Nor were the battles at home finished, battles whose cries were muffled or ignored during the war years. Recent critics, including John Carlos Rowe, Amy Kaplan, Laura Wexler, and Jonathan Hansen, have demonstrated the extent to which the voices of protest and progressivism were closed out of the rising tide of imperialist nationalism. From Jane Addams to W. E. B. Du Bois, the calls to attend to domestic crises were drowned out by the rallying cries to participate in the new imperial and interventionist American identity, an identity that was accepted as having been implicit from the time the first European foot trod on the land. Hansen identifies Woodrow Wilson's Second Inaugural speech (March 5, 1917) as marking the moment when Americans were positioned as united in the global work to come: " 'the greatest things that remain to be done must be done *with the whole world for our stage* [my emphasis] and in cooperation with the wide and universal forces of mankind, and we are making our spirits ready for those things' " (175). In the same year on Flag Day, Wilson insisted that America had only one choice: " 'Woe to the man or group of men that seeks to stand in the way in this day of high resolution when every principle we hold dearest is to be vindicated and made secure for the salvation of the nations" (176).

It is clear that despite initial debate and dissension, by 1918 the periodicals stood behind Wilson's call to consolidation, and the drama participated instrumentally in furthering an American imperial agenda, an agenda that favored Anglo-Saxon middle-class citizens, the readers whose private and public lives were played out, formed, tested, and reflected in the popular mass medium of the magazine and who just were beginning to see themselves as participants in a global, not narrowly national, landscape.

I began this study by invoking Raymond Williams, Benedict Anderson, and Etienne Balibar as guides to understanding the ways in which popular culture, the national imaginary, and fictive ethnicity worked in concert to produce a narrowly circumscribed national norm predicated on an insistent valuation of the "Larger England," a hegemonic construct I wanted to test. Though the overriding ideological stance of the periodicals may indeed be hegemonic, nonetheless the voices embody the anxiety and insecurity that marked them for me as those of "dis/contented" citizens. That this "dis/contentment" was played out in the varieties of dramatic experience is also significant because it proves that the hitherto neglected dramatic literature in periodicals held a prominent place in the national debate about everything from the most trivial domestic matters to international engagement with world war.

Appendix: Plays in Periodicals ~

Akins, Zoë. "The Magical City." *Forum* 55 (May 1916): 507–50.

Andrews, Mary Raymond Shipman. "A West Point Regulation." *McClure's Magazine* 23 (Aug 1904): 385–94.

———. "The Ditch." *Scribner's* 63 (Apr 1918): 405–14.

Anonymous. " 'Fanny's Second Play.' " *Bookman* 36 (Nov 1912): 284–86.

———. "A Woman's Luncheon." *Atlantic Monthly* 76 (Aug 1895): 194–205.

Bacon, Josephine Daskam. "The First of October." *Harper's Monthly* 109 (Oct 1904): 721–33.

———. "The Twilight of the Gods." *Forum* 53 (Jan 1915): 7–20.

Bangs, John Kendrick. "A Proposal under Difficulties." *Harper's Monthly* 91 (June 1895): 151–60.

———. "The Bicyclers." *Harper's Monthly* 91 (Nov 1895): 961–68.

———. "The Fatal Message." *Harper's Monthly* 92 (Feb 1896): 479–85.

———. "A Chafing-Dish Party." *Harper's Monthly* 94 (Dec 1896): 159–66.

———. "The Golfiacs." *Harper's Monthly* 95 (June 1897): 151–59.

Baunevji, Inar Prakas. "Gool and Bahar." *New England Magazine* 52 (Sept 1914): 19–30.

Bennett, Arnold. "What the Public Wants." *McClure's Magazine* 34 (Jan–Mar 1910): 300–15, 419–29, 499–517.

———. "The Honeymoon." *McClure's Magazine* 36 (Mar/Apr 1911): 688–706.

Boyce, Neith (Hapgood). "Maddalena Speaks: A Monologue." *Forum* 51 (Jan 1914): 103–07.

Briscoe, Margaret Sutton. "An I.O.U." *Scribner's Magazine* 14 (Sept 1893): 304–13.

Bynner, Witter. "Tiger." *Forum* 49 (May 1913): 522–47.

———. "The Little King." *Forum* 51 (Apr 1914): 605–32.

Cameron, Margaret. "The Committee on Matrimony." *McClure's Magazine* 21 (Oct 1903): 659–65.

Cowan, Sada. "Illumination: A Monologue." *Forum* 47 (Jan 1912): 71–73.

————. "In the Morgue." *Forum* 55 (Apr 1916): 399–407.

Dargan, Olive Tilford. "The Woods of Ida: A Masque." *Century* 74 (Aug 1907): 590–604.

Daskam, Josephine Dodge. "The Wanderers." *Century* 62 (Aug 1901): 583–89.

Dell, Floyd. "A Long Time Ago: A Fantasy." *Forum* 51 (Feb 1914): 261–77.

Dunbar, Newell. "Das Ewigweibliche (The Ever-Womanly)." *Arena* 31 (Feb 1904): 180–98.

Duncan, George. "A Proposal." *Harper's Monthly* 108 (Apr 1904): 796–801.

Eliot, Annie. "From Four to Six." *Scribner's* 6 (July 1889): 121–28.

Eliot, Annie (Annie Eliot Trumbell). "As Strangers: A Comedietta." *Scribner's Magazine* 20 (Aug 1896): 189–204.

Fisk, May Isabel. "Mis' Deborah Has a Visitor: A Monologue." *Harper's Monthly* 107 (June 1903): 156–59.

————. "Bill from the Milliner: A Monologue." *Harper's Monthly* 107 (Nov 1903): 973–76.

————. "A Woman in a Shoe-Shop: A Monologue." *Harper's Monthly* 108 (Dec 1903): 163–65.

————. "Her Tailor-Made Gown: A Monologue." *Harper's Monthly* 108 (Mar 1904): 649–52.

————. "The Invalid: A Monologue." *Harper's Monthly* 109 (Sept 1904): 649–51.

————. "Buying Theater Tickets: A Monologue." *Harper's Monthly* 129 (Sept 1914): 641–44.

Galsworthy, John. "The Little Dream." *Scribner's Magazine* 49 (May 1911): 531–40.

————. "Hall-Marked: A Satiric Trifle." *Atlantic Monthly* 113 (June 1914): 845–51.

Garland, Hamlin. "Under the Wheel." *Arena* 8 (July 1890): 182–228.

Garland, Robert. "The Double Miracle." *Forum* 53 (Apr 1915): 511–27.

Gilbert, Sir William S. "Trying a Dramatist." *Century* 83 (Dec 1911): 179–89.

Gleason, Elizabeth and Anne Gleason. "Signal Service." *New England Magazine* 7 ns. (Sept 1892): 101–06.

Goode, Kate Tucker. "A Princess of Virginia." *Lippincott's Monthly* 79 (June 1907): 817–48.

Green, Helen. "In Vaudeville." *McClure's* 34 (Feb 1910): 392–97.

Gregory, Lady Augusta. "MacDaragh's Wife." *Outlook* 99 (Dec 16, 1911): 920–25.

————. "The Bogie Man." *Forum* 49 (Jan 1913): 28–40.

Hibbard, George. "A Matter of Opinion." *Scribner's Magazine* 28 (Aug 1900): 233–45.

Hobbes, John Oliver (Pearl Mary Teresa Richards Craigie). "A Repentance." *Critic* 35 (Aug 1899): 691–704.

Hope, Anthony. "A Life Subscription." *McClure's Magazine* 17 (May 1901): 3–6.

Howells, William Dean. "A Letter of Introduction: A Farce." *Harper's Monthly* 84 (Jan 1892): 243–56.

———. "Evening Dress: A Farce." *Cosmopolitan* 13 (May 1892): 116–27.

———. "The Unexpected Guests." *Harper's Monthly* 86 (Jan 1893): 211–25.

———. "Bride Roses." *Harper's Monthly* 87 (Aug 1893): 424–30.

———. "A Masterpiece of Diplomacy: A Farce." *Harper's Monthly* 88 (Feb 1894): 371–85.

———. "A Previous Engagement." *Harper's Monthly* 92 (Dec 1895): 28–44.

———. "Indian Giver." *Harper's Monthly* 94 (Jan 1897): 235–52.

———. "Father and Mother: A Mystery." *Harper's Monthly* 100 (May 1900): 869–74.

———. "The Mother." *Harper's Monthly* 106 (Dec 1902): 21–26.

———. "After the Wedding." *Harper's Monthly* 114 (Dec 1906): 64–69.

———. "A True Hero: A Melodrama." *Harper's Monthly* 119 (Nov 1909): 866–75.

———. "Parting Friends." *Harper's Monthly* 121 (Oct 1910): 670–77.

———. "The Impossible. A Mystery Play." *Harper's Monthly* 122 (Dec 1910): 116–25.

———. "Self-Sacrifice: A Farce-Tragedy." *Harper's Monthly* 122 (Apr 1911): 748–57.

Jakobi, Paula. "Chinese Lily." *Forum* 54 (Nov 1915): 551–66.

James, Henry. "An Animated Conversation." *Scribner's Magazine* 5 (Mar 1889): 371–84.

Jenks, Tudor. "Parried." *Century* 58 (new series 36) (June 1899): 318–20.

———. "At the Door: A Little Comedy." *Century* 58 (new series 36) (Oct 1899): 857–58.

Jenks, Tudor and Duffield Osborne. "The Baron's Victim: A Mellow Drama." *Harper's Monthly* 96 (Mar 1898): 645–50.

Lady Gregory. "The Bogie Men." *Forum* 49 (Jan 1913): 28–40.

Lee, Albert. "A Prearranged Accident." *Harper's Monthly* 95 (Aug 1897): 477–83.

Luther, Lester. " 'Law.' " *Forum* 53 (June 1915): 776–79.

Manning, Marie. "Nervous Prostration." *Harper's Monthly* 125 (Sept 1912): 641–44.

McVickar, M. R. "A Society Tragedy." *Harper's Monthly* 84 (Jan 1892): 324–25.

———. "Sold." *Harper's Monthly* 84 (Mar 1892): 647–48.

Merington, Marguerite. "A Gainsborough Lady: A Christmas Masque." *Scribner's Magazine* 31 (Jan 1902): 65–67.

Meyer, Annie Nathan. "The Scientific Mother." *Bookman* 5 (July 1897): 381–82.

Middleton, George. "The Man Masterful." *Forum* 42 (1909): 369–82.

Neihardt, John G. "Eight Hundred Rubles." *Forum* 53 (Mar 1915): 393–402.

O'Brien, Edward J. "At the Flowing of the Tide." *Forum* 52 (Sept 1914): 375–86.

O'Rell, Max. "The Pleasures of Poverty (A Wife's Pleading)." *The North American Review* 169 (Aug 1899): 285–88.

Parker, Louis N. "A Minuet." *Century* 89 (Feb 1915): 370–76.

Peabody, Josephine Preston. "The Wings." *Harper's Monthly* 110 (May 1905): 947–56.

Phelps, Elizabeth Stuart. "Within the Gates." *McClure's Magazine* 17 (May– July 1901): 35–43, 142–49, 236–50.

Putnam, Nina Wilcox. "Orthodoxy." *Forum* 51 (June 1914): 801–20.

Rives, Amélie. "Athelwold." *Harper's Monthly* 84 (Feb 1892): 394–424.

Royle, Edwin Milton. "The Squaw-Man." *Cosmopolitan* 37 (Aug 1904): 411–18.

Shaw, George Bernard. "Androcles and the Lion." *Everybody's Magazine* 31 (Sept 1914): 289–311.

———. "Great Catherine." *Everybody's Magazine* 32 (Feb 1915): 193–212.

———. "Pygmalion." *Everybody's Magazine* 31 (Nov 1915): 577–612.

Sherwood, Margaret. "Vittoria." *Scribner's Magazine* 37 (Apr 1905): 497–504.

Stanwood, Louise Rogers. "The Progress of Mrs. Alexander." *New England Magazine* 43 ns. (Feb 1911): 529–60; 655–63.

Sutphen, Van Tassel. "First Aid to the Injured." *Harper's Monthly* 92 (May 1896): 965–70.

———. "Special Delivery: A Monologue." *Harper's Monthly* 108 (Feb 1904): 458–62.

———. "A House of Cards." *Harper's Monthly* 109 (Nov 1904): 901–10.

Symons, Arthur. "Cleopatra in Judea." *Forum* 55 (June 1916): 643–60.

Tadema, Laurence Alma. "An Undivined Tragedy." *Harper's* 88 (Mar 1894): 615–29.

———. "Love and Death." *Harper's Monthly* 90 (Dec 1894): 151–52.

———. "The Silent Voice." *Harper's Monthly* 93 (Aug 1896): 400–09.

Tagore, Rabindranath. "The Post Office." *Forum* 51 (Mar 1914): 455–71.

Tarkington, Booth. "Beauty and the Jacobin." *Harper's Monthly* 125 (Aug/Sept 1912): 390–99, 539–53.

———. "Mister Antonio." *Harper's Monthly* 134 (Feb 1917): 187–203, 374–87.

Thackeray, William M. "King Glumpus." *Bookman* 8 (Dec 1898).

Towne, Charles Hanson. "The Aliens." *McClure's Magazine* 47 (May 1916): 12–13, 76.

Vail, Laurence. "The Inconveniences of Being Neutral." *Forum* 59 (Jan 1918): 85–100.

Van Campen, Helen Green. " 'Life on Broadway.' " *McClure's Magazine* 40 (Dec 1912): 177–80.

———. "Elmer's Domestic Infelicities." *McClure's Magazine* 40 (Mar 1913): 35–40.

————. " 'Life on Broadway': The Musical Comedy Rehearsal." *McClure's Magazine* 41 (May 1913): 68–72.

————. " 'Life on Broadway': The Disillusions of Flossie." *McClure's Magazine* 41 (June 1913): 78–80.

————. "The Woes of Two Workers." *McClure's Magazine* 41 (Aug 1913): 190–98.

————. "The Woes of Two Workers." *McClure's Magazine* 41 (Sept 1913): 198–204.

————. "The Woes of Two Workers." *McClure's Magazine* 41 (Oct 1913): 216–28.

————. "The Woes of Two Workers." *McClure's Magazine* 42 (Nov 1913): 65–68.

————. " 'Life on Broadway': Master in His Own House." *McClure's Magazine* 42 (Dec 1913): 60–63.

Van Dyke, Henry. "The House of Rimmon." *Scribner's Magazine* 44 (Aug 1908): 129–47; 283–301.

Vibert, J. G. "The Sick Doctor." *Century* 51 ns. (Apr 1896): 944–47.

Welsh, Robert Gilbert. "Jezebel." *Forum* 53 (May 1915): 647–60.

Wendell, Barrett. "Rosamond." *Scribner's Magazine* 7 (June 1890): 783–88.

————. "Ralegh in Guiana." *Scribner's Magazine* 21 (June 1897): 776–84.

Wentworth, Marion Craig. "War Brides." *Century* 89 (Feb 1915): 527–44.

Wharton, Edith. " 'Copy:' A Dialogue." *Scribner's Magazine* 27 (June 1900): 656–63.

————. "Pomegranate Seed." *Scribner's Magazine* 51 (Mar 1912): 284–91.

Wilkins, Mary E. (Mary Wilkins Freeman). "Giles Corey, Yeoman." *Harper's Monthly* 86 (Dec 1892): 20–40.

Yeats, W. B. "The Shadowy Waters." *North American Review* 170 (May 1900): 741–29.

————. "The Hour-Glass." *North American Review* 177 (Sept 1903): 445–56.

————. "The Green Helmet." *Forum* 46 (1911): 301–21.

Works Cited ✌

Ackerman, Alan L., Jr. *The Portable Theater: American Literature & the Nineteenth-Century Stage*. Baltimore: The Johns Hopkins UP, 1999.

Adams, Henry. *The Education of Henry Adams*. New York: Viking, 1907.

Addams, Jane. *Newer Ideals of Peace*. New York: Macmillan, 1907.

Akins, Zoë. "The Magical City." *Forum* 55 (May 1916): 507–50.

Aldrich, Thomas Bailey. *Ponkapog Papers*. Boston: Houghton, Mifflin & Co., 1904.

Aly, Lucile. *John G. Neihardt: A Critical Biography*. Amsterdam: Rodopi, 1977.

Anderson, Benedict. *Imagined Communities: Reflections on the Origin and Spread of Nationalism*. London: Verso, 1983.

Anderson, Donald R. " 'Giles Corey' and the Pressing Past." *American Transcendental Quarterly* 14.2 (2000): 113–26.

Andrews, Benjamin E. "A History of the Last Quarter-Century in the United States." *Scribner's Magazine* 19 (Apr 1896): 469–89.

Andrews, Mary Raymond Shipman. "The Ditch." *Scribner's* 63 (Apr 1918): 405–14.

———. "A West Point Regulation." *McClure's Magazine* 23 (Aug 1904): 385–94.

Anonymous [Ellen Olney Kirk]. "A Woman's Luncheon." *Atlantic Monthly* 76 (Aug 1895): 194–205.

Anonymous. "An American Writer Who Just Missed Enduring Greatness." *Current Literature* 41 (Oct 1906): 404–05.

———. "Another Anglo-Indian Nobel Prizeman." *Literary Digest* 47 (Nov 1913): 1062.

———. "Arthur Schnitzler, the Austrian Hauptmann." *Current Literature* 39 (Nov 1905): 553.

———. "Bertha Von Suttner." *The Bookman* 33 (May 1911): 2403.

———. "Do Women Possess any Dramatic Ability?" *Poet-Lore* 7 (1895): 512–16.

———. "The Drama: Mr. Black's 'Picture Play.' " *The Critic* Oct 13, 1894: 249.

———. "Editorial." *McClure's Magazine* 1 (June 1893): 94–96.

———. "Editorial." *McClure's Magazine* 20 (Jan 1903): 336.

———. " 'Fanny's Second Play.' " *Bookman* 36 (Nov 1912): 284–86.

Anonymous. "A Hindu on the Celtic Spirit." *Review of Reviews* 49 (Jan 1914): 101–02.

———. "Notes and News." Editorial. *Poet-Lore* 1 (1889): 51.

———. "The Theatrical Muck-Raker Answered." *Current Literature* 46 (June 1909): 669–71.

———. "The Threatened Revolution in Spain." *Living Age* 217 (4 June 1898): 683–85.

———. "The Universal Appeal of the Nobel Prize Winner." *Current Opinion* 56 (Jan 1914): 50–51.

Anthony, Susan B. "The Status of Women, Past, Present, and Future." *Arena* 17 (May 1987): 901–08.

Archer, Melanie and Judith R. Blau. "Class Formation in the Nineteenth Century: The Case of the Middle Class." *Annual Review of Sociology* 19 (1993): 17–41.

Archer, William. "Real Conversations II.—with Mrs. Craigie (John Oliver Hobbes)." *Critic* 38 (May 1901): 405–12.

Auerbach, Nina. *Woman and the Demon: The Life of a Victorian Myth.* Cambridge: Harvard UP, 1982.

Bacon, Josephine Daskam. "The First of October." *Harper's Monthly* 109 (Oct 1904): 721–33.

———. "The Twilight of the Gods." *Forum* 53 (Jan 1915): 7–20.

Bailyn, Bernard et al. *The Great Republic.* Boston: Little, Brown and Company, 1977.

Baker, George P., ed. *The Collected Plays of Josephine Preston Peabody.* New York: Houghton Mifflin Co., 1927.

Balibar, Etienne. "The Nation Form: History and Ideology." *Race, Nation, Class: Ambiguous Identities.* Ed. Etienne Balibar and Immanuel Wallerstein. London: Verso, 1991. 86–106.

Bangs, John Kendrick. "The Bicyclers." *Harper's Monthly* 91 (Nov 1895): 961–68.

———. "A Chafing-Dish Party." *Harper's Monthly* 94 (Dec 1896): 159–66.

———. "The Fatal Message." *Harper's Monthly* 92 (Feb 1896): 479–85.

———. "The Golfiacs." *Harper's Monthly* 95 (June 1897): 151–59.

———. "A Proposal under Difficulties." *Harper's Monthly* 91 (June 1895): 151–60.

Banta, Martha. *Imaging American Women: Idea and Ideals in Cultural History.* New York: Columbia UP, 1987.

Barrish, Philip. *American Literary Realism, Critical Theory, and Intellectual Prestige, 1880–1995.* Cambridge: Cambridge UP, 2001.

Baunevji, Inar Prakas. "Gool and Bahar." *New England Magazine* 52 (Sept 1914): 19–30.

———. "Radindranath Tagore in India." *New England Magazine* 51 (Mar 1914): 23–25.

Bederman, Gail. *Manliness & Civilization: A Cultural History of Gender and Race in the United States, 1880–1917.* Chicago: University of Chicago Press, 1995.

Beisner, Robert L. *Twelve Against Empire: The Anti-Imperialists, 1898–1900.* New York: McGraw-Hill, 1968.

Bennett, Arnold. "The Honeymoon." *McClure's Magazine* 36 (Mar/Apr 1911): 688–706.

Black, Alexander. "The Camera and the Comedy." *Scribner's Magazine* Nov 1896: 605–10.

———. "Photography in Fiction: 'Miss Jerry,' the First Picture Play." *Scribner's Magazine* 18.3 (Sept 1895): 348–60.

Bledstein, Burton. "Storytellers to the Middle Class." *The Middling Sorts: Explorations in the History of the American Middle Class.* Ed. Burton J. Bledstein and Robert D. Johnston. New York: Routledge, 2001.

Blight, David W. *Race and Reunion: The Civil War in American Memory.* Cambridge, Mass.: Harvard UP, 2001.

Blumin, Stuart M. *The Emergence of the Middle Class: Social Experience in the American City.* Cambridge: Cambridge UP, 1989.

Boucicault, Dion. "The Future American Drama." *Arena* (Nov 1890): 641–52.

———. "The Future American Drama." *The Arena* 2 (Nov 1890): 641–52.

Boyce, Neith (Hapgood). "Maddalena Speaks: A Monologue." *Forum* 51 (Jan 1914): 103–07.

Bradley, Jennifer. "Zoe Akins and the Age of Excess: Broadway Melodrama in the 1920s." *Modern American Drama: The Female Canon.* Ed. June Schleuter. Rutherford, N.J.: Fairleigh Dickson UP, 1990. 86–96.

Brake, Laurel, Bill Bell, and David Finkelstein, eds. *Nineteenth-Century Media and the Construction of Identities.* Houndsmill, Basingstoke, Hampshire: Palgrave, 2000.

Brewster, Ben and Lea Jacobs. *Theatre to Cinema: Stage Pictorialism and the Early Feature Film.* New York: Oxford UP, 1997.

Briscoe, Margaret Sutton. "An I.O.U." *Scribner's Magazine* 14 (Sept 1893): 304–13.

Brodhead, Richard H. *Cultures of Letters: Scenes of Reading and Writing in Nineteenth-Century America.* Chicago: University of Chicago Press, 1993.

Brooks, Peter. *The Melodramatic Imagination: Balzac, Henry James, Melodrama and the Mode of Excess.* New York: Columbia UP, 1985.

Burke, Martin J. *The Conundrum of Class: Public Discourse on the Social Order in America.* Chicago: University of Chicago Press, 1995.

Butsch, Richard. *The Making of American Audiences: From Stage to Television, 1750–1990.* Cambridge: Cambridge UP, 2000.

Bynner, Witter. "The Little King." *Forum* 51 (Apr 1914): 605–32.

———. "Tiger." *Forum* 49 (May 1913): 522–47.

Bynner, Witter. "Tiger: Letter to the Editor of the Forum." *Forum* 51 (Apr 1914): 633–34.

Bzowski, Frances Diodato. *American Women Playwrights, 1900–1930: A Checklist.* Westport, Conn.: Greenwood Press, 1992.

Cameron, Margaret. "The Committee on Matrimony." *McClure's Magazine* 21 (Oct 1903): 659–65.

Carpenter, William H. "Ibsen's Latest Play." *Bookman* 5 (Mar 1897): 157–60.

Casper, Scott E. "Periodical Studies and Cultural History/Periodical Studies as Cultural History: New Scholarship on American Magazines." *Victorian Periodical Review* 29 (Fall 1996): 261–68.

Cheney, Sheldon. "The American Playwright and the Drama of Sincerity." *Forum* 51 (1914): 498–512.

Chudacoff, Howard P. *The Age of the Bachelor: Creating an American Subculture.* Princeton: Princeton UP, 1999.

Clayton, Douglas. *Floyd Dell: The Life and Times of an American Radical.* Chicago: Ivan Dee, 1994.

Cmiel, Kenneth. *Democratic Eloquence: The Fight Over Popular Speech in Nineteenth-Century America.* New York: William Morrow, 1990.

"Comment on Books." *The Atlantic Monthly* 75 (Apr 1895): 559–60.

Connelly, Mark Thomas. *The Response to Prostitution in the Progressive Era.* Chapel Hill: U of North Carolina P, 1980.

Corbin, John. "The Dawn of the American Drama." *The Atlantic Monthly* 99 (May 1907): 637–44.

———. "How the Other Half Laughs." *Harper's Monthly* 98 (Dec 1898): 30–48.

Cowan, Sada. "Illumination: A Monologue." *Forum* 47 (Jan 1912): 71–73.

———. "In the Morgue." *Forum* 55 (Apr 1916): 399–407.

Cross, Wilbur L. "Ibsen's Brand." *Arena* 3: 81–90.

Daly, Augustin et al. "American Playwrights on the American Drama." *Harper's Weekly* 33 (Feb 2, 1889): 97–100.

Dargan, Olive Tilford. "The Woods of Ida: A Masque." *Century* 74 (Aug 1907): 590–604.

Daskam, Josephine Dodge. "The Wanderers." *Century* 62 (Aug 1901): 583–89.

Davies, A. F. *Skills, Outlooks and Passions: A Psychoanalytic Contribution to the Study of Politics.* Cambridge: Cambridge UP, 1980.

Davies, Mary Carolyn. "Rabindranath Tagore: India's Shakespeare and Tasso in One." *Forum* 51 (Jan 1914): 140–44.

Dell, Floyd. *Homecoming: An Autobiography.* New York: Farrar & Rinehart, 1933.

———. "A Long Time Ago: A Fantasy." *Forum* 51 (Feb 1914): 261–77.

Demastes, William W. and Michael Vanden Heuval. "The Hurlyburly Lies of the Causalist Mind: Chaos and the Realism of Rabe and Shepard." *Realism and the American Dramatic Tradition.* Ed. William W. Demastes. Tuscaloosa: University of Alabama Press, 1996. 255–74.

Denison, John H. "The Survival of the American Type." *Atlantic Monthly* 75 (Jan 1895): 16–28.

Dijkstra, Bram. *Idols of Perversity: Fantasies of Feminine Evil in Fin-de-Siècle Culture.* New York: Oxford UP, 1986.

Dippie, Brian W. *The Vanishing American: White Attitudes & U.S. Indian Policy.* Lawrence, Kansas: U of Kansas P, 1982.

Donovan, Josephine. *After the Fall: The Demeter-Persephone Myth in Wharton, Cather, and Glasgow.* University Park: Pennsylvania University Press, 1989.

Draper, William R. "The Last of the Red Race." *Cosmopolitan* 32 (Jan 1902): 244–46.

Dresser, Horatio. "The Mental Cure in Its Relation to Modern Thought." *Arena* 16 (June 1896): 131–37.

———. "What Is the New Thought?" *Arena* 21 (Jan 1899): 29–50.

Dunbar, Newell. "Das Ewigweibliche (The Ever-Womanly)." *Arena* 31 (Feb 1904): 180–98.

Duncan, George. "A Proposal." *Harper's Monthly* 108 (Apr 1904): 796–801.

Dutta, Krishna and Andrew Robinson. *Rabindranath Tagore: The Myriad-Minded Man.* New York: St. Martin's, 1996.

Eliot, Annie (Annie Eliot Trumbell). "As Strangers: A Comedietta." *Scribner's Magazine* 20 (Aug 1896): 189–204.

Eliot, Annie. "From Four to Six." *Scribner's* 6 (July 1889): 121–28.

Elliot, Michael A. *The Culture Concept: Writing and Difference in the Age of Realism.* Minneapolis: U of Minnesota P, 2002.

Ellmann, Richard. *James Joyce.* New York: Oxford UP, 1965.

Elshtain, Jean Bethke. *Jane Addams and the Dream of American Democracy.* New York: Basic, 2002.

Engle, Sherry. "An 'Irruption of Women Dramatists': The Rise of America's Woman Playwright, 1890–1920." *New England Theatre Journal* 12 (2001): 27–50.

Erdman, Harley. *Staging the Jew: The Performance of an American Ethnicity, 1860–1920.* New Brunswick, N.J.: Rutgers UP, 1997.

Fahs, Alice. *The Imagined Civil War: Popular Literature of the North & South 1861–1865.* Chapel Hill, N.C.: U of North Carolina P, 2001.

"F." "Drama: 'Mister Antonio.'" *The Nation* 103 (Oct 5, 1916): 330.

Fearnow, Mark. "Theatre Groups and Their Playwrights." *The Cambridge History of American Theatre, 1870–1945.* Ed. Don B. Wilmeth and Christopher Bigsby. Cambridge: Cambridge UP, 1999. 343–77.

Filler, Louis. *The Muckrakers.* Stanford, California: Stanford UP, 1976. 1968.

Fisk, May Isabel. "Bill from the Milliner: A Monologue." *Harper's Monthly* 107 (Nov 1903): 973–76.

Fisk, May Isabel. "Buying Theater Tickets: A Monologue." *Harper's Monthly* 129 (Sept 1914): 641–44.

———. *The Eternal Feminine.* New York: Harper's, 1911.

———. "Her Tailor-Made Gown: A Monologue." *Harper's Monthly* 108 (Mar 1904): 649–52.

———. "Mis' Deborah Has a Visitor: A Monologue." *Harper's Monthly* 107 (June 1903): 156–59.

———. *The Talking Women.* New York: Harper's, 1907.

———. "A Woman in a Shoe-Shop: A Monologue." *Harper's Monthly* 108 (Dec 1903): 163–65.

Flint, Kate. *The Woman Reader 1837–1914.* Oxford: Clarendon Press, 1993.

Flower, B. O. "The Highest Function of the Novel." *Arena* 1 (Apr 1890): 628–30.

———. "An Interesting Representative of a Vanishing Race." *Arena* 16 (1896): 240–50.

Freedman, Jonathan. *The Temple of Culture: Assimilation and Anti-Semitism in Literary Anglo-America.* Oxford: Oxford UP, 2000.

Fussell, Paul. *The Great War and Modern Memory.* London: Oxford UP, 1975.

Gabler-Hover, Janet. "The North-South Reconciliation Theme and the 'Shadow of the Negro' in *Century Illustrated Magazine.*" *Periodical Literature in Nineteenth-Century America.* Charlottesville, Virginia: UP of Virginia, 1995. 239–56.

Galsworthy, John. "Hall-Marked: A Satiric Trifle." *Atlantic Monthly* 113 (June 1914): 845–51.

———. "The Little Dream." *Scribner's Magazine* 49 (May 1911): 531–40.

———. "Some Platitudes Concerning Drama." *Atlantic Monthly* 104 (Dec 1909): 768–73.

———. "The Sun." *Scribner's Magazine* 35 (May 1919): 513–16.

Garland, Hamlin. *Crumbling Idols: Twelve Essays on Art and Literature.* Gainesville, Florida: Scholars' Facsimiles & Reprints, 1952. 1894.

———. "The Future of Fiction." *Arena* 7 (Apr 1893): 513–24.

———. "Homestead and Its Perilous Trades." *McClure's Magazine* 3 (July 1894): 3–20.

———. "The Land Question, and Its Relation to Art and Literature." *Arena* 9 (Jan 1894): 165–75.

———. *Roadside Meetings.* New York: Macmillan, 1930.

———. "Under the Wheel." *Arena* 8 (July 1890): 182–228.

Garland, Robert. "The Double Miracle." *Forum* 53 (Apr 1915): 511–27.

Garvey, Ellen Gruber. *The Adman in the Parlor: Magazines and the Gendering of Consumer Culture, 1880s to 1910s.* Oxford: Oxford UP, 1996.

Gerstle, Gary. *American Crucible: Race and Nation in the Twentieth Century.* Princeton: Princeton UP, 2001.

Getz, John. " 'Eglantina': Freeman's Revision of Hawthorne's 'The Birth-Mark.' " *Critical Essays on Mary Wilkins Freeman*. Ed. Shirley Marchalionis. Boston: G. K. Hall & Co., 1991. 177–84.

Gilbert, Sir William S. "Trying a Dramatist." *Century* 83 (Dec 1911): 179–89.

Gillis, John R. "Memory and Identity: The History of a Relationship." *Commemorations: The Politics of National Identity*. Princeton, N.J.: Princeton UP, 1994. 3–26.

Glazener, Nancy. *Reading for Realism: The History of a U.S. Literary Institution 1850–1910*. Durham: Duke UP, 1997.

Gleason, Elizabeth and Anne Gleason. "Signal Service." *New England Magazine* 7 ns. (Sept 1892): 101–06.

Goode, Kate Tucker. "A Princess of Virginia." *Lippincott's Monthly* 79 (June 1907): 817–48.

Gramsci, Antonio. *The Modern Prince and Other Writings*. New York: International Publishers, 1959.

Grant, Madison. *The Passing of the Great Race, or the Racial Basis of European History*. New York: Charles Scribners' Sons, 1919.

———. "Race, Nationality and Language." *Geographical Review* 2 (Nov 1916): 354–60.

Grant, Robert. "The Conduct of Life." *Scribner's Magazine* 18 (1895): 581–92.

Green, Helen. "In Vaudeville." *McClure's* 34 (Feb 1910): 392–97.

———. "One Day in Vaudeville." *McClure's* 39 (Oct 1912): 637–47.

Gregory, Lady Augusta. "The Bogie Man." *Forum* 49 (Jan 1913): 28–40.

———. "MacDaragh's Wife." *Outlook* 99 (16 Dec 1911): 920–25.

Grinnell, George Bird. "The Wild Indian." *Atlantic Monthly* 83 (June 1899): 20–29.

Haenni, Sabine. "Visual and Theatrical Culture, Tenement Fiction and the Immigrant Subject on Abraham Cahan's 'Yekl.' " *American Literature* 71 (Sept 1999): 493–527.

Hall, Roger A. *Performing the American Frontier, 1870–1906*. Cambridge, England: Cambridge UP, 2001.

Hamilton, Clayton Meeker. "The Modern Social Drama." *Forum* 40 (Sept 1908): 265–73.

Hansen, Jonathan M. *The Lost Promise of Patriotism: Debating American Identity, 1890–1920*. Chicago: University of Chicago Press, 2003.

Harlow, V. T., ed. *The Discoverie of the Large and Beautiful Empire of Guiana by Sir Walter Ralegh*. London: The Argonaut Press, 1928.

Hatheway, Jay. *The Gilded Age Construction of Modern American Homophobia*. New York: Palgrave, 2003.

Hibbard, George. "A Matter of Opinion." *Scribner's Magazine* 28 (Aug 1900): 233–45.

Higham, John. *Strangers in the Land: Patterns of American Nativism, 1860–1925*. New Brunswick, N.J.: Rutgers UP, 1994.

Hobbes, John Oliver (Pearl Mary Teresa Richards Craigie). "A Repentance." *Critic* 35 (Aug 1899): 691–704.

Hodin, Mark. "The Disavowal of Ethnicity: Legitimate Theatre and the Social Construction of Literary Value in Turn-of-the-Century America." *Theatre Journal* 52 (May 2000): 211–26.

Holroyd, Michael. *Bernard Shaw: The Pursuit of Power*. New York: Random House, 1989.

Hope, Anthony. "A Life Subscription." *McClure's Magazine* 17 (May 1901): 3–6.

Howells, William Dean. "After the Wedding." *Harper's Monthly* 114 (Dec 1906): 64–69.

———. "Bride Roses." *Harper's Monthly* 87 (Aug 1893): 424–30.

———. "Evening Dress: A Farce." *Cosmopolitan* 13 (May 1892): 116–27.

———. "Father and Mother: A Mystery." *Harper's Monthly* 100 (May 1900): 869–74.

———. "The Fiction of John Oliver Hobbes." *North American Review* 183 (Dec 1906): 1251–61.

———. *A Hazard of New Fortunes*. New York: Penguin Meridian, 1994.

———. "The Impossible. A Mystery Play." *Harper's Monthly* 122 (Dec 1910): 116–25.

———. "Indian Giver." *Harper's Monthly* 94 (Jan 1897): 235–52.

———. "The Laureate of the Larger England." *McClure's* 8 (Mar 1897): 453–55.

———. "The Mother." *Harper's Monthly* 106 (Dec 1902): 21–26.

———. "Parting Friends." *Harper's Monthly* 121 (Oct 1910): 670–77.

———. "A Previous Engagement." *Harper's Monthly* 92 (Dec 1895): 28–44.

———. "Self-Sacrifice: A Farce." *Harper's Monthly* 122 (Apr 1911): 748–57.

———. "The Unexpected Guests." *Harper's Monthly* 86 (Jan 1893): 211–25.

Humphreys, Mary Gay. "The New York Working-Girl." *Scribner's Magazine* 20 (Oct 1896): 502–13.

———. "Women Bachelors in New York." *Scribner's Magazine* 20 (Nov 1896): 626–36.

Hutton, Laurence. "The American Burlesque." *Harper's Monthly* June 1890: 59–74.

Jacobson, Matthew Frye. *Barbarian Virtues: The United States Encounters Foreign Peoples at Home and Abroad, 1876–1917*. New York: Hill and Wang, 2000.

Jakobi, Paula. "Chinese Lily." *Forum* 54 (Nov 1915): 551–66.

James, Henry. "An Animated Conversation." *Scribner's Magazine* 5 (Mar 1889): 371–84.

James, William. "The Gospel of Relaxation." *Scribner's* 25 (Apr 1899): 499–507.

Jantz, Harold. "The Place of the 'Eternal-Womanly' in Goethe's Faust Drama." *PMLA* 68.4 (Sept 1953): 791–805.

Jenks, Tudor. "At the Door: A Little Comedy." *Century* 58 (new series 36) (Oct 1899): 857–58.

———. "Parried." *Century* 58 (new series 36) (June 1899): 318–20.

Jenks, Tudor and Duffield Osborne. "The Baron's Victim: A Mellow Drama." *Harper's Monthly* 96 (Mar 1898): 645–50.

John, Arthur. *The Best Years of the Century.* Urbana: U of Illinois P, 1981.

Jones, Eugene H. *Native Americans as Shown on the Stage, 1753–1916.* Metuchen, New Jersey: Scarecrow Press, 1988.

Jones, Gavin. *Strange Talk: The Politics of Dialect Literature in Gilded Age America.* Los Angeles: U of California P, 1999.

Jones, Maldwyn Allen. *American Immigration.* Chicago: University of Chicago Press, 1992.

Kaplan, Amy. *The Anarchy of Empire in the Making of U. S. Culture.* Cambridge: Harvard UP, 2002.

———. *The Social Construction of American Realism.* Chicago: University of Chicago Press, 1988.

Kauffman, Reginald Wright. "The Drama and Morality." *Forum* 51 (1914): 664–72.

Keating, Peter. *Kipling the Poet.* London: Secker & Warburg, 1994.

Kelly, Patrick J. "The Election of 1896 and the Restructuring of Civil War Memory." *The Memory of the Civil War in American Culture.* Ed. Alice and Joan Waugh Fahs. Chapel Hill, N.C.: U of North Carolina P, 2004. 180–212.

Kerber, Linda. *No Constitutional Right to Be Ladies: Women and the Obligations of Citizenship.* New York: Hill and Wang, 1999.

King, Desmond. *Making Americans: Immigration, Race, and the Origins of the Diverse Democracy.* Cambridge, Mass.: Harvard UP, 2000.

Kipling, Rudyard. " 'An American.' " *Rudyard Kipling's Verse.* New York: Doubleday, 1927. 210–12.

Kitch, Carolyn. *The Girl on the Magazine Cover: The Origins of Visual Stereotypes in American Mass Media.* Chapel Hill: U of North Carolina P, 2001.

Kraft, James. *Who is Witter Bynner?* Albuquerque: U of New Mexico P, 1995.

L. W. "Homestead as Seen by One of Its Workmen." *McClure's Magazine* 3 (July 1894): 161–69.

Lago, Mary M. *Rabindranath Tagore.* Boston: Twayne, 1976.

Latham, Sean and Robert Scholes. "The Rise of Periodical Studies." *Publications of the Modern Language Association of America* 121 (Mar 2006): 517–31.

Lee, Sidney. " 'The American West. III: The American Indian in Elizabethan England.' " *Scribner's* 42 (1907): 313–30.

Levine, Lawrence W. *Highbrow/Lowbrow: The Emergence of Cultural Hierarchy in America.* Cambridge, Mass.: Harvard UP, 1988.

Londré, Felicia Hardison. "Money without Glory: Turn-of-the-Century America's Playwrights." *The American Stage.* Ed. Ron Engle and Tice L. Miller. Cambridge: Cambridge UP, 1993. 131–40.

Lund, Michael. *America's Continuing Story: An Introduction to Serial Fiction, 1850–1900.* Detroit: Wayne State UP, 1993.

Luther, Lester. " 'Law.' " *Forum* 53 (June 1915): 776–79.

Lutz, Tom. *American Nervousness, 1903.* Ithaca: Cornell UP, 1991.

Mallet, Charles. *Anthony Hope and His Books.* Port Washington, N.Y.: Kennikat Press, 1968.

Maltby, Richard. "The Social Evil, the Moral Order and the Melodramatic Imagination, 1890–1915." *Melodrama: Stage, Picture, Screen.* London: British Film Institute, 1994. 214–30.

Manning, Marie. "Nervous Prostration." *Harper's Monthly* 125 (Sept 1912): 641–44.

May, Henry F. *The End of American Innocence.* New York: Columbia UP, 1959.

Mayer, David. *Playing Out the Empire: "Ben-Hur" and Other Toga Plays and Films, 1883–1908.* Oxford: Clarendon Press, 1994.

McConachie, Bruce. *Melodramatic Formations: American Theatre & Society, 1820–1870.* Iowa City, Iowa: U of Iowa P, 1992.

Mead, Sidney E. "American Protestantism since the Civil War: From Americanism to Christianity." *The Shaping of Twentieth-Century America.* Ed. Richard M. Abrams and Lawrence W. Levine. Boston: Little, 1965. 95–124.

Menand, Louis. *The Metaphysical Club: A Story of Ideas in America.* New York: Farrar, Straus and Giroux, 2001.

Merington, Marguerite. "A Gainsborough Lady: A Christmas Masque." *Scribner's Magazine* 31 (Jan 1902): 65–67.

Meyer, Annie Nathan. "The Scientific Mother." *Bookman* 5 (July 1897): 381–82.

———. "Woman's Assumption of Sex Superiority." *North American Review* 178 (Jan 1904): 103–09.

Middleton, George. *Embers and Other One-Act Plays.* New York: Henry Holt & Co., 1911.

———. "The Man Masterful." *Forum* 42 (1909): 369–82.

Millard, Thomas F. "The Passing of the American Indian." *Forum* 34 (Jan 1903): 466–80.

Moses, Montrose J. "The Drama, 1860–1918." *Cambridge History of American Literature.* Ed. Trent, Erskine, Sherman, and Van Doren. Vol. 3. New York: G. P. Putnam's Sons, 1921. 266–98.

Motley, Warren. "Hamlin Garland's *Under the Wheel*: Regionalism Unmasking America." *Modern Drama* 26 (Dec. 1983): 477–85.

Mott, Frank Luther. *A History of American Magazines, 1741–1905.* 5 Vols. Cambridge, Mass.: Harvard UP, 1930–1968.

———. *A History of American Magazines, 1905–1920.* Cambridge: Harvard UP, 1968.

———. "Literary Fevers of the Nineties." *Golden Multitudes: The Story of Best Sellers in the United States.* New York: Macmillan, 1947. 183–93.

Mott, Frank. *A History of American Magazines, 1885–1905.* Cambridge: Harvard UP, 1957.

Murphy, Brenda. *American Realism and American Drama, 1880–1940.* Cambridge: Cambridge UP, 1987.

———. "Plays and Playwrights: 1915–1945." *The Cambridge History of American Theatre, 1870–1945.* Ed. Don B. Wilmeth and Christopher Bigsby. Cambridge: Cambridge UP, 1999. 289–342.

Neihardt, John G. "Eight Hundred Rubles." *Forum* 53 (Mar 1915): 393–402.

Nelson, Dana D. *National Manhood: Capitalist Citizenship and the Imagined Fraternity of White Men.* Durham, N.C.: Duke UP, 1998.

O'Brien, Edward J. "At the Flowing of the Tide." *Forum* 52 (Sept 1914): 375–86.

O'Rell, Max (Léon Paul Blouet). "Petticoat Government." *The North American Review* 163 (July 1896): 101–14.

———. "The Pleasures of Poverty (A Wife's Pleading)." *The North American Review* 169 (Aug 1899): 285–88.

Odem, Mary E. *Delinquent Daughters: Protecting and Policing Adolescent Female Sexuality in the United States, 1885–1920.* Chapel Hill: U of North Carolina P, 1995.

Ohmann, Richard. *Selling Culture: Magazines, Markets, and Class at the Turn of the Century.* London: Verso, 1996.

Parker, Louis N. "A Minuet." *Century* 89 (Feb 1915): 370–76.

Peabody, Josephine Preston. "The Wings." *Harper's Monthly* 110 (May 1905): 947–56.

Pena, Carolyn Thomas de la. *The Body Electric: How Strange Machines Built the Modern American.* New York: New York UP, 2003.

Phegley, Jennifer. *Educating the Proper Woman Reader: Victorian Family Literary Magazines and the Cultural Health of the Nation.* Columbus: Ohio UP, 2004.

Phelps, Elizabeth Stuart. "Immortality and Agnosticism: 'The Gates Ajar'— Twenty-Five Years After." *North American Review* 156 (May 1893): 567–76.

———. "A Novelist's Views of Novel-Writing." *McClure's* 8 (Nov 1896): 77–85.

———. "Within the Gates." *McClure's Magazine* 17 (May–July 1901): 35–43, 142–49, 236–50.

Porter, Laura Spencer. "The Love Story of the First American Girl." *Ladies' Home Journal* 24 (May 1907): 10.

Postlewait, Thomas. "From Melodrama to Realism: The Suspect History of American Drama." *Melodrama: The Cultural Emergence of a Genre.* Ed.

Michael Hays and Anastasia Nikolopoulou. New York: St. Martin's, 1996. 39–60.

———. "The Hieroglyphic Stage: American Theatre and Society, Post–Civil War to 1945." *The Cambridge History of American Theatre, 1870–1945.* Ed. Don B. Wilmeth and Christopher Bigsby. Cambridge: Cambridge UP, 1999. 107–95.

Pratt, Helen Marshall. "A Newly Discovered Portrait of Pocahontas." *Harper's Weekly* 51 (29 June 1907): 958.

Pykett, Lyn. "Reading the Periodical Press: Text and Context." *Victorian Periodicals Review* 22 (Fall 1989): 100–08.

Quinn, Arthur Hobson. *A History of the American Drama from the Beginning to the Civil War.* New York: Irvington Publishers, Inc., 1979. 1923.

———. *A History of the American Drama from the Civil War to the Present Day.* New York: Irvington Publishers, 1980. 1936.

Reddin, Paul. *Wild West Shows.* Urbana: U of Illinois P, 1999.

Regier, C. C. *The Era of the Muckrakers.* Chapel Hill, N.C.: U of North Carolina P, 1932.

Riis, Jacob. "How the Other Half Lives." *Scribner's Magazine* 6 (Dec 1889): 643–62.

Ripley, William Z. "Races in the United States." *Atlantic Monthly* 102 (Dec 1908): 745–59.

Rives, Amélie. "Athelwold." *Harper's Monthly* 84 (Feb 1892): 394–424.

Roosevelt, Theodore. "An Introduction to 'With the American Ambulance in France.'" *The Outlook* (Sept 1915): 125–46.

———. "The Irish Players: Introduction." *Outlook* 99 (Dec 16, 1911): 915.

Rosen, Ruth. *The Lost Sisterhood——Prostitution in America, 1900–1918.* Baltimore: Johns Hopkins' UP, 1982.

Rowe, John Carlos. *Literary Culture and U. S. Imperialism: From the Revolution to World War II.* New York: Oxford UP, 2000.

Royle, Edwin Milton. "The Squaw-Man." *Cosmopolitan* 37 (Aug 1904): 411–18.

———. "The Vaudeville Theatre." *Scribner's Magazine* 26 (Oct 1899): 485–95.

Rusling, General James. "Interview with President William McKinley." *The Philippines Reader.* Ed. and comp. Daniel and Stephen Rosskamm Schirmer. Boston: South End Press, 1987. 22–23.

Salinger, Sharon V. *Taverns and Drinking in Early America.* Baltimore: Johns Hopkins UP, 2002.

Saxton, Alexander. *The Rise and Fall of the White Republic: Class Politics and Mass Culture in Nineteenth-Century America.* New York: Verso, 1990.

Scheckel, Susan. *The Insistence of the Indian: Race and Nationalism in Nineteenth-Century American Culture.* Princeton, N.J.: Princeton UP, 1998.

Schneirov, Matthew. *The Dream of a New Social Order: Popular Magazines in America 1893–1914*. New York: Columbia UP, 1994.

Schnitzler, Arthur. "The Wife. A Play by Schnitzler." *Current Literature* 39 (Nov 1905): 553–56.

Schueller, Malini Johar. *U. S. Orientalisms: Race, Nation, and Gender in Literature, 1790–1890*. Ann Arbor, Mich.: U of Michigan P, 2001.

Shaw, George Bernard. "Androcles and the Lion." *Everybody's Magazine* 31 (Sept 1914): 289–311.

———. "Great Catherine." *Everybody's Magazine* 32 (Feb 1915): 193–212.

———. "Neutrality is Nonsense." *Everybody's Magazine* 34 (Jan 1916): 12.

———. "Pygmalion." *Everybody's Magazine* 31 (Nov 1915): 577–612.

Sherwood, Margaret Pollock. *Coleridge's Imaginative Conception of the Imagination*. Wellesley: Wellesley Press, 1937.

Sherwood, Margaret. "Vittoria." *Scribner's Magazine* 37 (Apr 1905): 497–504.

Simon, Rita J. and Susan H. Alexander. *The Ambivalent Welcome: Print Media, Public Opinion and Immigration*. Westport, Conn.: Praeger, 1993.

Slotkin, Richard. *Gunfighter Nation: The Myth of the Frontier in Twentieth-Century America*. New York: Harper Collins, 1994.

———. *Regeneration through Violence: The Mythology of the American Frontier, 1600–1860*. Middletown, Conn.: Weslyan UP, 1973.

Sollors, Werner. *Beyond Ethnicity: Consent and Descent in American Culture*. Oxford: Oxford UP, 1986.

Spangler, Jacquelyn. "A Democracy of Letters: Best Short Stories and the Literary Aesthetic of Edward J. O'Brien." *Short Story* 9.1 (2001): 99–121

Stanwood, Louise Rogers. "The Progress of Mrs. Alexander." *New England Magazine* 43 ns. (Feb 1911): 529–60, 655–63.

Stephens, Ann S. *Malaeska; the Indian Wife of the White Hunter. Reading the West*. Ed. Bill Brown. New York: Bedford Books, 1997.

Stevens, Doris. *Jailed for Freedom*. New York. Liveright, 1920.

Stoneley, Peter. *Consumerism and American Girls' Literature, 1860–1940*. Cambridge: Cambridge UP, 2003.

Stott, Rebecca. *The Fabrication of the Late-Victorian Femme Fatale*. London: Macmillan, 1992.

Sutphen, Van Tassel. "First Aid to the Injured." *Harper's Monthly* 92 (May 1896): 965–70.

———. "A House of Cards." *Harper's Monthly* 109 (Nov 1904): 901–10.

———. *The Nineteenth Hole; Being Tales of the Fair Green*. New York: Harper & Brothers, 1901.

Suttner, Bertha von. "International Peace." *The Chautauquan* 70 (Mar 1913): 72–77.

———. "Making the Air Barbarous." *The Chautauquan* 70 (Mar 1913): 90–99.

Symons, Arthur. "Cleopatra in Judea." *Forum* 55 (June 1916): 643–60.

———. "The Decadent Movement in Literature." *Harper's Monthly* 87 (Nov 1893): 858–67.

———. *Studies in the Elizabethan Drama.* New York: E. P. Dutton & Company, 1919.

Tadema, Laurence Alma. "Love and Death." *Harper's Monthly* 90 (Dec 1894): 151–52.

———. "The Silent Voice." *Harper's Monthly* 93 (Aug 1896): 400–09.

———. "An Undivined Tragedy." *Harper's* 88 (Mar 1894): 615–29.

Tagore, Rabindranath. "Day's End." *Forum* 51 (Jan 1914): 145.

———. "The Post Office." *Forum* 51 (Mar 1914): 455–71.

———. *The Post Office.* Intro. by Anita Desai. New York: St. Martin's Press, 1996.

Tarkington, Booth. "Beauty and the Jacobin." *Harper's Monthly* 125 (Aug/Sept 1912): 390–99, 539–53.

———. "Mister Antonio." *Harper's Monthly* 134 (Feb 1917): 187–203; 374–87.

Taussig, Michael. *Mimesis and Alterity.* New York: Routledge, 1993.

Taylor, Welford Dunaway. *Amélie Rives (Princess Troubetzkoy).* New York: Twayne, 1973.

Tebbel, John. *The American Magazine: A Compact History.* New York: Hawthorn Books, 1969.

Tichi, Cecelia. *Exposes and Excess: Muckraking in America, 1900/2000.* Philadelphia: U of Pennsylvania P, 2004.

Tilton, Robert S. *Pocahontas: The Evolution of an American Narrative.* New York: Cambridge UP, 1994.

Tompkins, E. Berkeley. *Anti-Imperialism in the United States: The Great Debate, 1890–1920.* Philadelphia: U of Pennsylvania Press, 1970.

Towne, Charles Hanson. "The Aliens." *McClure's Magazine* 47 (May 1916): 12–13, 76.

Townsend, Kim. *Manhood at Harvard: William James and Others.* New York: W. W. Norton, 1996.

Trachtenberg, Alan. *The Incorporation of America: Culture and Society in the Gilded Age.* New York: Hill & Wang, 1982.

Traubel, Gertrude. "About 'Tiger.' " *Forum* 51 (Apr 1914): 583.

Tucker, Jackie. "Henry James." *American Playwrights, 1880–1945.* Ed. William W. Demastes. Westport, Conn.: Greenwood, 1995. 214–23.

Tylee, Claire M., ed. *War Plays by Women.* New Jersey: Routledge, 1999.

Vail, Laurence. "The Inconveniences of Being Neutral." *Forum* 59 (Jan 1918): 85–100.

———. "Untrammeled." *Forum* (Sept 1916): 350–54.

Vale, Charles. "Lord Dunsany's Gods." *Forum* 51 (May 1914): 782–90.

Valency, Maurice. *The Cart and the Trumpet: The Plays of George Bernard Shaw.* New York: Oxford UP, 1973.

Van Campen, Helen Green. " 'Life on Broadway': The Disillusions of Flossie." *McClure's Magazine* 41 (June 1913): 78–80.

———. " 'Life on Broadway': The Musical Comedy Rehearsal." *McClure's Magazine* 41 (May 1913): 68–72.

———. "The Woes of Two Workers." *McClure's Magazine* 41 (Sept 1913): 198–204.

———. "The Woes of Two Workers." *McClure's Magazine* 41 (Oct 1913): 216–28.

Van Dyke, Henry. "Fighting for Peace: Fair Weather and Storm-Signs." *Scribner's Magazine* 62 (Sept 1917): 280–89.

———. "Fighting for Peace: Stand Fast, Ye Free!" *Scribner's Magazine* 62 (Nov 1917): 517–32.

———. "Fighting for Peace: The Werewolf at Large." *Scribner's Magazine* 62 (Oct 1917): 387–98.

———. *Fighting for Peace.* New York: Charles Scribner's Sons, 1917.

———. "The House of Rimmon." *Scribner's Magazine* 44 (Aug 1908): 129–47; 283–301.

Veblen, Thorstein. *The Theory of the Leisure Class: An Economic Study of Institutions.* Intro. C. Wright Mills. New York: Mentor-New American Library, 1953.

Very, Alice, comp. *A Comprehensive Index of Poet-Lore 1889–1963.* Boston: Branden Press, 1966.

Vibert, J. G. "The Sick Doctor." *Century* 51 ns. (Apr 1896): 944–47.

Wainscott, Ronald H. *The Emergence of the Modern American Theater 1914–1929.* New Haven: Yale UP, 1997.

Wainscott, Ronald. "Plays and Playwrights: 1896–1915." *The Cambridge History of American Theatre. Volume II: 1870–1945.* Cambridge: Cambridge UP, 1998. 262–98.

Wakefield, Edward. "Nervousness: The National Disease of America." *McClure's* 2. (Feb 1894): 302–07.

Walker, Francis A. "Immigration and Degradation." *Forum* 11 (Aug 1891): 634–44.

Watts, Sarah. *Rough Rider in the White House.* Chicago: University of Chicago Press, 2003.

Welsh, Robert Gilbert. "Jezebel." *Forum* 53 (May 1915): 647–60.

Welter, Barbara. "The Cult of True Womanhood: 1820–1860." *American Quarterly* 18 (1966): 151–74.

Wendell, Barrett. "Ralegh in Guiana." *Scribner's Magazine* 21 (June 1897): 776–84.

Wendell, Barrett. "Rosamond." *Scribner's Magazine* 7 (June 1890): 783–88.
———. *Stelligeri and Other Essays Concerning America.* New York: Charles Scribner's Sons, 1893.

Wentworth, Marion Craig. "War Brides." *Century* 89 (Feb 1915): 527–44.

Westbrook, Peter D. *Mary Wilkins Freeman.* Rev. ed. Boston: Twayne, 1988.

Wexler, Laura. *Tender Violence: Domestic Visions in an Age of U.S. Imperialism.* Chapel Hill: U of North Carolina P, 2000.

Wharton, Edith. " 'Copy:' A Dialogue." *Scribner's Magazine* 27 (June 1900): 656–63.

———. "Pomegranate Seed." *Scribner's Magazine* 51 (Mar 1912): 284–91.

Whitlock, Brand. "The White Slave." *Forum* 51 (Feb 1914): 193–216.

Whitney, Blair. *John G. Neihardt.* Boston: Twayne, 1976.

Wilkins, Mary E. (Mary Wilkins Freeman). "Giles Corey, Yeoman." *Harper's Monthly* 86 (Dec 1892): 20–40.

Williams, Raymond. *The Long Revolution.* New York: Columbia UP, 1961.

———. *Marxism and Literature.* Oxford: Oxford UP, 1977.

Wilmeth, Don B. and Christopher Bigsby. *The Cambridge History of American Theatre: 1870–1945.* Cambridge: Cambridge UP, 1999.

Wilmeth, Don. "Noble or Ruthless Savage?: The American Indian on Stage and in the Drama." *Journal of American Drama and Theatre* 1 (Spring 1989): 39–78.

———. "Tentative Checklist of Indian Plays (1606–1987)." *Journal of American Drama and Theatre* 2 (Fall 1989): 34–54.

Wilson, Charles R. "Racial Reservations: Indians and Blacks in American Magazines, 1865–1900." *Journal of Popular Culture* 10 (1976): 70–79.

Wilson, Harold S. *McClure's Magazine and the Muckrackers.* Princeton: Princeton UP, 1970.

Woodress, James. *Booth Tarkington: Gentleman from Indiana.* New York: J. B. Lippincott, 1955.

Young, Philip. "The Mother of Us All: Pocahontas Reconsidered." *Kenyon Review* 24 (Summer 1962): 391–415.

Zboray, Ronald J. *A Fictive People: Antebellum Economic Development and the American Reading Public.* New York: Oxford UP, 1993.

Zuckerman, Mary Ellen. *A History of Popular Women's Magazines in the United States, 1792–1995.* Westport, Conn.: Greenwood Press, 1998.

Index ❧

Ackerman, Alan, xiv, 8, 25
Adams, Henry, 113
Addams, Jane, 12, 87, 189
  Newer Ideals of Peace, 182
Akins, Zoë, 69, 78, 119, 121, 128
  Magical City, The, 69, 119, 121,
    126, 128–29
Aldrich, Thomas Bailey, 121
Aly, Lucile, 133
"An American Writer Who Just Missed
    Enduring Greatness"
    (Anonymous), 169, 170
Anderson, Benedict, xiii, 2–3, 55, 168,
    169, 190
  Imagined Communities, 2, 169
Anderson, Donald, 150
Anderson, Maxwell, 132
Anderson, Sherwood, 183
Andrews, Benjamin, 53
Andrews, Mary Raymond Shipman,
    71, 99, 186
  The Ditch, 13, 178, 188
  West Point Regulation, A, 71, 99, 188
"Another Anglo-Indian Nobel
    Prizeman" (Anonymous), 142, 143
anti-war writings, 16, 162, 177–78,
    182–84, 186
Anthony, Susan B., 77
  See also suffrage, women's
Archer, Melanie, 18
Archer, William, 21, 26, 40, 170
Arena magazine
  Brodhead and, 153–54
  Cross and, 27
  Dunbar and, 86

Flower and, 5, 105, 151–52
Gardener and, 163
Garland and, 151–52
Herne and, 21
"Higher Thought" and, 49
individuality and, 59
O'Rell and, 85
Pokagon and, 105
Shaw and, 38
social issues and, 13, 59, 149, 159,
    163–64
Susan B. Anthony and, 77
"Arthur Schnitzler, the Austrian
    Hauptmann" (Anonymous), 28
Atlantic Monthly
  as "quality" periodical, 10, 35
  "*Atlantic* Group" and, 9
  conservatism of, 37
  cultural issues and, 100–1
  "fallen woman" and, 126
  Galsworthy and, 96, 118
  Howells and, 121–22
  James and, 25
  Native Americans and, 105
  popularity in America,
    4, 12
  Rives and, 123
  Schneirov on, 69
  Shaw and, 39
  social issues and, 158, 159
  Wendell and, 51
  Wharton and, 122–23
  Wilkins and, 150
  women and, 79–80
Auerbach, Nina, 126

Bacon, Josephine Daskam, 15, 156, 177, 184
  First of October, The, 15, 156
  Twilight of the Gods, The, 15, 177, 184
  Wanderer, The, 37, 169, 175
Bailyn, Bernard et al., 180
Baker, George Pierce, 110, 118, 127
Baker, Ray Stannard, 70, 113, 136
Balibar, Etienne, 2, 33, 190
Bangs, John Kendrick, 22, 67, 74–75, 95, 97, 98
  Bicyclers, The, 74, 75
  Chafing-Dish Party, A, 67
  Fatal Message, The, 22
  Golfiacs, The, 74, 75–76
  Proposal Under Difficulties, A, 95, 97, 98
Banta, Martha, 91
Barker, James Nelson, 134
Barrish, Philip, 18
Baunevji, Inar Prakas, 145–46
  Gool and Bahar, 145–46
  "Radindranath Tagore in India," 145
Bederman, Gail, 7, 102
  Manliness & Civilization, 7, 102
Beisner, Robert L., 179–80
Bennett, Arnold, 12, 29, 30, 71, 78, 92
  Honeymoon, The, 29, 30, 71, 92
  What the Public Wants, 71
"Bertha Von Suttner" (Anonymous), 128
Besant, Annie, 103
bicycles, 47, 48, 74–75, 83
Bigsby, Christopher, 15, 38
Black, Alexander
  Camera and the Comedy, The, 32
  Photography in Fiction: "Miss Jerry," 32
Blau, Judith, 18
Bledstein, Burton, 4
Blight, David, 3, 57, 158, 168
Blumin, Stuart M., 18

Bookman, 9, 27, 71, 83, 123, 182
Boucicault, Dion, 15, 20
  "Future American Drama, The" 20
Boyce, Neith
  Maddelena Speaks, 23–24
Boyesen, H.H., 73
Bradley, Jennifer, 128
Brewster, Ben, 32
Briscoe, Margaret Sutton, 99
Brodhead, Richard, 17, 35–36, 54, 76, 141, 153
Brooks, Peter, 121–22, 160
Brougham, John, 60–61, 134
  Pocahontas, 61
Bryan, Louise, 166, 183
Bryan, William Jennings, 168
Burke, Martin J., 19
Burlingame, Edward, 13
Butsch, Richard, 62
Bynner, Witter, 135–36, 162–63, 165, 183
  Little King, The, 135–36, 162
  Tiger, 13, 162, 164–66
Bzowski, Frances, 78

Cama, Bhikaji, 143
Cameron, Margaret, 45, 46, 71, 73, 97
  Committee on Matrimony, The, 45, 71, 73, 97
Carpenter, William, 27–28
Casper, Scott E., 35
Century
  advertisements in, 75
  as quality periodical, 4, 10
  Atlantic Group and, 9
  Dargan and, 122
  Daskam and, 175
  Garland and, 151–52
  Hibbard and, 15
  illustration in, 29, 30–31
  Jenks and, 92
  Kennerley and, 183
  Kipling and, 46

Mott and, 15
popularity, 13, 37
racial issues and, 55–56
social issues and, 69, 159
Wharton and, 123
Wilkins and, 150
Cheney, Sheldon, 160
Christy, Howard Chandler, 29
Chudacoff, Howard, 102–3
classes, classification of, 18–19
Clayton, Douglas, 183
Cleveland, Grover, 33, 53
Cmiel, Kenneth, 67
Connelly, Mark Thomas, 163–64, 167
Corbin, John, 16, 61–63, 64
"How the Other Half Laughs", 61, 64
Cosgrave, John O'Hara, 39
Cosmopolitan, 4, 9, 11, 16, 38, 69–70, 90, 103–6, 108–9, 152, 156
Cowan, Sada, 16, 23, 169, 173
Illumination, 16, 23
In the Morgue, 16, 169, 173
Cross, Wilbur, 27
Current Literature, 11–12, 27, 28

Dale, Alan, 104
Daly, Augustin, 20
Dargan, Olive Tilford, 30, 37, 121–22
Daskam, Josephine Dodge, see Bacon
Davies, Mary Carolyn, 143–44
Davis, John, 134
de Ivanowski, Sigismond, 30, 122
Dell, Floyd, 177, 183–84
Long Time Ago, A, 177, 183–84
Demastes, William, 9, 56
DeMille, Cecil B., 104, 162
Denison, John
"Survival of the American Type, The", 79
DeMille, William C., 15, 108
dialect, 23, 57–58, 73–74, 108, 153–58
dialogues, 26
Dijkstra, Bram, 126

Dippie, Brian, 104, 106
directed reading, 27–28
"Do Women Possess Any Dramatic Ability?" (Anonymous), 78
Doyle, Arthur Conan, 26, 70
Draper, William, 105
"Last of the Red Race, The," 105
Dreiser, Theodore, 48, 103
Dresser, Horatio
"Mental Thought in Its Relation to Modern Thought," 49
"What is the New Thought?," 49
Du Maurier, George, 155
Dunbar, Newell, 13, 86, 152
Ever-Womanly, The, (Das Ewigweibliche) 13, 86–90, 152
Duncan, George, 100
Proposal, A, 100

East India Company, 146
Eliot, Annie
As Strangers: A Comedietta, 93
From Four to Six, 93
Eliot, George, 88, 170
Eliot, T.S., 132
Elliot, Michael, 154
Ellmann, Richard, 187
Elshtain, Jean Bethke, 182
Emergency Quota Act (1921), 7
Engle, Sherry, 78
"Irruption of Women Dramatists," 78
Erdman, Harley, 62, 155
eugenics, 7, 55, 62, 100–2, 163
Everybody's magazine, 9, 15, 17, 29, 38–44, 74, 102
expansionism, American
Grover Cleveland and, 53
identity and, 2, 54, 169, 180
language and, 113
masculinity and, 51
Mowatt and, 112
Native Americans and, 134

expansionism, American—*continued*
  periodical literature and, 5, 76
  politics and, 168, 176–77
  Postlewait on, 21
  resistance to, 173, 179–80
  Tagore and, 143
  Woodrow Wilson and, 189
  See also Manifest Destiny;
    Orientalism

Fahs, Alice, 55
Fanny's Second Play (Anonymous), 22, 23
Fearnow, Mark, 183
Ferdinand, Franz, 39, 171
Fisk, May Isabel, 24, 58, 65, 82
  Bill from the Milliner, 82
  Buying Theatre Tickets, 82
  Eternal Feminine, 82
  Her Tailor-Made Gown, 82, 83
  Mis' Deborah Has a Visitor, 65
  Talking Women, 82
  Woman in a Shoe-Shop, 82
Fiske, Arthur Davison, 10, 162
Flint, Kate, 78
Flower, B.O.
  Arena and, 5, 151
  commitment to social issues, 87
  Gardener and, 163
  Garland and, 151–52
  "Highest Function of the Novel,"
    151
  "Interesting Representative of a
    Vanishing Race," 38, 105
  Pokagon and, 38, 105
Forum
  Akins and, 128
  Atlantic Group and, 9
  Boyce and, 23
  Bynner and, 165
  Cowan and, 16, 23, 169, 173
  Garland and, 152
  lack of illustrations, 29
  Neihardt and, 132, 133

O'Brien and, 141
politics and, 13
Putnam and, 16, 24
racial issues and, 100, 102, 105
social issues and, 36, 37–38, 59, 60,
    87, 149, 159–61
Tagore and, 143
Vail and, 186
Vale and, 28
Welsh and, 124
women and, 77
World War I and, 177–78, 182–83,
    184
Yeats and, 17, 140
Freedman, Jonathan, 155
Frost, A.B., 29, 176
  See also illustrations
Fussell, Paul, 6

Gabler-Hover, Janet, 55–56
Galsworthy, John
  criticism, 21
  "drama of sincerity" and, 160
  Hall-Marked, 16, 62, 96
  Little Dream, 16, 119
  morality in works of, 96
  on drama, 118–19
  publication in American periodicals,
    15, 16
  "quality" drama and, 13
  Strife, 11, 119
  The Sun, 16, 188–89
  women in works of, 78
Gardener, Helen, 163
Garland, Hamlin
  Arena and, 13, 86, 151–52
  Double Miracle, The, 130, 141
  Flower and, 151–52
  Future of Fiction, 154
  Homestead and Its Perilous Trades, 38
  Land Question, The, 154
  miracles and, 130, 141
  on period from 1898–1917, 7

politics and, 152–54
response to "Homestead and Its
   Perilous Trades," 38
Roadside Meetings, 7, 152
"Some Platitudes Concerning
   Drama," 96, 118
Under the Wheel, xiv-v, 13, 58, 86,
   151–54
vernacular and, 58
Garland, Robert, 130, 141
   Double Miracle, The, 130, 141
Garvey, Ellen Gruber, 75
Gerstle, Gary, 56, 57
Getz, John, 150
Gibson, Charles Dana, 29, 77
   See also illustrations
Gilbert, William S., 22, 37
   Trying a Dramatist, 22, 37
Gillis, John R., 55
Glackens, W., 29, 31
   See also illustrations
Glazener, Nancy, xiv, 9, 17, 154
Gleason, Anne, 31, 90, 119
   Signal Service, 31–32, 90, 119
Goode, Kate Tucker, 134–35
   Princess of Virginia, 134–35
Gow, M.I., 124
Grant, Madison, 62, 101–2
   "Passing of the Great Race," 62, 101
Grant, Robert, 81
   "Conduct of Life," 81
Green, Helen, 23, 29, 31, 58
   In Vaudeville, 23, 29, 31
Gregory, Lady Augusta, 13, 59, 140
   Bogie Man, 140
Grinnell, George Bird, 105
   "Wild Indian," 105

Haenni, Sabine, 65
Hall, Prescott F., 62
Hall, Roger, 108
Hamilton, Clayton, 21, 160, 161
   "Modern Social Drama," 160

Hansen, Jonathan, 189
Harlow, V.T., 50–51
Harper's
   as "quality" periodical, 10, 35
   "*Atlantic* Group" and, 9
   Bangs and, 67, 74–75, 97
   Boyce and, 24
   conservatism of, 37
   Corbin and, 61
   drama criticism and, 20
   Du Maurier and, 155
   Duncan and, 100
   Fisk and, 24, 82
   Garland and, 152
   Hibbard and, 15
   Howells and, 91, 154
   Hutton and, 60–61
   illustration in, 29, 44–45
   Manning and, 47, 49
   Mills and, 5
   Native Americans and, 133
   Peabody and, 126
   popularity in America, 4, 13
   popularity in England, 15
   Raleigh and, 44
   Rives and, 123
   social issues and, 158, 164
   Symons and, 124–25
   Tarkington and, 157, 173–74
   Wilkins and, 150
   women writers and, 78
Hatheway, Jay, 88
Hearst, William Randolph, 38, 44, 49,
   103–4
Hearst's magazine, 29
Hemmerde, Edward G., 12
Herne, James, 14, 15, 20–21, 153
Hibbard, George Abiah, 15, 68, 93
   Matter of Opinion, A, 15, 68, 93
Higham, John, 101
"Higher Thought," 47, 48–49
"Hindu on the Celtic Spirit, A"
   (Anonymous), 142

Hitchcock, Lucius, 63, 64
Hobbes, John Oliver, 26, 169–70, 172
    Repentance, A, 169–70
Hodin, Mark, 62, 63
Holroyd, Michael, 43
"Homestead as Seen by One of Its
    Workmen" (L.W.), 38
Hope, Anthony, 26–27
    Dolly Dialogues, 26–27
    Life Subscription, A, 26–27
Howard, Bronson, 20
Howells, William Dean
    After the Wedding, 119, 120
    blank verse plays, 120–21
    Bride Roses, 25, 58, 154
    *Cambridge History of English and
        American Literature* and, 15
    classism, 64–65, 95
    Cosmopolitan and, 104
    courtship fiction and, 94
    criticism, 21, 112
    Evening Dress, 156
    Father and Mother, 119, 120
    Hazard of New Fortunes, A, 64–65
    Hobbes and, 170
    Impossible, The, 25, 58, 155
    Indian Giver, 25, 91
    influence of, 73, 80
    Kipling and, 46
    "Larger England" and, xii, xv, 2, 36,
        112–13, 142
    "Laureate of the Larger England," 2,
        46, 112
    McClure's and, 73, 112
    Mother, The, 119, 120
    Parting Friends, 92, 94
    Previous Engagement, 25, 91
    racial difference and, 154–55
    regionalism and, 153
    Self-Sacrifice, 25, 92
    "tale dialogue" and, 25
    Unexpected Guests, 84, 95
    tragic sensibility and, 119
    vernacular and, 58

    women in works of, 84, 91
Humphreys, Mary Gay, 77
Hutton, Laurence, 60–61, 63
    American Burlesque, The, 60–61

Ibsen, Henrik, 7, 11, 16, 27–28, 38,
    80, 118, 119, 132, 152, 153
illustrations
    absence from *Atlantic Monthly,* 12
    Century and, 13
    class representation and, 97, 100
    fashion and, 24, 78
    Forum and, 13
    Harper's and, 13
    impact of, 69
    published plays and, 14, 18, 21, 29–33
    Shaw's plays and, 40–41, 43–44
immigration
    class and, 2, 64–66
    Emergency Quota Act and, 7
    fear of, 52, 54, 69, 126, 149
    Garland and, 152–54
    identity and, 3, 51
    language and, 157–58
    racism and, 52, 81, 100–3, 163
    Roosevelt and, 102
    social problems and, 60–62
    women and, 77
imperialism, American
    See expansionism, American
India, 142–46

Jacobs, Lea, 32
Jacobson, Matthew Frye, 176
Jakobi, Paula, 38, 55, 165–67
    Chinese Lily, 13, 38, 55, 165–67
James, Henry, 25, 27, 111
    Animated Conversation, 25, 27
James, William, 2, 48, 102, 180
    "Gospel of Relaxation," 48
Jantz, Harold, 86
    "Place of the 'Eternal-Womanly'," 86
Jenks, Tudor, 22, 37, 81, 92
    Baron's Victim, 22

John, Arthur, xiii, 37
Jones, Eugene, 107
Jones, Gavin, 57, 157
Jones, Henry Arthur, 21, 39
Jones, Maldwyn Allen, 52

Kaplan, Amy, 5, 189
Kaufmann, Reginald, 161, 164
  House of Bondage, 161, 164
Keating, Peter, 112–14
Kelly, Patrick J., 168
Kennerley, Mitchell, 183
Kerber, Linda, 79
King, Desmond, 7, 55
Kipling, Rudyard
  American, An, 111–12
  Cameron and, 45–46, 98
  "Larger America" and, 110
  McClure's and, 26, 70
  Mowatt and, 111, 112
  popularity, 46, 143
Kitch, Carolyn, 4
Kirk, Ellen Warner Olney,
    79–80
Knoblauch, Edward, 12

"Larger England," xii, xv, 2, 17,
    36, 46, 76, 107, 112–13,
    142, 190
Levine, Lawrence, 17, 117
Leyendecker, J.C., 133
Lippincott's magazine, 9, 24, 46, 80,
    123, 134–35, 143
Locke, Edward, 12
Lodge, Henry Cabot, 180
London, Jack, 48, 103
Londré, Felicia, 78
Lund, Michael, 17
Luther, Lester, 16, 177, 185
  Law, 16, 177, 185
Lutz, Tom, 47–48

MacKaye, Steele, 14, 15, 20
Maltby, Richard, 159

Manifest Destiny, 106, 107, 172–73,
    177, 180
  See also expansionism, American
manliness, 52–53
Manning, Marie, 45, 47, 48–49
  Nervous Prostration, 45, 47, 49
May, Henry F., 4–5, 179, 183
McClure's
  advertising in, 36
  Atlantic Group and, 9–10
  Bennett and, 71, 92
  Boyce and, 24
  Bynner and, 162–63
  founding of, 4
  Garland and, 152
  Hope and, 26, 27
  illustrations and, 29, 30, 31, 68
  Kipling and, 45–46
  marriage and, 73, 74, 90, 97
  popularity, 4, 70
  religion and, 136
  social issues and, 38, 39, 48, 69, 99,
      113, 136–37, 159, 164
  Tagore and, 143
  Van Campen and, 23, 66
  women and, 137
McConachie, Bruce, 22
McKinley, William, 168, 172
Mead, Sidney E., 138
Menand, Louis, 7, 56, 57
Merington, Marguerite, 13, 24, 31, 78,
    82, 119
  Gainsborough Lady, A, 13, 24, 31,
      82, 119
Meyer, Annie Nathan, 83–84
  Scientific Mother, 83–84
  "Women's Assumption of Sex
      Superiority," 84
Middleton, George, 38, 161–62
  Embers and Other One-Act Plays, 161
  Man Masterful, The, 38, 161
Millard, Thomas, 105
  "Passing of the American
      Indian," 105

Mills, Henry Alden, 5
miscegenation, 100, 103, 106, 108, 134
monologues, 23–24
Moody, William Vaughn, 11, 126, 132
Morgan, Wallace, 67, 68
    See also illustrations
Moses, Montrose, 8, 14, 21
Motley, Warren, 152–53
Mott, Frank
    on American periodicals in England,
        15
    on European war, 177
    on Flower, 151
    on *Forum*, 183
    on Grover Cleveland, 53
    on growth of American periodicals,
        xiii, 4, 13, 39, 103
    on growth of Protestant churches, 138
    on Hearst, 38
    on "Higher Thought" publications, 49
    on Kipling, 46
    on *McClure's*, 70
    reflection theory, 35
Mowatt, Anna Cora, 111
muck-raking, 11–12, 39, 54, 113, 160
Munsey's magazine, 4, 9, 39, 69, 70, 90
Murphy, Brenda, xiv, 25, 132, 153

Native Americans
    Christianity and, 133
    literary romanticizing of, 133–35
    Manifest Destiny and, 106
    Royle and, 104–8
    U.S. policy toward, 54, 104–5
nativism, 7, 11, 17, 52, 59–60, 100–2,
        158, 163, 167
Neihardt, John G., 132–33, 183
    Black Elk Speaks, 132
    Eight Hundred Rubles, 132–33, 141
    Passing of the Lion, 132
Neilson, Francis, 12
Nelson, Dana, 79, 106, 108
"Nervousness," 47–48

New England Magazine, 9, 90, 109,
        119, 145, 152
Newell, Peter, 40, 44
    See also illustrations
Norris, Frank, 39, 48
North American Review, 9, 17, 20, 84–85,
        102, 137, 139–40, 151, 182
Norton, Charles Eliot, 180

O'Brien, Edward J., 140–41
    At the Flowing of the Tide, 140
Odem, Mary E., 163
Ohmann, Richard, xiii–iv, 17, 19, 74,
        90, 94, 97
Olney, Ellen Warner, 79
Olney, Richard, 53
O'Rell, Max, 78, 84–86
    "Petticoat Government," 85–86
    Pleasures of Poverty, 84–86
Orientalism, 178
Outlook magazine, 53, 59, 138, 140,
        152, 159

Page, Thomas Nelson, 153
Parker, Louis, 37, 169, 175
    Minuet, A, 37, 169, 175
Paulding, James Kirke, 20
Peabody, Josephine Preston, 78,
        117–18, 121, 126
    Wings, The, 117–18, 121, 126–27
Penfield, Edward, 29, 98
    See also illustrations
Phegley, Jennifer, 78
Phelps, Elizabeth Stuart, 71, 137–39
    "Immortality and Agnosticism," 137
    "Novelist's View of Novel-Writing," 71
    Within the Gates, 71, 137, 138
Pocahontas, popular interest in,
        133–35
Poet-Lore, 8, 10–11, 51, 78
Pokagon, Simon, 38, 105
Portor, Laura, 133
Postlewait, Thomas, 8, 13–14, 21

Pratt, Helen, 133
Preston, May Wilson, 23, 41, 42, 44, 72
  See also illustrations
prostitution, 13, 38, 55, 149, 151,
  159–60, 162–68
Putnam, Nina Wilcox, 13, 16, 24
Pykett, Lyn, 5

Quinn, Arthur Hobson, 8, 15, 108, 126

race
  drama and, 35, 56–57
  identity and, 3, 5, 59
  Kipling and, 143
  language and, 2
  marriage and, 95
  nationalism and, 18, 33
  women and, 77, 86, 166–68
racism, 62, 65, 69, 74, 100–3, 105,
  107, 118, 146, 163, 180
  race suicide, hysteria about, 7, 52,
    100, 126
  racial degeneration, hysteria about, 7
Raleigh, Henry, 43–44
  See also illustrations
Regier, C.C., 87
regionalism, 141, 151, 153–54
Riis, Jacob, 157
  How the Other Half Lives, 157
Ripley, William Z., 100–2
  "Races in the United States," 100–1
Rives, Amélie, 78, 121, 123
  Athelwold, 78, 121, 123–24
Roosevelt, Theodore
  American writers and, 140
  bicycles and, 75
  Everybody's Magazine and, 40
  immigration and, 102
  loss of presidency, 48
  masculinity and, 102–3
  muckraking and, 39
  O'Brien and, 140
  Outlook and, 59

  Saxton on, 8
  Shaw and, 39
  Spanish-American War and, 8, 53,
    172, 180
  Wendell and, 53–54
Rosen, Ruth, 163, 166
  Lost Sisterhood, The, 166
Rowe, John Carlos, 112, 189
Royle, Edwin Milton
  depiction of American West, 104–6,
    108–9
  miscegenation and, 69, 103
  social class and, 95
  Squaw-Man, The, 58, 69, 95, 103–9
  vaudeville and, 62–63
  vernacular and, 58
Rusling, General James, 172

Salinger, Sharon, 137
Saturday Evening Post, 15, 16, 44, 158,
  171
Saxton, Alexander, 7–8, 100
Scheckel, Susan, 134
Schneirov, Matthew, xiv, 69–70, 74, 76
Schnitzler, Arthur, 10, 11, 27, 28
  Wife, The, 27, 28
Schueller, Malini, 178
Schultz, Alfred P., 62
Scribner's
  Andrews and, 53
  anti-war writings and, 177–79
  as "quality" periodical, 10, 12–13
  "Atlantic Group" and, 9
  Briscoe and, 99
  Eliot and, 93
  Frost and, 29
  Galsworthy and, 188
  Grant and, 81
  Hibbard and, 15, 93
  illustration in, 29, 32
  James and, 25, 27, 48
  McClure's and, 4
  Merington and, 82

Scribner's—continued
  morality and, 37
  Peabody and, 126
  popularity in England, 15
  Royle and, 62
  Schneirov on, 69
  social issues and, 157–59
  Van Dyke and, 178–79
  Wendell and, 50
  Wharton and, 16, 26, 122–23
Shaw, George Bernard
  Androcles and the Lion, 17, 38,
    39–40, 44
  blacklisting, 39–40
  "drama of sincerity" and, 160
  Everybody's Magazine and, 38–43
  Fanny's First Play, 12, 23
  gentlemen and, 43
  Great Catherine, 17, 38, 43–44
  "Neutrality is Nonsense," 40
  publication in American periodicals,
    15, 16–17
  Pygmalion, 17, 38, 41, 42, 44
  Raleigh's illustrations and, 45
  Roosevelt and, 39
Sherwood, Margaret, 13, 130, 131–32
  Vittoria, 13
Shinn, Everett, 29, 176
Simon, Rita J., 158
slavery, 71, 126, 137, 143
  industrial, 149, 152
  white slavery, 159, 162–65, 167–68
Slotkin, Richard, 7, 106
Smith, Hopkinson, 153
Social Darwinism, 8, 11, 62, 138, 180
Sollors, Werner, 134
Spangler, Jacquelyn, 141
Spanish-American War, 7, 53–54, 169,
    172, 176, 180
Stanwood, Louise Rogers, 109, 113
  Progress of Mrs. Alexander, 69, 79,
    109–14
Steele, Frederic Dorr, 29, 30
  See also illustrations

Steffens, Lincoln, 70, 74, 137
Stephens, Ann, 106
Stevens, Otheman, 38
Stoneley, Peter, 78
Stott, Rebecca, 126
suffrage, women's
  drama and, 71, 78, 114
  image of "happy wife" and, 86
  Jakobi and, 165–66
  Kirk and, 80
  men's support for, 162
  opposition to, 83, 165
  peace movement and, 181
  Preston and, 41
  Susan B. Anthony and, 77
  What the Public Wants and, 71
Sutphen, Van Tassel, 24, 29, 74–76, 94
  First Aid to the Injured, 29, 74, 76
  House of Cards, A, 94
  Nineteenth Hole, 76
Suttner, Bertha von
  "International Peace," 182
  Lay Down Your Arms, 182
  "Making the Air Barbarous," 182
Symons, Arthur, 21, 121, 124–25
  Cleopatra in Judea, 121, 124–26
  "Decadent Movement in Literature,"
    125

Tadema, Laurence Alma, 78, 95, 119, 120
  Love and Death, 119–20
  Post Office, 143–45
  Silent Voice, 119–20
  Undivined Tragedy, 95–96
Tagore, Rabindranath, 13, 142–46
tale dialogue, 25
Tarbell, Ida M., 70
Tarkington, Booth
  Beauty and the Jacobin, 157, 169,
    173–75
  French Revolution and, 173–75
  Mr. Antonio, 157, 158–59
  publication in periodicals, 157, 169
  vernacular and, 58

Taussig, Michael, 58, 68, 90
  Mimesis and Alterity, 58, 68, 90
Tebbel, John, xiii
"Theatrical Muck-Raker Answered"
  (Anonymous), 12
"Threatened Revolution in Spain, The"
  (Anonymous), 171–72
Theatrical Syndicate, 20
Tichi, Cecelia, 160
Tilton, Robert, 135
Tompkins, E. Berkeley, 179–80
Towne, Charles Hanson, 71
  Aliens, The, 71–73
Townsend, Kim, 51
Trachtenberg, Alan, 58
Traubel, Gertrude, 165
Tylee, Claire, 182

"Universal Appeal of the Nobel
  Prize Winners, The"
  (Anonymous), 142

Vail, Laurence, 38, 178, 186–87
  Inconveniences of Being Neutral, 13,
    38, 178, 186–88
  Untrammeled, 186
Vale, Charles, 28
  "Lord Dunsany's Gods", 28
Valency, Maurice, 39, 41, 43
Van Campen, Helen, 22–23, 58,
  66–67
  Disillusions of Flossie, The, 67, 68
  Life on Broadway, 22–23, 66, 68
  Woes of Two Workers, 66
Van Dyke, Henry, 177–80
  Fighting for Peace, 179–80
  House of Rimmon, The, 177–78, 180
Vanden Heuvel, Michael, 9, 56
vaudeville, 23, 43, 58, 60, 62–63,
  156, 157
Veblen, Thorstein, 72, 111
Vibert, Jehen George, 30–31, 37
  Sick Doctor, The, 31, 37
Vrooman, Charles, 113

Wainscott, Ronald, xii, xiv, 57,
  176–77, 186
Wakefield, Edward, 48
  "Nervousness," 48
Walker, Francis Amasa, 100–2
  "Immigration and Degradation,"
    100–1
Walker, John Brisben, 103
Welsh, Robert Gilbert, 121, 124
  Jezebel, 121, 124, 126
Welter, Barbara, 77
Wendell, Barrett, 45, 49–54, 119
  Ralegh and Guiana, 45, 49–51,
    119
  Rosamond, 50
Wentworth, Marion Craig, 37, 177,
  181–82
  Flower Shop, The, 181
  War Brides, 37, 177–78, 181–82
Westbrook, Peter, 150
Wexler, Laura, 189
Wharton, Edith
  Copy: A Dialogue, 16, 26
  Cosmopolitan and, 103
  Kirk and, 80
  Pomegranate Seed, 16, 121,
    122–23
  publication of short stories, 16
  Scribner's and, 13, 16
Wheeler, Edward, 11
Whitlock, Brand, 164
  White Slave, The, 164
Whitney, Blair, 132
Wilkins, Mary E., 150–51
  Giles Corey, Yeoman, 78, 150–51
Williams, Raymond, xv, 1, 5, 190
  Marxism and Literature, 1
  The Long Revolution, 1
Wilmeth, Don, 38, 104, 108
Wilson, Charles, 105
Wilson, Harold, xiii, 71, 73
Wilson, John Grovesnor, 20
Wilson, Woodrow, 48, 179, 189
womanliness, 89, 90

Woman's Luncheon (Anonymous), 79,
    108, 114
World War I, 6, 168–69, 184, 190
    See also anti-war writings

Yeats, William Butler
    Dell and, 183–84
    Forum and, 13

introduction to *Gitanjali,* 142
publication in American periodicals,
    15, 16, 139–40
Tagore and, 142, 142
Young, Philip, 134

Zboray, Ronald, 6, 17
Zuckerman, Ellen, 10